# GUIDE TO

# MISSOURI VEGETABLE GARDENING

Cool Springs Press
P.O. Box 2828
Brentwood, Tennessee 37024

EAN: 9781591864042

Managing Editor: Billie Brownell
Art Director: Karen Phillips
Illustrator: Bill Kersey
Copyeditor: Dimples Kellogg
Horticultural Nomenclature Editor: Greg Stack
Production Artist: S. E. Anderson

First Printing 2001
Printed in the United States of America
10 9 8 7 6 5 4 3 2

Visit the Cool Springs Press website at **www.coolspringspress.com**

GUIDE TO

# MISSOURI VEGETABLE GARDENING

JAMES A. FIZZELL

COOL SPRINGS PRESS
*Growing Successful Gardeners™*
Brentwood, Tennessee

# Dedication and Acknowledgments

*To our Grandchildren: Aaron, Elaina, Andy, Alicia, Benjamin, Jim, Timothy, Katie, Colin, Thomas, Christina Jane, and Elizabeth Anne.*

No one who writes a book can claim credit for everything in it. It takes the effort of lots of people who provide time and expertise to make the dream a reality. *The Midwest Fruit and Vegetable Book: Missouri Edition* is no exception.

The following friends have been especially helpful in the preparation of this book: Dr. William F. Whiteside, *Vegetable Crops Specialist, U of IL Cooperative Extension Service,* has been a friend and colleague for nearly 45 years. I have relied on his advice and his friendship since beginning my horticulture career. William Shoemaker, *U of IL Experiment Station, St. Charles* grows all of the crops mentioned in this book. He was kind enough to review the manuscript and offer suggestions on varieties suited to this part of the country. Greg Soulje, *Meteorologist, LaGrange Park, IL* provides our office with long-range weather information and supplied much of the frost date information. Dr. Robert M. Skirvin, *Fruit Crop and Viticulture Specialist, U of IL, Urbana* is always available to provide answers to questions regarding fruit production. (He also takes time to send notes of encouragement.) Gregory R. Stack, *Horticulturist, U of IL, Matteson,* is a friend and fellow horticulturist at the University of Illinois. Greg is an outstanding horticulturist who lent his expertise by reviewing the botanical nomenclature and offering many suggestions on the technical aspects of the book. Last, but far from least is (Adrienne) Jane Fizzell, my wife and business partner. The hours and hours it takes to write a book are hours we could have spent together. Without any thought for her own time, she read copy, edited, researched, fended off impatient clients, and offered to help in any way she could to make this book possible. (Many of the recipes are from Aunt Jane's kitchen.) A sincere thank you to all of my wonderful friends.

Also, a sincere thanks is due to Cool Springs Communications—Roger Waynick for making this book possible; and Hank McBride, Billie Brownell, and Dimples Kellogg for the many hours they have spent on editing, layout, production, and distribution.

# CONTENTS

# GARDENING IN MISSOURI

Soils and the weather make gardening in Missouri challenging. Soils differ throughout the state, and most gardeners agree, "If you don't like the weather, wait a day or so. It will change!"

## Soil Texture

To determine soil texture, (the relative proportion of particle sizes and amounts), perform the following simple test:

- Fill a clear quart jar ⅔ full of clean water. Keep the lid handy.
- Collect and mix samples of soil from areas in your garden. Add enough of the sample to the jar of water to fill it, leaving ½ inch of air space, and screw on the lid. Shake vigorously until the soil is broken up and suspended in the water.
- Allow the mixture to settle for exactly one minute and mark the level on the side of the jar. This is the amount of sand.

SOIL TEXTURE CLASSIFICATIONS

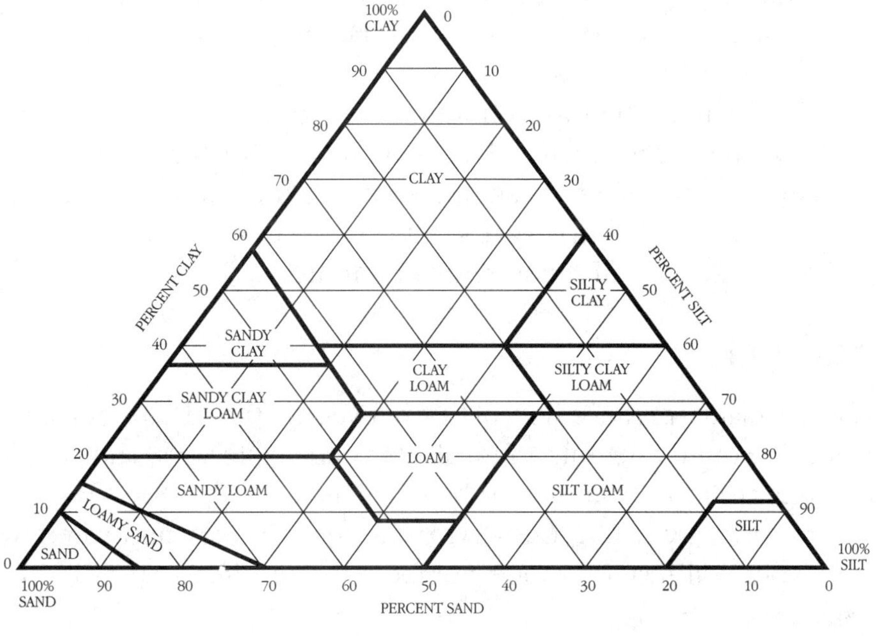


Source: Soil Science Society of America

Allow the suspension to settle for 24 hours and again mark the amount that settled out. This is the amount of silt. After another 24 hours, mark the next layer, which is the amount of clay in the mixture.

The relative percentage of each layer indicates the type of soil you have. Use the Soil Texture Classification chart to determine the type. It indicates the 12 soil classifications based on sizes of soil particles. Loams are the bext kinds of soils. They have about 50% sand, 30% silt, and 20% clay. See page 22 in the Introduction to learn how to handle your soil to get the most out of it, even if it isn't a loam.

## Soil Structure

The physical condition of soil is called structure. It is determined by the distribution of pore spaces in the soil (compaction). To determine the infiltration rate of your soil, which will provide information about the compaction of your soil, try this test:

- Cut the top and bottom off a large coffee can. Starting about 2 inches from the bottom, using a permanent marker, mark off each half-inch to the top of the can.
- Firmly push the can into the ground about one inch. Hammer with a block of wood if necessary. Do not water the soil. It will interfere with the test.
- Fill the can to the top with water, then for ten minutes measure how long it takes each inch of water to drain out of the can. (You may need to refill the can and continue the test if the soil is in excellent condition.) Add the total inches of water and divide by 10 to find the infiltration rate per minute.

## Soil pH

Garden plants prefer a soil pH of between 6.0 and 7.0, but most plants are quite tolerant. A few plants need acidic soils, and certain diseases are more common if the pH is high.

Your County Extension Service can tell you how and where to have your soil tested. Phone numbers for all offices are listed on page 15.

## Soil Temperatures

| Soil Temperature | Effect on Plant Growth |
|---|---|
| Less Than 40 degrees F | Little growth. Certain disease organisims capable of attacking roots and seeds. |
| 40 to 65 degrees F | Roots of cold-tolerant plants and some seeds able to develop. |
| 65 to 70 degrees F | Most seeds germinate rapidly; roots make their greatest growth. |
| 70 to 85 degrees F | Roots and seeds of hot-weather plants continue to develop. Development of cool weather plants inhibited. |
| Above 85 degrees F | Little if any growth of roots or seeds, underground parts of plants begin to deteriorate. |

## The Weather

To help you make your gardening plans, I included maps showing the average dates of the last frost in spring and the first frost of fall, as well as the Frost/Freeze Occurrence Table. These maps and table indicate when to expect the first and last frost (about 36 degrees) and freezes (28 degrees) each year.

I have also included a map showing the average annual precipitation you can expect in your part of Missouri.

Finally, the USDA Hardiness Zone map for Missouri indicates the lowest expected annual temperatures and is provided on page 14. This is important in determining what plants will survive our winters.

Of course, these are all averages. It is important to keep records and to compare them with the tables and maps, which will give you a good idea how much your garden differs from the averages for your area. To learn more about the weather, see page 21 in the Introduction.

Information adapted from: Thomsen, K.D., 1999. Soil Types and Testing. LA County Department of Public Works, Environmental Programs Division. Retrieved from the Internet January 2001.

# Missouri
# Average First Frost

**Median Dates**

- Oct. 20 - 24
- Oct. 25 - 29
- Oct. 30
- Oct. 30 - Nov. 4
- Nov. 5 - 9
- Nov. 10 - 14
- Nov. 15 - 19
- Nov. 20 - 24

# MISSOURI AVERAGE LAST FROST

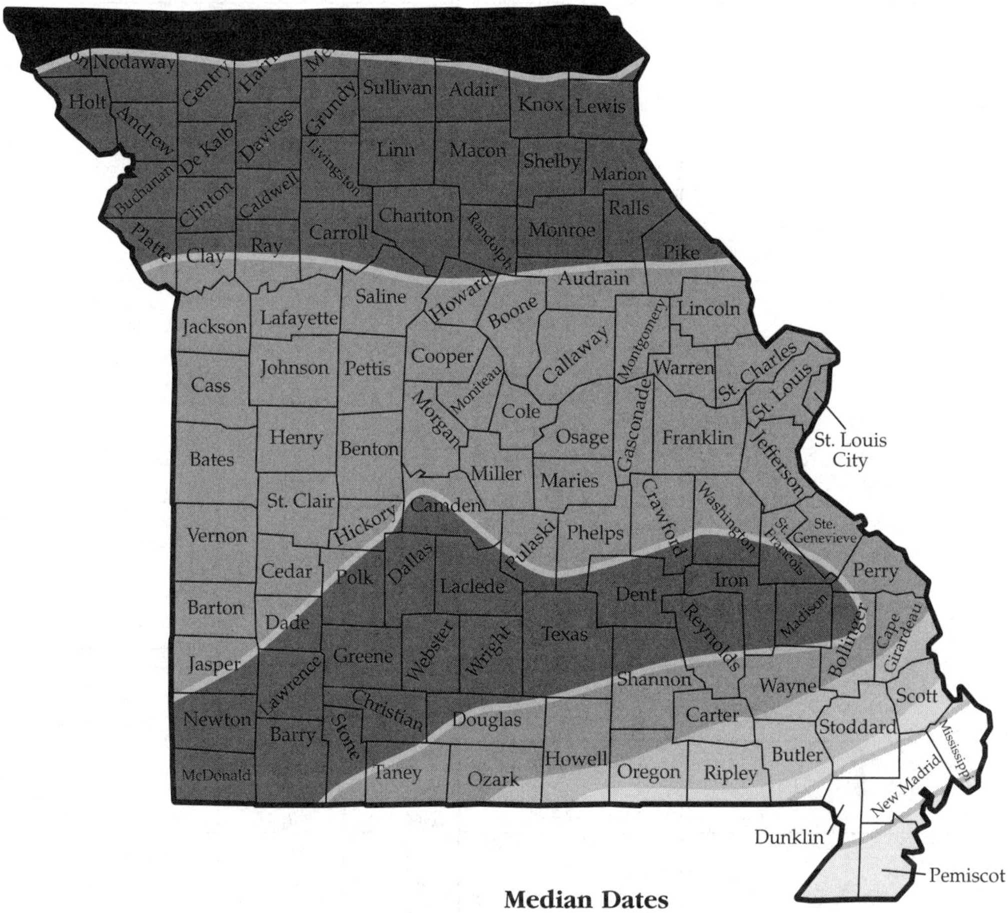


**Median Dates**

| | |
|---|---|
| | Apr. 15 - 11 |
| | Apr. 10 - 6 |
| | Apr. 5 - 1 |
| | Mar. 31 - 27 |
| | Mar. 26 - 22 |
| | Mar. 21 - 17 |
| | Mar. 17 - 13 |

# Missouri Freeze/Frost Occurrence Table

| Station Name | Temp Threshold (Degrees F) | 50% Probability | | |
|---|---|---|---|---|
| | | Fall Freeze | Spring Freeze | Freeze Free Period |
| Bolivar | 36 | Oct 12 | Apr 30 | 165 |
| | 32 | Oct 19 | Apr 20 | 181 |
| | 28 | Oct 30 | Apr 04 | 208 |
| Boonville | 36 | Oct 18 | Apr 21 | 180 |
| | 32 | Oct 30 | Apr 10 | 202 |
| | 28 | Nov 06 | Apr 01 | 219 |
| Farmington | 36 | Oct 02 | May 06 | 148 |
| | 32 | Oct 10 | Apr 24 | 168 |
| | 28 | Oct 17 | Apr 12 | 187 |
| Harrisonville | 36 | Oct 11 | Apr 25 | 167 |
| | 32 | Oct 23 | Apr 15 | 190 |
| | 28 | Nov 02 | Apr 08 | 207 |
| Joplin | 36 | Oct 17 | Apr 21 | 178 |
| | 32 | Oct 26 | Apr 10 | 198 |
| | 28 | Nov 07 | Mar 27 | 224 |
| Kirksville | 36 | Oct 02 | May 05 | 149 |
| | 32 | Oct 11 | Apr 22 | 171 |
| | 28 | Oct 25 | Apr 11 | 196 |
| Saint Charles | 36 | Oct 14 | Apr 21 | 172 |
| | 32 | Oct 21 | Apr 15 | 189 |
| | 28 | Nov 01 | Apr 02 | 213 |
| St. Joseph | 36 | Oct 04 | Apr 29 | 157 |
| | 32 | Oct 15 | Apr 19 | 179 |
| | 28 | Oct 27 | Apr 05 | 204 |
| Sikeston | 36 | Oct 15 | Apr 17 | 180 |
| | 32 | Oct 29 | Apr 07 | 204 |
| | 28 | Nov 07 | Mar 25 | 227 |
| Vichy | 36 | Oct 17 | Apr 26 | 173 |
| | 32 | Oct 28 | Apr 12 | 198 |
| | 28 | Nov 05 | Apr 01 | 217 |
| West Plains | 36 | Oct 09 | May 01 | 160 |
| | 32 | Oct 18 | Apr 20 | 180 |
| | 28 | Oct 29 | Apr 08 | 203 |

To use this table, locate the recording station nearest you. Using 32 degrees F as an example, and assuming the .5 probability noted in the table (which is a 50/50 chance), this means that five years out of ten, a temperature as cold or colder than 32 degrees is expected to occur later than the date indicated for spring. Conversely, for fall, there is a chance five years out of ten of experiencing temperatures as cold or colder than 32 degrees before the date indicated. This table can be used to determine the chance of the first or last frosts/freezes of the seasons and their relative severity. The period of frost-free days for which the temperature exceeds the specified temperature is also noted. (Source: National Climatic Data Center)

# MISSOURI TOTAL ANNUAL PRECIPITATION IN INCHES

Averaged from 1961 to 1990

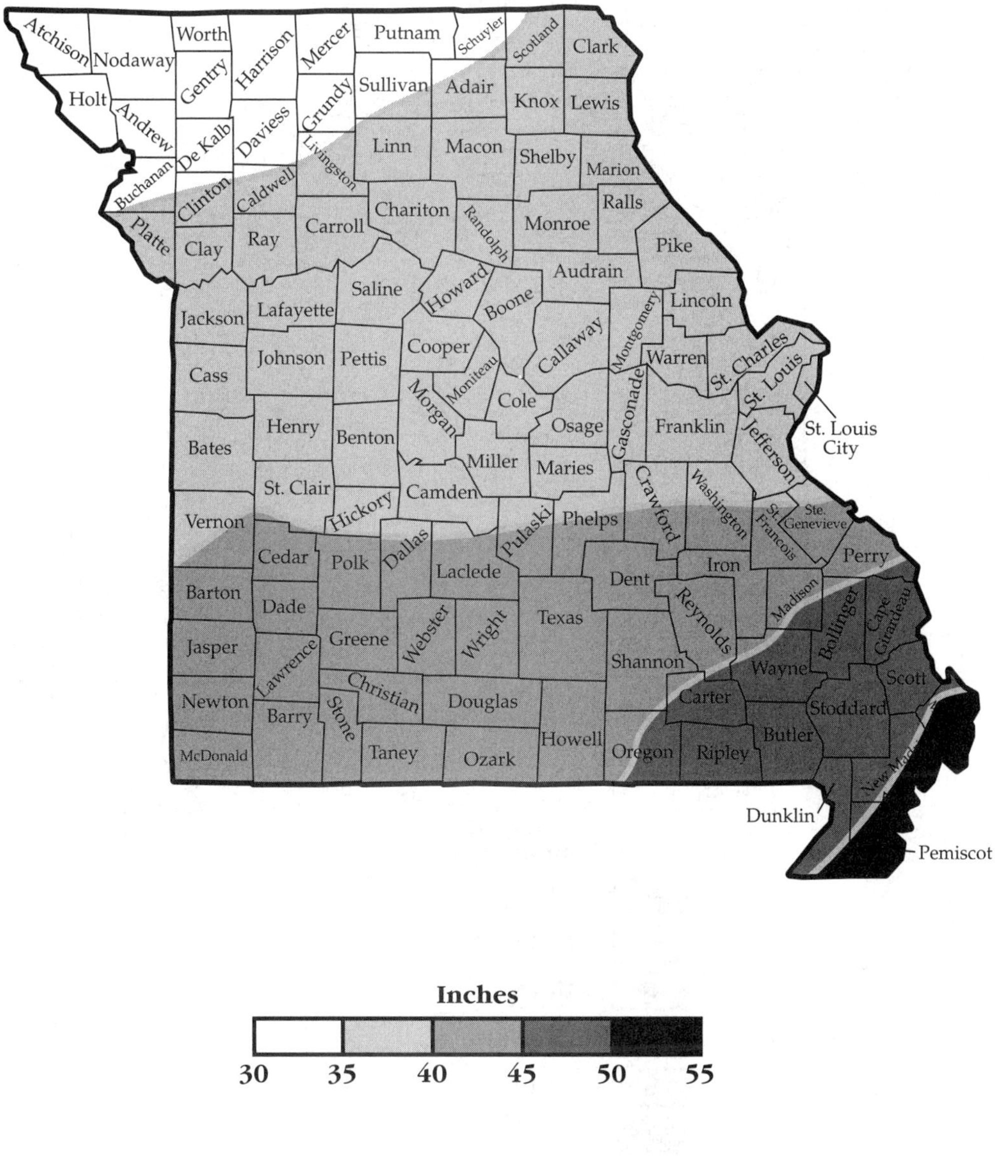


Data from the Midwestern Regional
Climate Center, Champaign, Illinois

# MISSOURI USDA HARDINESS ZONES

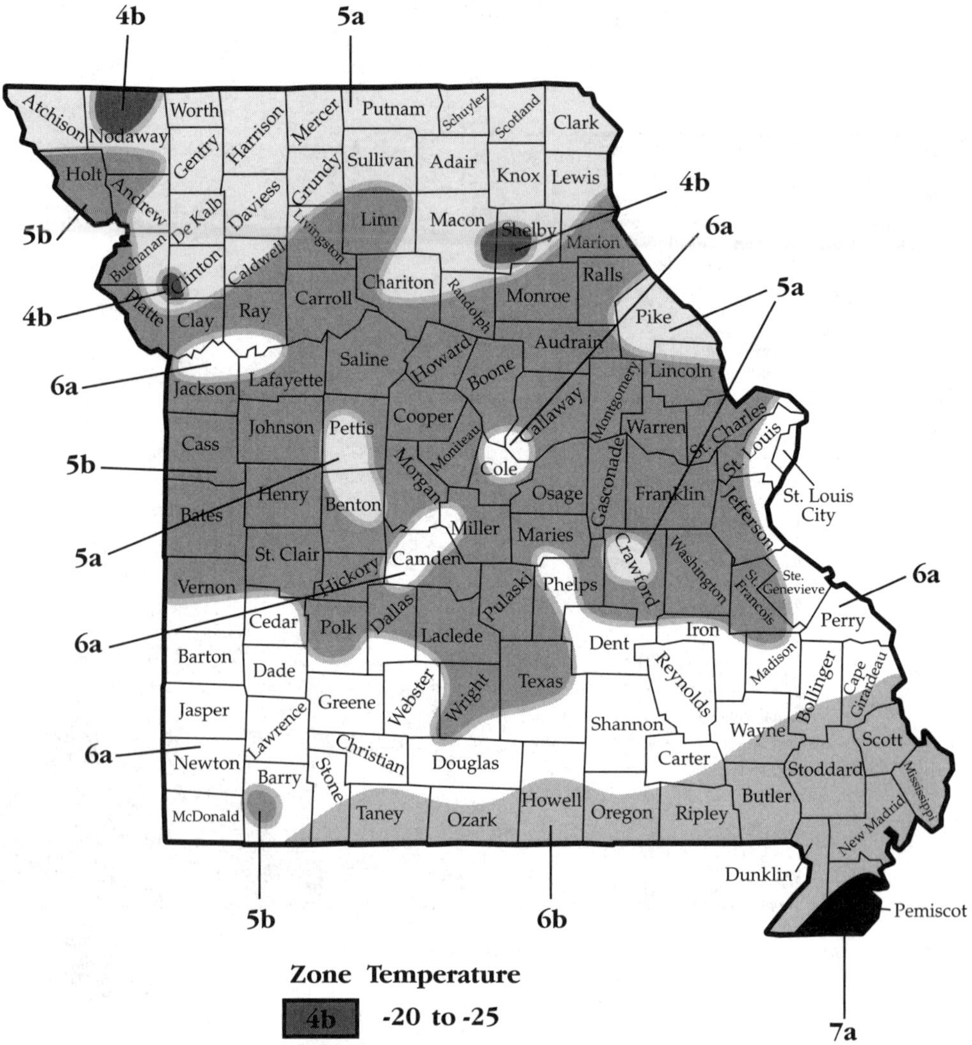


| Zone | Temperature |
|---|---|
| 4b | -20 to -25 |
| 5a | -15 to -20 |
| 5b | -10 to -15 |
| 6a | -5 to -10 |
| 6b | 0 to -5 |
| 7a | 5 to 0 |

# MISSOURI COUNTY EXTENSION TELEPHONE NUMBERS

| | |
|---|---|
| Adair | 660-665-9866 |
| Andrew | 816-324-3147 |
| Atchison | 660-744-6231 |
| Audrain | 573-581-3231 |
| Barry | 417-847-3161 |
| Barton | 417-682-3579 |
| Bates | 660-679-4167 |
| Benton | 660-438-5012 |
| Bollinger | 573-238-2420 |
| Boone | 573-445-9792 |
| Buchanan | 816-279-1691 |
| Butler | 573-686-8064 |
| Caldwell | 816-586-2761 |
| Callaway | 573-642-0755 |
| Camden | 573-346-2644 |
| Cape Girardeau | 573-243-3581 |
| Carroll | 660-542-1792 |
| Carter | 573-323-4418 |
| Cass | 816-380-8460 |
| Cedar | 417-276-3313 |
| Chariton | 660-288-3239 |
| Christian | 417-581-3558 |
| Clark | 660-727-3339 |
| Clay | 816-792-7760 |
| Clinton | 816-539-3765 |
| Cole | 573-634-2824 |
| Cooper | 660-882-5661 |
| Crawford | 573-775-2135 |
| Dade | 417-637-2112 |
| Dallas | 417-345-7551 |
| Daviess | 660-663-3232 |
| De Kalb | 816-449-2101 |
| Dent | 573-729-3196 |
| Douglas | 417-683-4409 |
| Dunklin | 573-888-4722 |
| Franklin | 636-583-5141 |
| Gasconade | 573-437-2165 |
| Gentry | 660-726-5610 |
| Greene | 417-862-9284 |
| Grundy | 660-359-5643 |
| Harrison | 660-425-6434 |
| Henry | 660-885-5556 |
| Hickory | 417-745-6767 |
| Holt | 660-446-3724 |
| Howard | 660-482-2272 |
| Howell | 417-256-2391 |
| Iron | 573-546-7515 |
| Jackson | 816-252-5051 |
| Jasper | 417-358-2158 |
| Jefferson | 636-797-5391 |
| Johnson | 816-747-3193 |
| Knox | 660-397-2179 |
| Laclede | 417-532-7126 |
| Lafayette | 660-584-3658 |
| Lawrence | 417-466-3102 |
| Lewis | 573-767-5273 |
| Lincoln | 636-528-4613 |
| Linn | 660-895-5123 |
| Livingston | 660-646-0811 |
| Macon | 660-385-2173 |
| Madison | 573-783-3303 |
| Maries | 573-422-3359 |
| Marion | 573-769-2177 |
| McDonald | 417-223-4775 |
| Mercer | 660-748-3315 |
| Miller | 573-369-2394 |
| Mississippi | 573-683-6129 |
| Monroe | 660-327-4158 |
| Montgomery | 573-564-3733 |
| Morgan | 573-378-5358 |
| New Madrid | 573-748-5531 |
| Newton | 417-455-9500 |
| Nodaway | 660-582-8101 |
| Oregon | 417-778-7490 |
| Osage | 573-897-3648 |
| Ozark | 417-679-3525 |
| Pemiscot | 573-333-0258 |
| Perry | 573-547-4504 |
| Pettis | 660-827-0591 |
| Phelps | 573-364-3147 |
| Pike | 573-324-5464 |
| Platte | 816-858-2165 |
| Polk | 417-326-4916 |
| Pulaski | 573-774-6177 |
| Putnam | 660-947-2990 |
| Ralls | 573-985-3911 |
| Randolph | 660-269-9656 |
| Ray | 816-776-6961 |
| Reynolds | 573-663-2251 |
| Ripley | 573-996-2921 |
| Saline | 660-886-6908 |
| Schuyler | 660-457-3469 |
| Scotland | 660-465-7255 |
| Scott | 573-545-3516 |
| Shannon | 573-226-5544 |
| Shelby | 573-633-2640 |
| St. Charles | 636-970-3000 |
| St. Clair | 417-646-2419 |
| St. Francois | 573-756-4539 |
| St. Louis | 314-615-2911 |
| Ste. Genevieve | 573-883-3548 |
| Stoddard | 573-568-3344 |
| Stone | 417-357-6812 |
| Sullivan | 660-265-4541 |
| Taney | 417-546-2371 |
| Texas | 417-967-4545 |
| Vernon | 417-448-2560 |
| Warren | 636-456-3444 |
| Washington | 573-438-2671 |
| Wayne | 573-224-3035 |
| Webster | 417-859-2044 |
| Worth | 660-564-3363 |
| Wright | 417-741-6134 |

# Roots of Midwest Gardening

## A History

Fruit and vegetable gardening in the Midwest started as a necessity. The earliest settlers found wooded rolling hills in the East, then flatlands and grassy prairies as they moved farther west. The open prairies were perfect to produce corn, grains, and forages for horses and cattle. These were in direct contrast to the mountains and forests through which pioneers had carved out trails and small farms. The flood of European immigrants in the 1800s found the land very similar to what they left at home; the soil was dark, fertile, and productive. But even before crops could be grown and harvested, pioneer women fed the family from the garden.

Gardening was women's work. The housewife located the garden next to the house where she could keep an eye on it, and she fenced the garden to keep out wild animals and wandering livestock. There she grew all the vegetables, fruits, and herbs to feed her family. Along with the food crops, she grew all the necessities for making medicine, flavoring foods, freshening the air, and repelling vermin and bugs. And she always had room for a few flowers to add a little joy to the otherwise harsh pioneer life.

Typical pioneer gardens can be seen today around the restored buildings in the Garfield Farm Museum, La Fox, Illinois; Old World, Wisconsin; and other locations throughout the Midwest. Amish settlements preserve the flavor of pioneer gardens in a contemporary setting; some examples can be found in the Shipshewana area in LaPorte County, Indiana; the Arcola area in Douglas and Coles Counties, Illinois; and especially

Millersburg, Sugarcreek, and Walnut Creek in Tuscawaras and Holmes Counties, Ohio.

Gardens were planted to provide fresh produce during the growing season, but it was equally important to provide enough to feed the family through the long, hard Midwest winter. Potatoes, carrots, beets, winter squash and pumpkins, onions, dried beans, legumes, and corn were basics. Later, apple, peach, and pear trees were planted. Wild grapes and brambles provided berries for those fortunate enough to find them.

The settlers dug pits or root cellars to store the harvest for later use. These were simple holes in the ground into which the produce was layered, or they could be quite elaborate with a trapdoor and enough space for entry to retrieve the needed items. Various means were employed to insulate the structures against the cold from above; for example, boards were covered with bales of straw, piles of topsoil, or piles of manure. The soil temperatures kept the pit at approximately 50 degrees Fahrenheit if it was adequately protected. These pits served as storm cellars as well to protect settlers from the "cyclones" peculiar to the plains.

## The Changing Land

As the land was increasingly settled, farms replaced the homesteads, and nearly all the tillable land was eventually occupied. Farming consisted of mostly corn, oats, wheat and pasture, and livestock. The garden and often chickens remained the responsibility of the women of the family. Backyard gardens provided fresh produce for people who moved to towns and cities. Nearly everyone had a garden producing asparagus, rhubarb, horseradish, beans, squash, tomatoes, carrots, beets, onions, various greens, and herbs.

Surrounding the larger towns, specialized agriculture developed to provide fresh produce for townspeople, especially those living in apartments and tenements. Often the entrepreneurs farmed small pieces of land, which they cropped intensively. Many were recent immigrants trying to get started in the new land who harvested their produce early in the morning and delivered it to town markets or to stores and restaurants.

Often the vegetables they grew were specialized because of the ethnic origins of their customers. The truck farms surrounding Chicago and St. Louis offered cabbages, beets, potatoes, and onions. Some smaller growers produced pickles and squash, and specialty items such as dill and horseradish. Until the 1960s, Illinois was the largest producer of horseradish and onion sets in the country. Grand Rapids, Michigan, was a center of summer lettuce production. The lettuce variety 'Grand Rapids', selected for its adaptability to Midwest conditions, is still grown today. Tomato producers near larger communities—Chicago, Indianapolis, Detroit, Milwaukee, and Cleveland—provided tomatoes for the fresh market and also for processing into ketchup.

## Gardening Growth in the 20th Century

During the 1920s, large greenhouses were constructed near larger cities to produce year-round vegetables for fresh consumption. Crops included tomatoes, cucumbers, Bibb lettuce, radishes, and other high-value salad items. Many of these facilities later converted to flower production and remain in operation today.

Between World War I and World War II, interest in gardening was stimulated by the Land Grant College system and the Cooperative Extension Service. Begun to help farmers adopt improved methods, the service expanded to assist rural homemakers and, through the 4-H program, young people. Gardening was an important part of both the homemaker and the 4-H programs. Concurrently, seed companies began supplying improved varieties of familiar garden vegetables and new kinds of plants.

When the Great Depression intensified in the early 1930s with multitudes out of work and unable to support their families, gardening became a necessity for many. Those fortunate enough to have yards took full advantage of them to feed their families.

I distinctly remember Grandma's garden at the farm during that time, with rows of new (to me) plants such as cauliflower, eggplant, dill, potatoes, and onions. Coming from an apartment in the city, I was familiar with leaf lettuce, radishes, beans, and carrots that could be grown in tiny plots along the railroad tracks. I also remember the evening the cow got into Grandma's onion patch. We youngsters were catching lightning bugs. Chasing from the front yard, where family members were visiting, around to the back, we were startled by Bossie contentedly munching the tops off the onions. Even after the milk had been poured on the ground for several days, it still provided a touch of onion to the cereal at breakfast time.

At the onset of World War II, we were fortunate to move to a large old house in town. It had an oversized yard, just right for the Victory Gardens that soon proliferated throughout the country. The Victory Gardens were part of a national drive to produce food for the war effort and to enhance the diet of the general population while most food items were rationed. For many of us, it was the first serious gardening we had done. Canning fruits, vegetables, jams, and jellies became a regular summer pastime.

Following World War II, housing was in short supply as returning vets married and sought homes to start families. A tremendous housing boom resulted in conversion of hundreds of acres of farmland into neighborhoods. Tiny houses on 10,000-square-foot lots left room for plantings, yet vegetable gardening was not the rage. Most had money to buy new foods being offered in the markets: pre-prepared things, frozen foods, and, a little later, TV dinners. Young families had more than enough to do without tending to vegetable gardens. They had time only to tend to landscape plants and annual flowers that filled most of the gardens.

With the increasing value of land, many local truck farmers sold out, and fresh market production moved farther from towns. The construction of the Dwight D. Eisenhower highway system improved transportation so that growers in remote locations could send fresh produce into Midwest markets in only a day or two. Shippers in Florida, Texas, Arizona, and the West Coast quickly replaced many local producers.

While the produce was certainly available, many consumers began to miss the fresh-picked quality and taste. At the same time, with the "back to nature" movement of the 1960s and 1970s, green things became popular again. And as the baby boomer generation matured and found time for hobbies, it wasn't long before someone figured out that gardening was a great hobby, and homegrown produce was the tastiest obtainable.

## Gardening in the 21st Century

Today gardening is the number one hobby in the United States. (To help you as you learn more about gardening, I have provided a glossary and lists of some garden suppliers at the back of the book.) Home vegetable gardens, and community gardens for those living in high-rises or condos without sufficient space, provide fresh food for the table. But more than that, gardens provide exercise, a place to work off the adrenaline from hectic work schedules. Garden clubs in every community unite folks of similar interests, providing fellowship and help, sharing extra plants, and supplying answers to vexing questions. Gardening offers something of common interest among neighbors, something to talk about. And gardening is fun.

## What Is Unique About Gardening in the Midwest?

### The Seasons

The Midwest has a moist, temperate, continental climate. Spring is often cool and wet, and snow is common in the northern parts until the end of April. Spring weather is quite changeable with temperatures in the 70-degree Fahrenheit range in March followed by highs in the 30-degree range a few days later. Rainfall occurs in spring storms, although extended periods of wet weather are common.

The average date of last frost (frost-free date) varies from about April 5 in the southernmost part of the Midwest to May 25 in northern Wisconsin and Michigan. The latest date of last frost is 2 or 3 weeks later; that is the date after which no frost occurs.

Summers are generally hot, except in the northernmost parts, and sometimes dry. Daily high temperatures can be expected in the 90-degree Fahrenheit range throughout most of the lower third of the Midwest, in the 80s through the midsection, and in the 70s to the north. Along the shores of the Great Lakes, lake-effect winds often cause temperatures to be much lower than in inland areas. (The lake effect is more pronounced in the spring when shoreline gardens may be as much as 2 or 3 weeks behind gardens well inland.) Water temperatures at that time of the year are generally in the 50- to 60-degree Fahrenheit range, and breezes off the lakes are quite cool.

Summer rain occurs as warm fronts and low pressure areas pull warm, humid air up from the Gulf of Mexico. Where the warm air and cool, high-pressure fronts meet, storms break out, sometimes accompanied by severe weather. Summer storms can be spotty with some locations receiving inches of rain while nearby areas receive little or none. Rainfall throughout the summer months averages less than 1 inch per week. For maximum production in vegetable gardens, supplemental watering can be very helpful when the season is dry.

The first frost in fall puts an end to the gardening season around Labor Day in the north, and about mid-October in the far south part of the Midwest. The frost-free season is about 200 days in the southernmost parts of the Midwest, and about 95 days in the northern parts.

### Understanding Soils

The basis for gardening is the soil. The most productive parts of the world are blessed with good, fertile soils. Our country developed as an agricultural society, and as old soils wore out, pioneers moved west to find better land. Here in the Midwest, we are blessed with some of the best soils in the world, and it is important for you to understand why and to know how to make the best use of them.

Soils are produced by the weathering and aging of rock. Soils throughout much of the Midwest were developed by glaciers; the debris from rocks over which the glaciers passed was left as they receded. Glacial till, the material left in place by the glaciers, is a mixture of various sizes of soil particles, gravel, rocks, and sometimes boulders of various sizes. Glacial outwash soils are mixtures as well, but often are stratified in layers.

Throughout the Midwest, loess soils are the most common. Loess soils were created by the wind, which picked up finer soil particles from the beds of rivers created by the retreating glaciers. These particles were blown east from the Missouri, Mississippi, Wisconsin, Illinois, and other rivers. The heavier particles fell out first. Then the finer particles, silts and clays, blew the farthest east. The Dust Bowl days of the 1930s were a continuation of the processes that created our soils.

Soils are named according to the sizes of the particles. *Sands* have comparatively large particles; the grains are visible to the naked eye. Sandy soils are well drained and tend to be infertile because nutrients are easily washed from the soil by rains or irrigation. Sands are often the soils found in river valleys.

*Silt soils* are made up of small particles, too tiny to be seen without magnification. Silt soils are usually poorly drained and become compacted by their own weight, but silt soils hold nutrients well. Properly managed silts can be quite productive. For instance, the soils of the Salinas Valley in California are granitic silts, and the farmers have learned to fluff these soils up into hills and grow their crops before the hills collapse. Much of our winter lettuce comes from these farms.

*Clay soils* are the most productive types, but they can be very frustrating. If they are mistreated—for example, they are worked when too wet or too dry, they are kept too wet, or they are walked on so that they compact—they become like modeling clay. But if they are properly handled, they become friable and workable. Clay particles are microscopic in size; they are so small that they have electrical charges and will stick to each other, making little clusters or crumbs called aggregates. Calcium promotes this tendency, but before adding calcium to your soil, test it first. Most of our Midwest soils have more than enough calcium in them, and adding unneeded gypsum or lime can be very harmful to them. With good structure, clays hold lots of water inside the aggregates (and lots of fertilizer materials, too), but the large spaces between the crumbs let air in. Clays can be well drained and still provide plenty of water and nutrients for plants.

*Loam soils* have the proper mix of sand (20 to 80 percent), silt (40 to 60 percent), and clay (10 to 30 percent) so they have the good features of each kind of soil type.

### The Value of Organic Matter

Organic matter comes from things that were alive, such as dead garden plants, leaves, peat moss, cottonseed meal, compost, and manure, among others. Coarse organic matter opens the soil so that air can get in, which improves heavy soils. Particles of organic matter act as sponges to hold lots of water and improve light, sandy soils. Soil microorganisms break down organic matter, recycling the nutrients. The microorganisms also help cement soil particles together, improving aggregation of clay soils. An abundance of organic matter is essential for a healthy, productive soil, so try to get as much organic matter as you can to add to your garden. There is no need to throw any away.

### Composting

Any organic matter resulting from the garden, such as grass clippings, fallen leaves in autumn, plant tops, spent plants, and kitchen scraps (but no meat scraps), can be recycled by composting. Naturally occurring organisms—bacteria, fungi, worms, and other creatures—digest the organic matter and turn it into a dark brown, crumbly, earthy-smelling material that is compost.

A compost heap must be large enough to heat internally. The most convenient size for most gardens is about 3 feet high, wide, and deep. A pile can be built up on the ground, but a container, such as a bin made of concrete blocks, fence wire, or boards, is usually easier to handle. Construct the compost pile starting with a 6- to 8-inch layer of coarse organic matter. Moisten the matter so that it is damp. Cover that with about 2 inches of garden soil, which will add the organisms needed to start the process. Repeat alternating layers of organic matter and soil until the pile is 3 feet high. Sprinkle each layer with a couple of handfuls of nitrogen fertilizer such as ammonium nitrate or urea, needed by beneficial organisms. Finally, level the top.

In a properly constructed compost pile, the internal temperature should reach 140 to 160 degrees Fahrenheit in a few days. You can tell when it is working because the pile will settle noticeably. After a month, fork the pile over, turning the outside of the old pile to the middle of the new pile. Then moisten it if necessary. The compost should be ready for use in 4 to 5 months.

Some communities do not allow open composting because of the potential for causing odor and attracting rodents. If your community bans the practice, buy a composting drum. Composting drums are usually constructed so they can be turned occasionally to mix the compost. Fill yours by alternating garden refuse and soil.

Composting works the best with the right carbon (C) to nitrogen (N) ratio, the right mix of dry and green plant material. A C:N ratio of about 30:1 is ideal. A mix of 1 part high-carbon dry leaves or something similar to 2 parts high-nitrogen grass clippings is just about right. The proper C:N ratio with sufficient moisture will result in hotter, faster composting, and the heat will kill off the insects and diseases that might be hiding in the plant parts.

The most common problem with composting is the odor. For a compost pile that smells bad, turn it to aerate it, and add dry material if the pile is too wet. A pile needs to remain moist, however, and rainfall usually provides adequate moisture. A pile that will not heat is too small or has insufficient nitrogen. Remember to make the pile at least 3 feet high, wide, and deep. Add 1 or 2 handfuls of high-nitrogen fertilizer.

The following chart gives you an idea of the kinds of things that need to be mixed to get the proper ratios in a compost pile.

**Carbon to Nitrogen Ratios**

| | | | |
|---|---|---|---|
| Alfalfa Hay | 12:1 | Cornstalks | 60:1 |
| Food Wastes | 15:1 | Leaves | 60:1 |
| Grass Clippings | 20:1 | Straw | 80:1 |
| Rotted Manures | 20:1 | Sawdust | 500:1 |
| Fruit Wastes | 35:1 | Wood | 700:1 |

## Soil Chemistry

The soil provides most of the fertilizer elements needed by plants, and productive soils generally have enough of the elements in forms available to plants. (Carbon, oxygen, and hydrogen come from the air and water.) The correct soil acidity and sufficient air and water are necessary for these elements to be available. The major elements (those needed in larger amounts by plants) are nitrogen, phosphorus, potassium, calcium, magnesium, and sulfur. Minor elements (those needed in smaller amounts) include iron, manganese, boron, zinc, copper, molybdenum, cobalt, and chlorine. Native soils are rarely deficient in minor elements. The minerals that make up our loamy soils usually provide adequate calcium, magnesium, and potassium as well. They are part of the chemical makeup of the rocks from which these soils came.

### Major Elements—Nitrogen (N), Phosphorus (P), Potassium (K)

You probably recognize the N, P, and K from fertilizer packages. These elements are most commonly found in fertilizers because they are most often lacking in garden soils since they are the elements used the most by plants.

#### NITROGEN

Plants need nitrogen for the proteins that make up the plant tissues. While the air we breathe is about 80 percent nitrogen, plants can't use it in that form. Soil organisms capture atmospheric nitrogen and convert it into forms that plants can use. Most of the nitrogen in the soil is part of the soil organic matter. As it decomposes, nitrogen is released and recycled by the plants and soil organisms. It really does not matter what kind of nitrogen you add to your soil—organic, inorganic, or natural. Soil organisms convert it sooner or later to forms plants can use. Plants never know where it came from, so don't worry about what kind of nitrogen fertilizers you buy.

### PHOSPHORUS

Elemental phosphorus is a flammable, white material that is quite poisonous. Of course, plants cannot use it in that form. Phosphorus combines with hydrogen and oxygen in the soil, depending on the soil pH, creating usable forms. Rock phosphate has been added over the years to soils that have been farmed, so there is a lot of it in the soil. But much of it is held tightly in the soil, and plants can't absorb it. Phosphorus fertilizers need to be incorporated into the soil because those applied to the soil surface are tied up before they get to the plant roots. Soluble phosphorus applied in solution works best. Plants need phosphorus for good roots, flowers, and fruits. Transplant starter fertilizers often have an analysis, such as 10-52-17 or 10-30-10, very high in soluble phosphate. The phosphorus is necessary for the rapid development of healthy roots.

### POTASSIUM

Potassium keeps plants sturdy and helps them develop flowers and fruits. Potassium is part of the chemistry of clay particles; chemically, clays are potassium, magnesium, aluminum, and iron silicates. Because most of the potassium in soils is held firmly so plants can't absorb it, adding potassium to the soil before it is tilled is recommended. Soluble potassium applied in solution is more available to plant roots.

## Soil Alkalinity/Acidity—pH

The soil pH is a measure of acidity or alkalinity. Soil is neutral at a pH of 7.0. Above 7.0, the soil is alkaline; below 7.0, the soil is acidic. Most garden plants prefer a pH of 6.0 to 7.0. Midwest soils tend to be alkaline, however, and a pH as high as 8.0 is fairly common. Soils with high pH are quite difficult to change.

Fortunately, most garden plants will grow at the higher pH if they are given enough soluble fertilizers and water. Lime (calcium carbonate) or gypsum (calcium sulfate) are often recommended for application to garden soils. *You must test your soil* before adding either of these materials because additional calcium can increase the alkalinity and may cause deficiencies of other needed elements. Sulfur applications are better for alkaline soils because they reduce the alkalinity.

### Understanding Fertilizers

Fertilizers supply the essential elements needed by plants. As I noted, the elements needed in greatest amounts are nitrogen, phosphorus, and potassium. Most garden fertilizers contain all of these, and the amounts are listed on the label as percentage by weight of N (nitrogen), P-2-O-5 (phosphate), and K-2-O (potash). A fertilizer with an analysis of 10-6-4 contains 10 percent nitrogen, 6 percent phosphate, and 4 percent potash. It is a complete fertilizer containing all 3 of the major elements. A complete fertilizer containing equal amounts of the 3 elements is called a balanced fertilizer; for example, an analysis of 20-20-20 is balanced.

A soil test determines the amount of additional fertilizer that your soil requires. To have your soil tested, collect several cupfuls from various areas of the garden. Mix them thoroughly in a bucket, and spread the soil on a newspaper overnight to air-dry. Package 1 pint of this blend in a paper bag, and send it to a local soil testing laboratory. Most extension service offices will provide directions for testing and the addresses of the labs. The testing lab will suggest a fertilizer analysis for your soil.

If you do not have a soil test done, it is probably best to apply a balanced fertilizer to the soil prior to tilling. Usually, the standard rate is 1 pound of actual nitrogen per 1000 square feet of garden, so 5 pounds of 20-20-20 (that is, 20 percent of 5 pounds is 1 pound) or 6¼ pounds of 16-16-16 (that is, 16 percent of 6¼ pounds is 1 pound) spread on 1000 square feet of garden will supply 1 pound of actual nitrogen. The other elements, phosphate and potash, are provided just in case they are deficient.

Applying fertilizer directly to growing crops would burn them. To avoid this damage, side-dress growing crops by applying fertilizer next to the rows of plants at about half the normal rate. Sidedressing is usually applied midseason after the preplant fertilizers have begun to run out.

Transplant starters are soluble fertilizers containing a high percentage of phosphorus. Common analyses are 10-52-17, 10-50-10, and 10-30-10. These materials are applied following transplanting to stimulate rapid development of new roots. Mix starter fertilizer according to label instructions, and use 1 cup per plant.

### Soils for Container Gardens

Container soils present special problems. Containers filled with garden soil are poorly drained because they lack the deep, natural soil profile through which the water can percolate down, and the water simply stays in the pot. A good soil mix for general use consists of ⅓ garden soil, ⅓ coarse organic matter (such as shredded leaves, compost, or peat moss), and ⅓ coarse sand. Make sure the containers have drainage holes.

Prepared soil mixes available from garden centers consist of brown peat moss, composted bark (or some other organic material) and an aggregate such as perlite or Styrofoam beads. These mixes are very light and tend to dry out very quickly. For pots and small planters, they work quite well. For very large planters such as tree pits, they are too expensive and probably need replacing each season. Your homemade soil mix will probably not need replacing every year in large planters, and it is certainly much more economical than prepared soil mixes.

## Understanding Garden Plants

### How Plants Grow

Garden plants are divided into 2 main kinds, annuals and perennials. Annual plants start from seed, grow, flower, and produce a fruit and seeds in 1 season. Tomatoes, lettuce, corn, and beans are examples of annuals. Perennial plants grow from seed, develop a plant for the first year or so, and then flower and produce fruit and seeds each year thereafter. Rhubarb, strawberries, and apple trees are examples of perennials. The first 2 are herbaceous perennials; that is, the tops die down every fall, but the plants grow again in spring. Trees are woody perennials; that is, only the leaves die, and the rest of the above-ground parts live from year to year.

A third kind of plant, biennial, grows a rosette of foliage from seed the first year, produces a flower, fruit, and seed the second year, and dies. Several biennials are grown as garden plants, but they are usually handled as annuals. The leaves or roots are used, and the plants are discarded after the first year before they bolt (flower). Parsley, angelica, and carrots are examples of biennials.

### Parts of a Plant

Plants consist of above-ground parts and below-ground parts. Generally, everything above ground is a shoot, and below-ground parts are roots. There are some exceptions, however. Occasionally, roots develop above ground, such as aerial roots on wandering fig trees, philodendrons, or orchid plants; and some shoot parts, such as tubers or rhizomes, develop below ground. Roots anchor the plants, absorb water and fertilizer nutrients, and often store sugars and starches for use by the plants later. Above ground, stems transport water and nutrients, and support the leaves, flowers, and fruits. Some stems store sugars and starches as the roots do. Leaves photosynthesize to produce sugars using water from the soil and carbon dioxide from the air.

Flowers produce seeds and fruits. Pollination of flowers by insects or by the wind causes seeds to begin to develop. Then fruits develop around the seeds. Some kinds of plants such as the vines (squash and melon) have separate male and female flowers on the same plant. Male flowers have straight stems, while female flowers have tiny undeveloped fruits below the petals. (See page 78.) Technically, many vegetables are really fruits. Any plant part that develops from a flower is a fruit, so tomatoes, zucchini, and pumpkins are fruits, just as apples and strawberries are fruits. Peas, beans, and corn are seeds that develop inside the fruits. Vegetables are the leaves, stems, or roots that we eat. Lettuce, asparagus, carrots, and potatoes are vegetables. Common usage has confused this distinction so that any plant part with a sweet taste is considered a fruit, and the rest are vegetables. Although a tomato or a sugar pea is a fruit, we call it a vegetable. Is a pumpkin a fruit, or is it a vegetable? I often hear that question each fall. Now you can answer it too. The answer is yes!

## Let's Get Started!

Gardening is a skill. We learn it by doing, making mistakes, correcting them, and going on. Those of us who have been gardening a long time have made a lot of mistakes and have learned from them. If you are not as successful as you would like to be the first year, don't be discouraged. Even the best gardeners have good years and bad years. It is important to record your experiences as you garden—what you planted, when you planted, what the weather was like, and how the crops turned out. Doing this will allow you to evaluate each season and make changes so that the next season will be even better. The remainder of this book describes vegetables, herbs, and fruits that are suited for growing in the Midwest and helps you to get the most enjoyment from them.

# Growing Vegetables in the Home Garden

## Location

The food garden should be located where it is accessible, but where it does not intrude on the living area in your yard. The food garden tends to be messier than a flower garden because it is utilitarian, not aesthetic. Set it in an area that receives full sun if at all possible. (Full sun means there is from 8 to 10 hours daily of direct or full sunlight.) Many crops can be grown in less than full sun, but the result may be less than a full crop. Avoid locations next to large trees or shrubs that will shade the garden and send roots into it; try to plant your garden a distance from trees and shrubs at least equal to the height of the plants. Choosing a site with a nearby water source will also make gardening easier for you in those inevitable dry spells.

Good soil drainage is essential for most garden plants. Some plants tolerate slow drainage, but other plants deteriorate and eventually die. To check the drainage, dig a hole 1 foot wide and deep, then fill it with water. After it drains, fill it again. Repeat the process a third time. If the hole

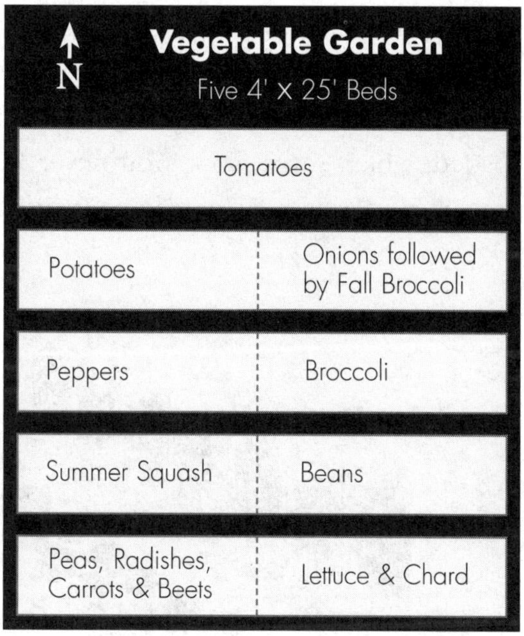


Vegetable Garden Plan

drains out in 12 hours, the drainage is good. If it does not, install drain tiles or build raised beds to improve drainage.

## Size

Make the garden only as big as you can tend it comfortably. A 10-by-10-foot garden is a good starter size. If you can rely on help from other family members, a larger garden may be fine, but do not plan on getting much help from the kids. Soccer, swimming, and friends will soon occupy their time and you will be stuck with weeding by yourself.

## Rows versus Beds

There are several factors to consider when deciding whether to plant in rows or beds. Large gardens are usually laid out in rows because rows are easier to plant, cultivate, and harvest using mechanical equipment. Small gardens are much easier to handle when laid out in beds, which are suited to hand tilling. Rows use space less efficiently than beds. Rows require 1 aisle per row while beds require aisles only every $3^1/_2$ to 4 feet. Rows necessitate spading the entire garden; only the beds are spaded, which saves work. You never walk on the soil in beds, and organic matter and soil amendments go only in the beds—there is no

Raised Beds

waste! With beds, more of the area is available for production than in rows, and the part that is not used for growing does not need fertilizing, weeding, or watering.

If you decide to make raised beds, begin the first bed 18 inches from an edge of the garden. Set a pair of stakes to indicate 2 corners. Measure the width of the bed, 36 to 48 inches depending on the size of your garden and your reach, then set another pair of stakes at the other corners. These stakes mark out the first bed. Next, measure 18 inches to identify an aisle, measure the width of the next bed, and set another pair of stakes. Continue to delineate the rest of the beds. Rototill or spade the beds only, not the aisles. Work from the aisles, never walking on the beds. After you have worked up the soil, open furrows across the beds to plant. Placing boards or edging materials around each bed to contain the soil is not necessary.

"Double Row" Rows

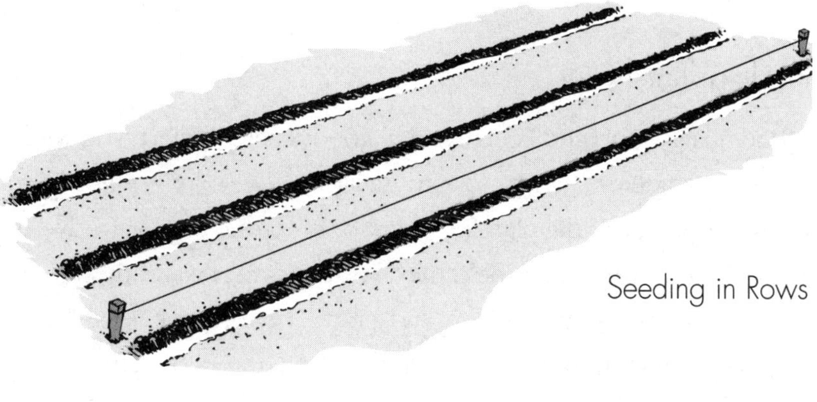

Seeding in Rows

## Hotbeds and Cold Frames

If you grow your own transplants, space will be at a premium every spring. Using hotbeds or cold frames provides space to protect plants until it is time to set them in the garden. (A hotbed is a cold frame provided with a heat source, such as electric cables or hot water heat.) Garden catalogs offer all kinds of cold frames, but they do not need to be fancy. I use a portable one made of plywood that I can set up in the part of the garden that will be planted last. It is the size of an old storm window: it is 30 by 60 inches inside and holds 9 10-by-20-inch flats. Four pieces of 2-by-4 make the corners. The back is 15 inches high, and the front is 10 inches high. The sash sits on it, and I can slide it back to work on the plants or to let in air. I may put hinges on it this year.

Cold Frame

## Garden Tools

Buy good quality tools and keep them in good repair. To start, you will need a flat garden spade or spading fork to turn over the soil, a round shovel to move soil around or to dig planting holes for fruit trees, and a sturdy garden rake to level the garden. Also helpful will be a trowel, a watering can, stakes and string for laying out the garden, and a forked garden cultivator. Keep the shovel, spade, and hoe well sharpened. Clean the tools after use, and wipe them with an oily rag to keep them from rusting. I still use tools that were my grandfather's, and except for replacing handles, they are in nearly original shape.

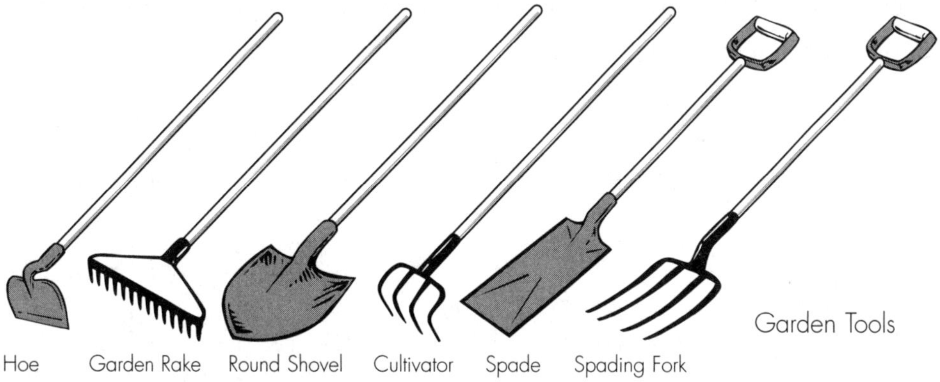

Garden Tools

## Vertical Gardens

Make the most of the space in a small garden by growing anything that can be trained on supports, stakes, cages, trellises, poles, and fencing. Peas and tomatoes are commonly grown on supports, and you may want to try squash, pole beans, or cucumbers. You can grow watermelons on a trellis if you provide each developing melon with a cloth parachute under it to keep it from pulling the vine down. A great deal of discussion concerns orien-

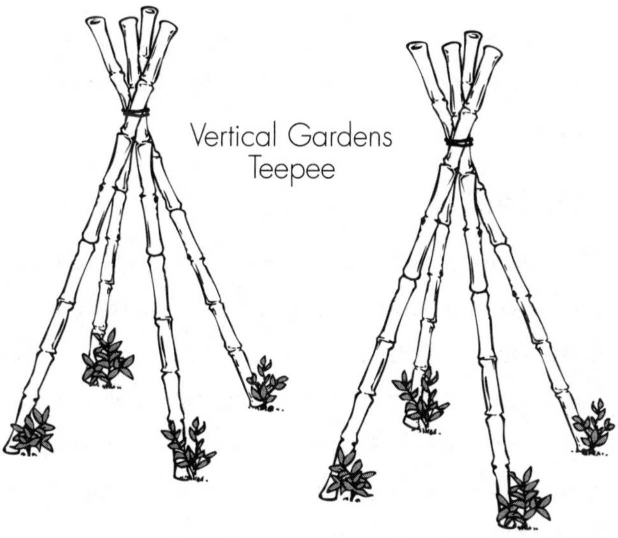
Vertical Gardens Teepee

tation of the beds in vertical gardens. Usually, an east-west orientation is preferred because it allows the shorter plants to be planted to the south, and taller ones to the north. If you contemplate an extensive vertical garden, give it a north-south orientation so both sides of the structures receive some direct light during the day.

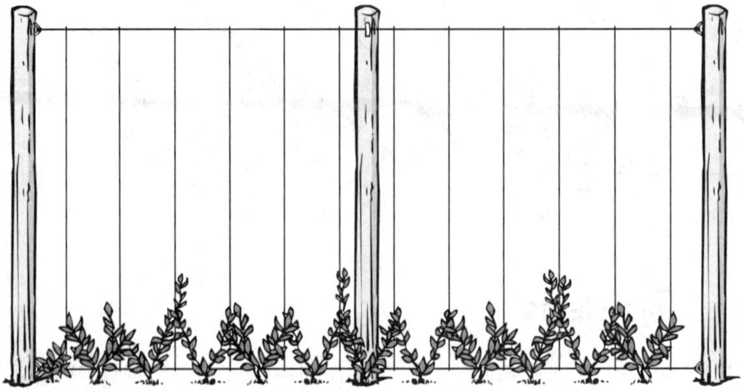

Vertical Gardens—Stakes and Wires

## Container Gardens

Cliff dwellers, condo owners, and other gardeners without yards can grow vegetables in containers. Many kinds of vegetables are available to fit any situation. Containers must have good drainage, and the soil needs to be made specifically for containers. (See "Soils for Container Gardens" on page 29 in the introduction.)

## Selecting Varieties

In this book I list varieties of plants suggested for growing in the Midwest. They have been grown here and can be trusted to perform well. New varieties for the home garden are being developed each year, and catalogs are full of them. Many are worth trying, but before you devote your entire garden and a pile of money to something new, try it on a small scale. If the new variety performs better for a couple of seasons than the variety you have been growing, making a change may be safe.

Home gardeners grow many old standards. Some of them have the same name, but have been improved over the years. The 'Big Boy' tomatoes of the 1940s are not the same as those you are planting now. Improved disease resistance, plant habit, production, and weather tolerance have been added. Heirloom varieties, available from seed specialists, have become popular. These varieties have not been improved and may not have the disease resistance of newer varieties, but they retain the wonderful characteristics that made them popular in the past. These varieties may do very well in your garden if it is free of certain diseases.

All-America Selections (AAS) are awarded to varieties that have given outstanding performance in trial gardens throughout the country. These varieties, indicated by the letters AAS in the text, are worth trying in your garden.

## Starting Transplants from Seed

To grow your own transplants, you'll need to plan your garden well in advance. Garden plants such as tomatoes, peppers, onion stick-outs, broccoli, and cauliflower profit from an early start indoors. If you're successful, your well-grown transplants will be compact, 4 to 6 inches tall, and have about 6 fully developed leaves. To start transplants from seed, you will need various materials. You will need containers in which to start seeds and to grow transplants. At your local garden center, obtain some 10-by-20-inch plastic flats and miscellaneous containers for transplanting. If you intend to grow vine crops from seed indoors, you will need peat pots or peat pellets. Buying at least 1 seedling starter tray is a good investment. It has 20 rows of depressions or grooves to fill with artificial planting mix and fits into a standard 10-by-20-inch flat; seeds are then sown in the depressions. You will need artificial potting soil for seed-starting trays. Any of the commercial mixtures, such as Jiffy Mix™ or Pro Mix™, will work, but do not use the moist black "potting soil." This "potting soil" is too light and fluffy; it dries out and will not rewet properly. Moisten the soil in a bucket, and use the moistened soil to fill the depressions in the starter tray.

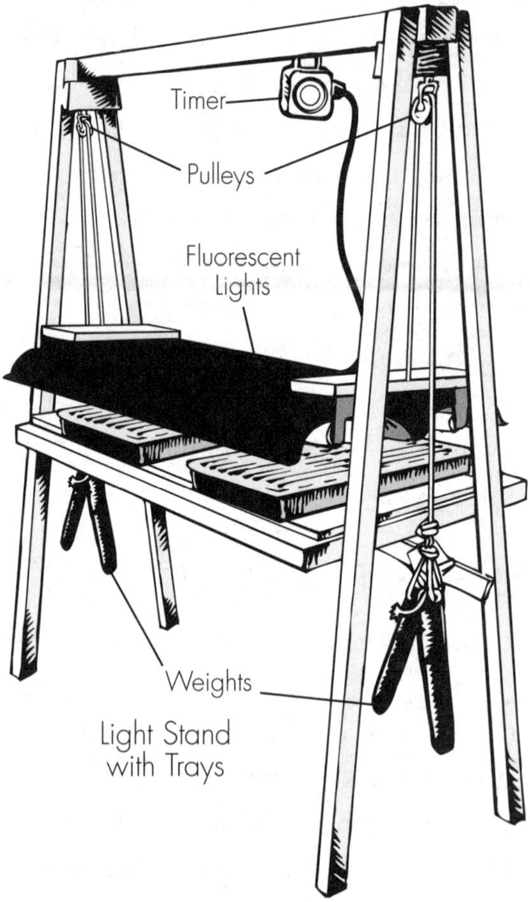

Light Stand with Trays

Most of the difficulties in starting seeds and growing transplants indoors stem from a lack of sufficient light. Growing plants in a bright window is seldom successful. Tall, spindly plants that fall over before you can get them planted are the result. The problem of insufficient light can be solved by growing your plants under lights. A greenhouse would be best, but if that is not an option for you, you probably have a place to set up an artificial light plant stand. The stand can be specially constructed for the purpose, or it can be a work bench or boards placed over saw horses. It should be at least 4 feet long and 2 feet wide to accommodate 4 standard 10-by-20-inch flats.

For the lights, you will need two, 2-tube, 40-watt fluorescent shop lights. Attach them side by side to a piece of 3/4-inch plywood or two 1-by-4s to make a fixture that will light the four 10-by-20-inch flats. Cool white fluorescent tubes are okay; plant lights are not necessary. To suspend the lights so that they can be raised and lowered as needed, hang chains on hooks from the ceiling, or construct a system of pulleys and weights using old sash weights or bricks for counterbalances. Keep the lights on for 18 hours out of each 24. Plugging the lights into a timer will simplify this task.

Although nearly any container will suffice, sow seeds (other than those of vines, which are difficult to transplant) in the 20-row, seed-starting inserts. Sow the seeds on the moistened soil mix, and cover them lightly. Caution: some extremely tiny seeds and seeds that need light to germinate cannot be covered. The seed packs provide this information, and the profiles in this book indicate seeds that need to be treated in this way. Enclose the container with clear plastic wrap to keep it from drying out, and make sure to label the rows so you can tell what you planted. Set the tray on the plant stand, and lower the lights to about 1 inch above the surface. This will provide all the heat and light needed. The temperature should be as close to 70 degrees Fahrenheit as you can keep it. You may not be able to use some spaces, such as an unheated garage, because of this temperature requirement.

Sow 3 or 4 seeds of vine crops in individual peat pots or peat pellets, then cover them with clear plastic wrap. Once the seedlings are up, thin to 1 plant in each. Clip the extras instead of pulling them to avoid damaging the remaining seedling.

## Transplanting Seedlings

When they are big enough to handle, transplant the seedlings into plastic cell-packs, the kind commercial growers use (these fit into flats, too), or

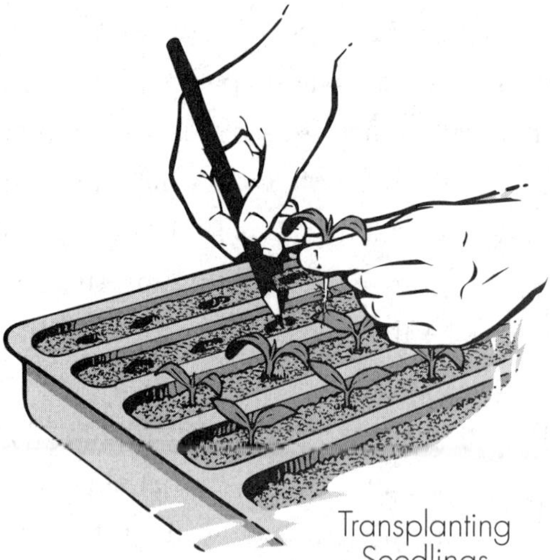

Transplanting Seedlings

into another convenient container. Keep the lights just above the plant tops, or move the plants into a cold frame or greenhouse until it is safe to set them in the garden. Apply liquid fertilizer at the recommended rate after the plants start to grow, and maintain temperatures in the range of 60 to 70 degrees Fahrenheit.

Harden off transplants grown indoors under lights by setting them in the containers outside for a few days, but be prepared to move them if unusually cold temperatures are predicted. (You may want to start the process by setting them outside during sunny days.) Exposure to the elements will harden them so they will more easily tolerate transplanting into the garden. Plants that are excessively hardened off, or allowed to harden off during the growing season, may not develop properly, sometimes blooming prematurely on tiny plants or remaining stunted all season. Set transplants—whether they are ones you have grown or ones you have purchased at a garden center—in well-prepared soil. If the soil is properly prepared, you can set the plants by hand without using any tools.

## Direct Seeding

Most vegetables can be seeded directly in the garden. Some do not take transplanting very well, and others start so easily and quickly from direct seeding that there is no advantage to starting them indoors. Work the soil to produce a fine seedbed. Mark out the rows, and stretch a string to keep the rows straight. The plants don't care, but anything worth doing is worth doing correctly. Prepare a shallow furrow along the string, and sow the seeds,

spaced as indicated on the seed pack. Cover them lightly with soil, and firm the soil with your hand or the back of a hoe held vertically. Some seeds such as lettuce will not germinate in the dark, so do not cover them. (Again, the seed packs should provide this information, and the profiles in this book will indicate plants with this requirement.) Sow them on the surface, and firm them down gently.

*To seed in beds*, run the rows across the beds, then run the string down the middle of the beds. Use a measuring stick to find the correct spacing between rows. I use an 8-foot furring stick marked every 6 inches. *To plant in hills*, sow several seeds in the same spot. Then sow several more seeds in another spot about 5 feet farther down the row. There is no need to make a hill of soil in each spot. Squash and pumpkins are planted with this method. *To broadcast seed*, scatter the seed evenly over a section of bed. This method is commonly used for seeding mustard, lettuce, or arugula.

## Buying Transplants

The easiest way to start a garden is to purchase transplants from a greenhouse, a garden center, or a mass merchandiser. Well-grown transplants are compact, 4 to 6 inches tall, and have about 6 fully developed leaves. Make sure the plants you buy have a good green color and have no pests on them. A reliable local outlet is the safest source for plants because it carries only varieties that grow in your area, and the plants are hardened off. In addition, the plants will be correctly labeled with the actual variety, and they will be free of insects or diseases. The managers know that you will come back to their center only if you are satisfied.

## Soil Preparation

Kill grasses and weeds that have started in the garden. Spade them over and fallow the garden, hoe them out, or kill them with herbicides. Apply Roundup®, which kills underground parts as well as tops, to perennial grasses such as quackgrass and Kentucky bluegrass. Roundup is deactivated as soon as it hits the ground or is absorbed by the weeds, so there is no danger to plants later on. Keep it off perennial garden plants or any other plants that you want to save, however.

Add as much organic matter as you can acquire, such as compost, well-rotted manure (aged a year or so), old plant tops, or leaves. Usually, about 2 inches evenly spread over the area is as much as a gardener can acquire or handle at one time. Spread a complete fertilizer such as 1 pound of 10-10-10 per 100 square feet of garden. To prepare rows, spade or till to at least a depth of 6 inches, and break up any lumps or clods. To prepare beds, double-dig to the depth of 2 garden spades, usually 12 to 18 inches, incorporating organic matter throughout. Rake the rows or each bed to level for planting.

# Planting

## When to Plant

The timing of planting depends on the kinds of plants and the average date of the last frost (also called the frost-free date) in your area. See pages 10–12 for these dates. Some vegetables are completely hardy and can stand winter weather. Perennial vegetables and herbs such as asparagus and thyme are in this category. Annual vegetables are classified as very hardy, frost-tolerant, tender, or hot weather. Very hardy varieties can stand a freeze, and they can be planted as soon as the ground can be worked in the spring. Seeds of some of these plants can be sown in the fall and will germinate in spring much earlier than the soil can be worked, giving them a tremendous head start. Frost-tolerant vegetables can stand light frost. They and the very hardy are cool-season crops that grow and develop best in cool weather. Some are intolerant of heat and deteriorate quickly when warm weather arrives. Tender vegetables do poorly in cool weather and are killed by a frost. Hot-weather kinds need warm soil and hot weather to do their best. They will not stand any freezing and are severely delayed by cool weather.

Here are examples of cool-season vegetables:

**VERY HARDY**

(Direct seed or plant 4 to 6 weeks before average date of last frost.)

| | | | |
|---|---|---|---|
| Asparagus | Cabbage | Lettuce | Rhubarb |
| Broccoli | Horseradish | Onion | Rutabaga |
| Brussels | Kale | Parsley | Spinach |
| Sprouts | Kohlrabi | PeaPotato | Turnip |

**FROST-TOLERANT**

(Direct seed or plant 2 to 3 weeks before average date of last frost.)

| | | | |
|---|---|---|---|
| Beet | Cauliflower | Chinese Cabbage | Parsnip |
| Carrot | Chard | Mustard | Radish |

Here are examples of warm-season vegetables:

**TENDER**

(Direct seed or plant on the average date of last frost.)

| | | |
|---|---|---|
| Bean | Summer Squash | Tomato |
| New Zealand Spinach | Sweet Corn | |

**HOT WEATHER**

(Direct seed or plant after the latest date of last frost.)

| | | | |
|---|---|---|---|
| Cucumber | Muskmelon | Pepper | Watermelon |
| Eggplant | Okra | Pumpkin | Winter Squash |

### How to Plant

For your method of planting, you may choose rows or hills. Plants may be set in rows, spaced evenly, or in hills, with several plants in one place at widely spaced intervals. Set transplants you grow or buy in well-prepared soil. If you have properly prepared the soil, you can set the plants without using any tools. Dig your hand into the soil, pull open a hole big enough for the ball of soil on the plant, and set the plant in the hole at the same depth it was growing. Push the soil back around the plant, and firm it down, using your thumb and forefingers to push the soil down next to the plant. Apply a transplant starter fertilizer in solution, and water the soil to settle it. If the soil was not well prepared, you will need a trowel to plant your vegetables. The process is the same, but it is slower.

## General Care

### Watering

Garden plants need about 1 inch of water per week. If rain does not fall, or if the plants begin to wilt, apply a measured inch of water. For a reliable way to determine when 1 inch has been applied with a sprinkler, set coffee cans in the garden, and run the water until there is 1 inch of water in each can. Do not water again until the plants begin to wilt. If you water with a soaker, dig down to see how far the water has gone; it should soak at least the top

6 inches of the soil. Many types of drip or trickle watering systems that are available to home gardeners are especially efficient for large gardens. Various kinds of emitters apply water exactly where the plants need it. What time of day is best to water? Water as the daytime temperature rises.

Measuring 1 inch of Water

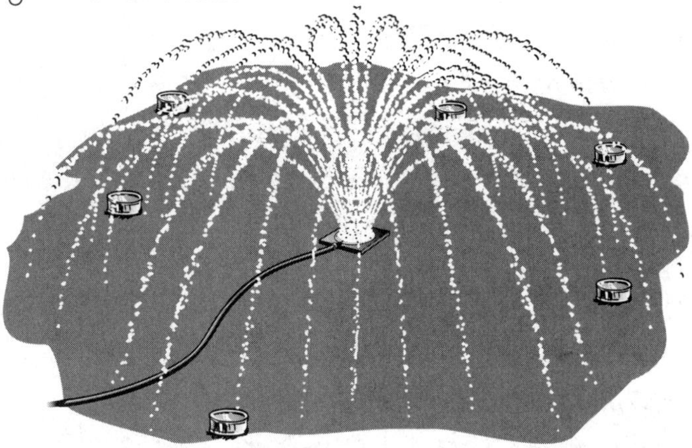

Container gardens need more frequent watering, maybe as often as twice every day in hot weather. Check the plants in the morning and again in the afternoon. Water the plants when they wilt and do not recover overnight. Thoroughly soak the soil in the container so that water runs out the drain holes. If the soil is allowed to dry out completely, it may be hard to rewet. Stage watering (applying a little water several times so that it stays in the container until the soil is once again wet) may be necessary to remedy the situation.

## MULCHING

Mulches help control weeds, conserve water, warm the soil in the spring and cool the soil in the summer, and keep the produce off the ground.

*Organic mulches* consist of plant residues, such as straw, hay, leaves, crushed corncobs, grass clippings, or compost. These materials also decompose over the season, adding needed organic matter to the soil and recycling the nutrients. Organic matter addition is the primary means of improving soil tilth (physical condition of the soil). The recommended application is 2 to 4 inches deep on weed-free soil. Since organic mulches tend to keep the soil cool, apply them after the soil has warmed sufficiently in spring and the plants are growing well. Later in the season, some plants benefit from the cooling effects of the mulch.

*Black plastic mulch* is beneficial in the spring for warming the soils. It also keeps weeds from germinating. Lay the mulch after preparing the soil for planting, and plant through holes cut in the mulch. In the fall, remove the black plastic mulch and dispose of it.

## Fertilizing

Side-dressing

Apply fertilizer according to soil test recommendations. Or if you did not have a soil test done, apply 1 pound of complete balanced fertilizer such as 10-10-10 per 100 square feet of garden. About midseason, after the plants have become well developed, making another application of fertilizer may be beneficial. Side-dress the plants with the same fertilizer at half the recommended rate, then water in thoroughly after application to wash fertilizer off the plants and to activate the fertilizer. Liquid fertilizers in solution can be applied according to the directions on the container.

## Insect and Disease Problems

Control insects as they appear. Specific pests of certain garden varieties are described under the profiles for the plants. If root maggots

## Suggested Controls of Common Vegetable Pests

| INSECTS | CONTROLS |
|---|---|
| Aphids, mites, thrips—tiny, slow-moving insects that affect shoot tips or foliage of most garden crops. | *Apply insecticidal soap. Pick off infested shoots.* |
| Bean leaf beetles—affect beans. | *Apply Sevin when damage (small holes eaten in leaves) is noticed.* |
| Beetles, cutworms, grasshoppers, leafhoppers—affect most crops. | *Apply Sevin, rotenone, or permethrin when insects are observed on the plants.* |
| Cabbage worms—green worms that affect all cole crops and related herbs eating holes in leaves. | *Apply* Bacillus thuringiensis *Kurstaki when white butterflies are seen in the garden.* |
| Colorado potato beetles—affect potatoes, tomatoes, eggplant. | *Apply* Bacillus thuringiensis *'San Diego'. Handpick from plants.* |
| Corn borers—affect sweet corn, tomatoes, peppers. | *Apply Sevin insecticide when damage (holes eaten in stems or in fruit) is noticed.* |
| Corn earworms—affect sweet corn. | *Apply Sevin insecticide when damage is noticed on tips of the ears.* |
| Cucumber beetles—affect vine crops. | *Cover plants with floating row covers until bloom begins. Apply Sevin insecticide.* |
| Earwigs—nocturnal insects with pincers on posterior end eat holes in leaves. | *Apply Sevin, rotenone, or permethrin when insects are observed on the plants or damage is noticed.* |
| Potato leafhoppers—affect potatoes, beans. | *Apply Sevin when damage (brown spots in leaves or brown dry leaf margins) is noticed or when leafhoppers are seen.* |
| Slugs—slimy, snail-like creatures eat holes in leaves or fruit of all crops. | *Remove mulches and debris. Pick slugs when seen. If damage is severe, apply metaldehyde bait.* |
| Soil insects, maggots—affect all crops by fly larvae damaging stems or roots. | *Cover rows with screen after sowing seed and until seedlings are sizable.* |
| Squash bugs—affect squash, pumpkins. | *Trap them under boards. Apply sabidilla.* |
| Squash vine borers—affect squash by shredding stems at soil line. | *Cover plants with floating row covers until bloom begins. Apply Sevin insecticide.* |
| Whiteflies—affect tomatoes, squash. | *Apply insecticidal soap when adults are seen in garden (clouds of tiny white insects scatter when the plants are disturbed).* |

*Insecticides are safe to use on food crops if you follow the directions on the label.* Be sure to wear the proper protection when mixing the materials, and keep the containers securely locked where children cannot get to them. Sevin® is a wettable powder that is not absorbed by plants. This chemical applied at the recommended rate breaks down in the time between application and harvest.

## Suggested Controls of Common Vegetable Diseases

| DISEASES | CONTROLS |
| --- | --- |
| Leaf spots, anthracnoses—affect most vegetable crops. | *Apply maneb, Bravo, or copper fungicide when noticed.* |
| Mildew—covers leaves late in the season with a white powdery fungus. | *Apply sulfur when noticed.* |
| Virus diseases—cause distortion of leaves and fruits. | *Grow only resistant varieties; avoid touching solanaceous crops after handling tobacco products. Rogue out affected plants.* |
| Wilts—cause plants to wilt and die because of fungus or bacterial diseases. | *Grow only resistant varieties.* |

These fungicides are labeled for use on vegetables: chlorothalonil—Bravo®, Terranil®, and others; copper—Bordeaux mixture, copper sulfate, many brand names; and maneb—many brand names. PCNB (Terraclor) is applied to soil or incorporated as soil is tilled.

have been a problem in the past and your previous crops have suffered damage, cover rows with screening or floating row covers after planting and leave them in place until plants are sizeable because fly larvae may damage roots or stems. Pick off shoots infested with a few aphids, and pick off Japanese beetles. Supply protection from cutworms by placing foil collars around individual plants. Cut 4-inch-wide strips of aluminum foil, and wrap the stems with them. Make sure to push the foil into the soil so that the cutworms can't get under it.

## Weed Control

Weeds have destroyed more gardens than any other problem. The difference between gardeners and the also-rans is their ability to keep weeds from taking over. If the garden is too big, or if the weed problem gets ahead of a new gardener, it is too easy to give up. Most who quit once are reluctant to try again, and that is a shame because each season becomes easier after weeds are controlled. There are fewer seeds and fewer weeds each year. Starting with a weed-free garden will be a big advantage in keeping it weed-free. As weeds germinate, hoe them out. They are easy to remove when they are small, but very difficult to keep under control after they have a chance to get established.

## Author's Caution

From time to time in this book, I recommend the use of pesticides. The use of such pest controls, however, must remain the choice of each individual gardener. It may not always be necessary to use pesticides to control insects or diseases. A particular pest or disease may not be harmful to your particular plants.

If pest control does become a problem, you should consider the use of alternative means. These include the use of resistant varieties, the use of botanical and microbial insecticides or soaps, encouraging predators and parasites, mechanical means such as screening, hand picking, and improving botanical practices.

If you do find it necessary to use traditional chemical pest controls, first consult your local authorities such as your extension service office for correct pest identification and control recommendations. Once you have decided to use a specific pest control product, you must read and follow label directions carefully.

## Organic Gardening

Organic gardening is nothing new, and the benefits of large amounts of good organic matter in the soil cannot be denied. All gardeners rely on many so-called organic methods. The difference is that organic gardeners are reluctant to use synthetic materials such as fertilizers or pesticides.

### Animal Pest Controls

Animals such as rabbits and birds are best controlled with mechanical barriers. Use fences to keep rabbits out. Netting over blueberry bushes or cherry trees will eliminate losses from birds. (See illustration on following page.)

Rabbit Fence

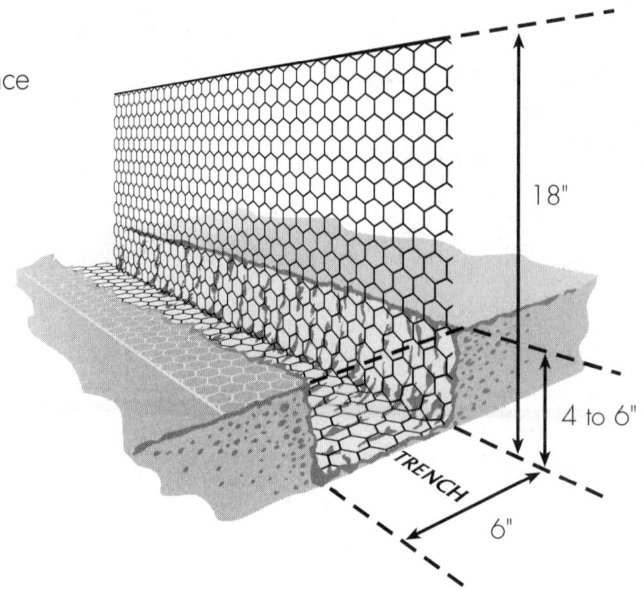


## Soil Preparation and Fertilization

Prepare the soil as you would for a regular vegetable garden (see page 68). Fertilizers may be derived from manures, cotton seed, other organic sources, greensand, rock phosphorus, and many other naturally occurring minerals.

## Soil Amendments

Abundant organic matter provides most of the needed soil amendments. Add sulfur to correct alkaline soil or you can add lime to correct acidic soil after a soil test is performed.

## Physical Controls

Use traps, baits, and attractants to lure insects from the garden. Handpicking insects or diseased leaves and quickly eliminating infected plants can protect the others from the problem. Companion plantings reduce the chances that pests will find the plants they need for food. Companion plantings include intercropping in which 2 crops are grown in the same space and plantings of several different varieties are grown next to each other to reduce insect problems. For example, radishes are often sown in the same rows as carrots. The quick-germinating radishes are up to mark the rows and are harvested about the time the carrots begin to sprout. Winter squash vines are sometimes grown in the sweet corn patch. The corn is harvested long before the squash plants cover the ground. This is more of an intensive gardening technique, but it may help reduce pests too. Some people think that planting chives or garlic in the rows of tomatoes will prevent attack by spider mites, or that planting tomatoes will protect asparagus from asparagus beetles. Try it and see if it works for you. I have grown onions next to tomatoes and have not had mite problems; of course, I never had mites in the tomatoes anyway. Marigolds can be grown to reduce the numbers of root knot nematodes in the soil and will protect susceptible plants grown later. Root knot nematodes are not common in the Midwest, however, and marigolds are magnets for spider mites.

## Biological Controls

Predators, parasites, and microbials are available to counter pest invasions. These organisms live off the pests and will keep pest populations to a tolerable level. If they entirely eliminated the pests, they would run out of food and move on. Lady bugs, several kinds of flies, wasps, nematodes, or diseases can be acquired from suppliers of these products. All of these methods are effective. The lack of pests in a garden, whether the gardener follows strict organic practices or not, may be due to naturally occurring beneficials doing what comes naturally. Encouraging these creatures by avoiding routine chemical applications often will keep pest injuries to a minimum.

## Insecticides

Many insecticides, including nicotine, pyrethrum, and piperonyl butoxide, are derived from various plants. Others are derived from naturally occurring toxins; *Bacillus thuringiensis* Kurstaki is an example. These materials are used successfully by organic gardeners and by other gardeners too.

## Others

Putting screens and row covers over susceptible plants prevents insect damage, such as leaf miners attacking Swiss chard or cucumber beetles feeding on vine crops. Screens can be made out of common screen wire bent or folded to fit plants, or cheesecloth can be stretched over hoops to cover plants. Floating row covers are mats of spun-bound polypropylene that are very light, needing no supports, so they do not smash the plants under them. Squash vine borer damage can be prevented with mesh tents over the plants, but the covers will eliminate bees as well. You will have to pollinate the plants by hand if fruit is to develop; that involves collecting pollen from the male flowers and applying it to the female flowers. This extra effort is a good tradeoff for freedom from this damaging insect.

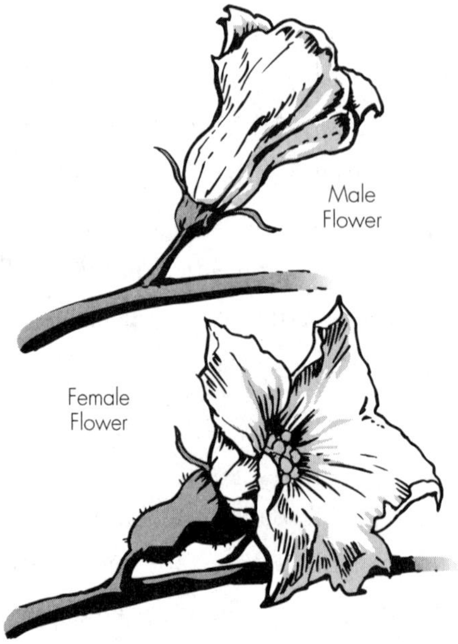


Male and Female Flowers on the Same Vine

## Preventive Measures

Planting insect- and disease-resistant varieties is a simple way to eliminate some pest problems. Being careful about where you obtain your plants is another way to prevent introduction of many kinds of pests.

## Site Location

Situating a garden where it is less likely to be exposed to pests and where it gets the optimum growing conditions will go a long way toward achieving success with organic gardening. Set it next to a community garden or a poorly kept backyard garden, and it will be next to impossible to control invasions by pests. Some avid organic gardeners have relocated to other parts of the country where there are no other gardeners. I know of one who moved to a remote part of northern Wisconsin for just that reason. If moving to a remote location is out of the question for you, site the garden hundreds of feet away from other gardens.

## Identifying Problems

Organic gardening requires great familiarity with pests and quick identification of a problem to limit damage. Knowledge of insects and their life cycles and diseases affecting each crop gives you an advantage in attacking each at its weak point.

## Cultural Practices

Reduce many pest problems by: proper timing of planting; keeping the plants vigorously growing; providing the optimum conditions for the plants; keeping foliage dry; and not working in the garden when the foliage is wet. Some thought is necessary to take advantage of the many cultural details that make organic gardening successful.

## Sanitation

The most important cultural practice for any kind of gardening is maintaining a sanitary garden. In this case, sanitation refers not to keeping it clean but to keeping out any sources of contamination. Do not bring insect-infested or diseased plants into the garden. Do not bring in soil with weed seeds or soil-borne diseases. Collect organic matter in a compost pile, and allow it to heat before using the material in the garden.

Now let's get into the vegetable garden!

# ARUGULA

***Eruca vesicaria* var. *sativa***

Looking for something to add zip to your salads? Try arugula, a relative of mustard and cabbage that has a biting, pungent taste, somewhat like horseradish. It is also known as roquette, rocket salad, and pepper. Like all the members of the cabbage family, arugula is a hardy, cool-weather crop; it bolts (sends up a seed stalk) and becomes bitter when warm daily temperatures arrive.

## When to Plant

Plant arugula early, and harvest it before hot weather arrives. Unless you want lots of arugula at one time, however, make several seedings to spread out the harvest. A little goes a long way, and a few plants are enough for most gardens. Seed is available in early spring, and you can order it from catalogs as well as find it in the garden center. Sow seed directly in the garden as early as the soil can be worked. Some gardeners prepare the soil in the fall and broadcast the seed over the frozen ground. To have the earliest production, start with transplants. Indoors, sow the earliest seed for arugula about 2 months before the frost-free date (the average date of last frost). Grow the plants under lights about 18 hours per day or in the greenhouse, and transplant them into the garden when they are large enough to handle, usually about 3 or 4 weeks before the frost-free date. Since arugula will finish producing edible leaves by midsummer and the harvest will be complete, plan to replace it with a fall crop. Sow seed directly in the garden or sow seed indoors about August 10; then set the seedlings in the garden about August 31. Arugula can stand a freeze, and mild fall weather may last until Thanksgiving. Gardeners in the milder parts of the Midwest who sow arugula in late fall will have a crop very early the next spring if they carefully mulch the small seedlings so that they can survive the winter.

## Where to Plant

Arugula prefers a location in full sun (8 to 10 hours will suffice). If you want to extend its production into the hot summer months, plant it in partial shade (filtered sun all day or shade part of the day) to keep it cooler. The plants need lots of water for vigorous growth, but they require excellent drainage. Their roots cannot stand soggy soils.

## How to Plant

Apply a complete garden fertilizer, such as 10-10-10, at the rate of $1^1/_2$ pounds per 100 square feet of garden. Then spade or rototill the garden. (See "Soil Preparation" in the introduction to the vegetable garden.) For transplants, space them 6 inches apart in beds. (You will have 6 to 8 plants across a standard 48-inch bed.) Set the plants at the same depth they were growing. For direct seeding, sow arugula in rows 6 inches apart across the bed, or broadcast the seed. Thin seedlings to 4 to 6 inches in each direction. You can recognize arugula seedlings because they will be in rows and all look the same; weeds will be randomly spaced, and all will look different.

## Care and Maintenance

Water as needed to keep the plants growing; they require about 1 inch of water per week. Hoe or pull weeds to control them while the plants are small. Be careful as you weed because arugula plants are shallowly rooted and easily uprooted. Watch out for cabbage worms and root maggots that will attack arugula. (See the pest control chart in the introduction to the vegetable garden.)

### Additional Information

Harvest arugula by snipping off outer leaves as soon as they are large enough to use, about 6 inches long. When the entire plants are large enough to harvest, cut every other one, leaving more room for the others. As soon as the plants begin to bolt, harvest all that remain before they are spoiled, and pull up the plants. For variety, grow arugula with other cool-season greens, such as spinach, lettuce, and mustard.

# Asparagus

***Asparagus officinalis***

Asparagus is a perennial garden vegetable that is well adapted to the Midwest climate. Its tender spears, which arise from the crowns in the spring, make it an appetizing product of the home garden. Asparagus is native to Europe and Asia where it has been cultivated for more than 2,000 years. The earliest settlers brought it to America, and abandoned plantings can still be found around old farmsteads and in volunteer patches along roadsides and railroad rights-of-way.

## When to Plant

Planning is essential for these plants because a well-prepared asparagus bed can last a lifetime. The asparagus planting will take a few years to get into full production, so you will not want to move the bed around. Plant asparagus as soon as the ground can be worked in the spring. Asparagus plants consist of a crown with many dormant buds and several fleshy roots. One-year-old crowns are preferred, but 2- and 3-year-old crowns are available. They are more expensive, but produce earlier.

## Where to Plant

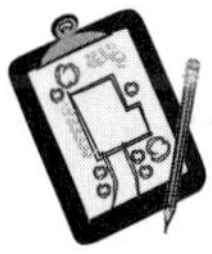

Position the bed in a full-sun (8 to 10 hours will suffice) location away from trees or shrubs that may send roots into the bed. A poorly drained bed will deteriorate, and the plants will rot and eventually die out. Asparagus prefers sandy soil, which is generally better drained, warms up earlier in spring, and makes harvesting easier. Any well-prepared and well-drained soil will suffice, however.

## How to Plant

Prepare the soil by spading it over and incorporating organic matter. (See "Soil Preparation" in the introduction to the vegetable garden.) Open a trench 6 inches deep and 15 inches wide, the length of the bed. Set the plants in the trench about 1 foot apart with the buds pointing up, then spread the roots in a uniform pattern around each crown. Replace 2 inches of the soil from the trench over the crowns, and water the plants thoroughly to settle the soil. Reserve the remaining soil to gradually cover the crowns as the plants grow during their first year; all of the soil is to be used in the first year.

## Care and Maintenance

In the first year, the plants will produce weak, spindly growth. As the root system develops, the spears will become larger each year, but the spears are not ready for harvesting until the *third* season. As soon as you complete the harvest, apply a complete garden fertilizer, such as 10-10-10, at the rate of 2 to 3 pounds per 100 square feet of bed. The nitrogen stimulates the growth of the ferns that replenish the roots for the next year. Water the plants to provide about 1 inch per week during the season. Weed control is the most challenging part of growing any perennial plant, and asparagus is no different. Weeds compete with the asparagus for water and nutrients and make harvesting difficult. Because the bed is always occupied, there is no good time to get rid of the weeds without the chance of damaging the plants. Hoe or pull weeds as they appear, remove grasses with Fusilade® or Take-Away®, and use 2,4-D Amine® to defeat broadleaf weeds. After they are clean, keep the beds that way by applying Treflan® to prevent germination of weed seeds. Pests pose another problem. Asparagus beetles can destroy the ferns or damage spears as they emerge. Control them by handpicking, or spray with Sevin, Malathion®, or rotenone if populations exceed 5 to 10 adults per 100 crowns during harvest. You must wait 24 hours after treatment before resuming the harvest and be sure to carefully wash all asparagus. Following harvest, treat the ferns if you notice 1 or more beetles per plant. (See the pest control chart in the introduction to the vegetable garden.) No serious diseases affect asparagus.

### Additional Information

Harvest asparagus spears beginning in the third season, and limit harvesting to 3 weeks after the start of harvest. The following year and thereafter, harvest spears from the time they appear in spring until late May or June. Cut the spears when they are 6 to 8 inches long; discontinue harvesting when spears become noticeably smaller. Europeans and recent immigrants to the U.S. prefer blanched asparagus. They hill the plants with sand carefully packed over the developing spears. When spears begin to emerge, cracks appear in the sand, and they pull back the sand to reveal the white spears. After they cut the spears, they replace the sand and pack it down again. They often peel the spears to remove any fiber and make them very tender additions to a meal.

## VARIETIES

Asparagus plants are either male or female. The female plants produce more but smaller spears than the male plants. The female plants produce seeds, an activity that takes energy that could be stored up in the plants for better production the next year. Male plants direct the energy into making spears. The old-line varieties such as 'Waltham' or the 'Washingtons—Mary and Martha'—are still available but are mixed male and female plants. They are not nearly as productive as the newer kinds. Recent introductions are either mostly male or all male. Syn 53, Syn 4-362, UC-157, Viking KBC, Jersey Knight, Jersey Prince, and Jersey Giant are vastly improved varieties derived from a selection that produces only male plants. Try to plant the latest introductions; the bed will last a long time, so it pays to plant the very best.

| Varieties | Comments |
|---|---|
| Jersey Giant | Hybrid, good yield, mostly male. |
| Jersey Knight | Good producer, disease resistant, mostly male. |
| Jersey Prince | Mostly male, cold tolerant, hybrid. |
| Syn 4-362 | Mostly male, hybrid, large spears. |
| Syn 53 | Newer, mostly male, hybrid. |
| UC-157 | Large yield, male, hybrid. |
| Viking KBC | Hybrid, mostly male, good producer. |

# Crunchy Almond Asparagus

*Wash and cut 1 pound fresh asparagus into ¾-inch pieces. Cook in 1 cup lightly salted water until tender-crisp. Drain asparagus, reserving liquid. Combine 2 cups seasoned dressing mix and 8 ounces shredded Cheddar cheese; set aside. Combine 1 can cream of chicken soup (10½ ounces), reserved liquid and asparagus. Layer half of crumb mixture in a buttered 2 quart casserole. Top with half of asparagus. Repeat. Toss ½ cup chopped almonds with 1 tablespoon melted butter; sprinkle over casserole. Bake at 350 degrees for 30 to 35 minutes.*

# Bean

***Phaseolus vulgaris***

Beans may be the most diverse garden vegetables, ranking second only to tomatoes in popularity. Common beans are probably native to South America and were grown there for centuries before Europeans began growing them. All beans are members of the legume family, *Leguminosae,* which can extract and use nitrogen from the air. Most beans are grown for their seeds and pods. The tender pods, which are used before the seeds mature, are called snap beans because the pods snap easily when bent. Snap beans may be green or yellow (wax beans). Shell beans, such as limas, are harvested before maturity, and the seeds are removed, or shelled. Dry beans are grown for the seeds, which are allowed to mature before harvest and are shelled from the pods for use. Bean plants may be either bush types or runners. The runners are called pole beans; they may be allowed to vine along the ground, but gardeners usually grow them on supports.

## When to Plant

Sow seeds about 2 weeks before the latest date of last frost; these tender plants cannot tolerate a freeze. Planting seeds every 3 weeks until the beginning of August will assure a continuous supply of fresh snap beans.

## Where to Plant

A location with at least 6 hours of sunlight a day and well-drained soil will produce healthy beans for you. Giving them a full-sun location (8 to 10 hours will suffice) will make them even happier. Beneficial bacteria are necessary for nitrogen fixation, and if beans have never been grown in the garden, you may need to add beneficial bacteria to the soil. Garden stores or garden catalogs list them as legume inoculants.

## How to Plant

Prepare the soil for planting. (See "Soil Preparation" in the introduction to the vegetable garden.) Sow seeds of **bush beans** 2 to 3 inches apart, and cover them with 1 inch of soil. Sow seeds of **pole beans** 6 inches apart in rows along a fence or trellis, or sow them in hills of 6 seeds around poles set 3 feet apart; then cover the seeds with 1 inch of soil. You may need to help pole beans get started on their supports—they twine counterclockwise. I grow them up wooden furring strips tied at the top to make a teepee, or you may prefer to drive poles securely into the ground in each hill. Where soil insects have been troublesome—damaging roots or stems before they emerge—you may have to apply a soil insecticide, such as Diazinon, to protect the seeds as they germinate. Mix Diazinon in water according to label directions, and use it as a drench after sowing the seeds. Beans may not germinate well if they are kept too wet so I cannot overemphasize the importance of good drainage. Moisten them at planting time but do not keep them constantly soaked.

## Care and Maintenance

Beans require little care except regular weeding and adequate water if the weather is dry. The plants need about 1 inch of water per week. Pests may affect the plantings, but rotating the bean plantings to a different place in the garden each year reduces pest problems. Applying Sevin insecticide will control numerous bean leaf beetles, which will eat holes in the leaves. Planting disease-resistant varieties will go a long way toward producing a good bean crop. To avoid spreading disease, do not work in the beans when they are wet. Diseases include bean mosaic disease (affected plants turn yellowish green and do not produce beans) and bacterial blight, evidenced by brown spots on the leaves or water-soaked spots on the pods. (See the pest control chart in the introduction to the vegetable garden.)

### Additional Information

Pole beans are much easier to harvest than bush beans because they are up in the air and no bending over is involved. They also produce longer from a single seeding than the bush types. In exceptionally hot weather, pollination may be poor, resulting in few beans. The pollen fails to grow a pollen tube through the pistil and the unfertilized ova fail to grow. Don't be alarmed, however; production will resume when the weather moderates. Harvest snap beans when the pods are firm and fully elongated, but before the seeds begin to swell. Pick beans regularly to keep the plants producing. Expect to be able to harvest bush beans 2 or 3 times, and then discard the planting. Pick pole beans all season; they will continue to produce if kept picked clean. Pick lima beans when the seeds are tender, green, and fully developed. If you wait until they are overly ripe, they will be tough and mealy. Limas can be left to mature and harvested as dry beans, although dry beans are rarely grown in home gardens because they are so inexpensive to buy. If you do choose to grow them, harvest them after the pods dry and begin to split open. Pull up mature plants, and hang them in a dry place until the pods split.

## VARIETIES

| Varieties | Days to Maturity | Comments |
|---|---|---|
| **Dry** | | |
| Dark Red Kidney | 95 days | Use in soup, chili. |
| Great Northern | 90 days | Half runner, white. |
| Pinto | 90 days | Standard in Mexican cuisine, half runner |
| White Kidney | 90 days | Bush, white, kidney-shaped beans. |
| **Green Bush** | | |
| Blue Lake | 58 days | Mosaic resistant. |
| Bush Kentucky Wonder | 57 days | Long, flat pods. |
| Contender | 50 days | Mosaic resistant. |
| Derby | 57 days | AAS. |
| Jade | 53 days | Long, slender pods. |
| Labrador | 57 days | Best in cooler climates. |
| Tendercrop | 55 days | Mosaic resistant. |
| Tendergreen Improved | 54 days | Mosaic resistant. |
| Topcrop | 50 days | Meaty. |
| **Lima Bush, Large Seeded** | | |
| Fordhook 242 | 75 days | AAS. |
| **Lima Bush, Small Seeded** | | |
| Baby Fordhook | 70 days | Small beans. |
| Eastland | 70 days | Heavy yield. |
| Henderson | 65 days | Flat pods. |
| Jackson Wonder | 65 days | Purple spots. |
| Thorogreen | 66 days | Tall plants. |
| **Lima Pole** | | |
| King of the Garden | 88 days | Tasty. |
| Prizetaker | 90 days | Giant seeds. |
| Sieva | 72 days | Baby lima. |

## VARIETIES

| Varieties | Days to Maturity | Comments |
|---|---|---|
| **Pole** | | |
| Blue Lake | 65 days | Mosaic resistant. |
| Kentucky Blue | 65 days | AAS; heavy producer, long season. |
| Kentucky Wonder | 65 days | Good flavor. |
| Kentucky Wonder Wax | 68 days | Yellow. |
| Purple Pod | 65 days | Heavy crop. |
| Romano | 60 days | Flat pods. |
| Scarlet Runner | 70 days | Novelty. |
| **Purple Bush** | | |
| Royalty | 55 days | Original purple bush beans. |
| **Romano** | | |
| Bush Romano | 56 days | Delicious broad, flat pods. |
| Jumbo | 55 days | Big Italian type. |
| Roma II | 53 days | Broad, flat pods. |
| Romano 942 | 57 days | Hybrid. |
| Wax Romano | 59 days | Yellow. |
| **Wax Bush** | | |
| Cherokee Wax | 50 days | Mosaic resistant. |
| Goldcrop | 54 days | AAS. |
| Golden Wax | 50 days | Stringless. |
| Goldkist | 56 days | Rust resistant. |
| Pencilpod Wax | 58 days | Round, pencil-like pods. |
| Slender Wax | 55 days | Early coloring. |

# Succotash

*Give this down-to-earth recipe a try when your vegetables are plentiful in your garden. Combine 2 cups shelled fresh lima beans and salt to taste with just enough water to cover in a saucepan. Simmer for 15 to 20 minutes or until the lima beans are tender, stirring occasionally.*

*Stir in 2 cups fresh corn kernels, chopped onion to taste, and chopped red and green bell peppers to taste. Simmer for 15 minutes or until most of the liquid has evaporated, stirring occasionally. Stir in 1/3 cup milk, 1 tablespoon butter, 1/2 teaspoon salt and black pepper to taste. Simmer just until heated through, stirring occasionally.*

# BEET

***Beta vulgaris***

Garden beets are closely related to sugar beets and to Swiss chard. All are the same species and are members of the goosefoot family. Beets originated in the maritime regions of Europe, and gardeners hybridized them in Germany and England in the middle of the sixteenth century. Beets are the main ingredients in borscht, but that is certainly not the only way to enjoy them. People love beets both for their globe-shaped roots and their leafy tops.

## When to Plant

Because beets will stand a frost, you may sow them 1 month before the frost-free date (the average date of last frost). Make successive plantings at 20-day intervals until midsummer to have a continuous supply of fresh beets.

## Where to Plant

These root crops require well-prepared loamy soil. Beets do best in a soil that is neutral to alkaline, which is common in the Midwest. (Remember that a pH of 7.0 is neutral; above 7.0, the soil is alkaline; below 7.0, the soil is acidic.) If soil tests point to acidic soil, add lime. *Do not* apply lime or gypsum to garden soils unless they have been tested to determine whether they need the added calcium. The soil should also have a high potassium level, essential for good root development. Drainage is important, especially if you desire to start the plants early, so that the soil is dry enough to work. Plant beets in a full-sun location (8 to 10 hours will suffice), and they will reward you with a full crop.

## How to Plant

Apply a complete garden fertilizer, such as 10-10-10, at a rate of 1½ pounds per 100 square feet of garden. Work the soil into a fine seedbed (make sure that the soil is finely broken up; see "Soil Preparation" in the introduction to the vegetable garden). Poor germination will result from soil that is not well prepared. In rows, sow beet seeds 1 inch apart, and allow 12 to 15 inches between rows. In a raised bed, sow the rows 8 to 10 inches apart across the bed. Cover the seeds with ½ inch of fine soil. For summer seedings, place a board over each row to keep the soil from drying or from being compacted by pounding rain. Check twice a day to see whether the seedlings have begun to emerge, and remove the board as soon as you notice them. Beet seeds are actually dried-up fruits; each contains 2 or more seeds, so don't plant them too close together. When the seedlings are large enough to handle, thin them to 1 to 3 inches apart. You can recognize the beet seedlings because they will appear in rows and all look the same; weed seedlings will appear at a random spacing, and all will look different. If you wait until the seedlings are about 3 inches tall, you can cook them as greens.

## Care and Maintenance

These plants require little care. Hoe or pull the weeds so that they don't compete with the beets for water and nutrients. If no rain falls for 7 to 10 days, apply 1 inch of water; beets that develop in dry weather will be fibrous and woody. Pests and diseases may affect the plantings. If you want to use the tops, protect them from leaf miners with Diazinon, or cover the plants with netting or row covers. Prevent leaf spot diseases by applying maneb. Soil-borne maggots may damage the roots. If they may pose a problem, mix Diazinon in water according to label directions, and apply it to the furrows as you plant the seeds. (See the pest control chart in the introduction to the vegetable garden.)

### Additional Information

Red beets are notorious for "bleeding" all over the counter and sink. The yellow and white varieties don't have this problem. Harvest tops when they are 6 inches high, and use them as you would use spinach. Harvest roots when they are 1½ to 2 inches in size. Beets allowed to grow more than 3 inches in diameter will be tough and woody. Dig late-season beets, and store them in pits of sand or in boxes of sand in a cool place, such as a garage. Or store them in plastic bags with air holes. Keep them at a temperature just above freezing; don't let them freeze.

## VARIETIES

The old standby varieties are open pollinated (inbred). Inbred varieties are not necessarily inferior, and they include a recent AAS winner. More recent varieties include hybrids, which are not necessarily better, just newer (and costlier).

| Varieties | Days to Maturity | Comments |
|---|---|---|
| **Hybrid** | | |
| Avenger | 57 days | Greens. |
| Big Red | 55 days | Late season. |
| Gladiator | 48 days | Good for canning. |
| Pacemaker | 50 days | Early. |
| Red Ace | 53 days | Good in hot weather. |
| **Inbred** | | |
| Crosby's Egyptian | 56 days | Uniform, sweet, dark red. |
| Detroit Dark Red | 58 days | Tender. |
| Early Wonder | 52 days | Flattened. |
| Ruby Queen | 60 days | Top quality. AAS. |
| Sangria | 56 days | Keeps shape even when crowded. |
| Sweetheart | 58 days | Tops good for greens. |
| **Specialty** | | |
| Bull's Blood | 35 days | Red tops. |
| | 55 days | Roots. |
| Burpee's Golden | 55 days | Yellow. |
| Cylindra | 60 days | Long, cylindrical. |
| Green Top Bunching | 65 days | Superior tops for greens. |
| Little Ball | 50 days | 1½ inches at maturity. |

# Harvard Beets

*Cook and drain 3 medium-size beets; reserve ⅓ cup liquid. Peel and slice beets. In medium saucepan, combine 2 tablespoons sugar, 1 tablespoon cornstarch, and ¼ teaspoon salt. Stir in reserved beet liquid, ¼ cup vinegar, and 2 tablespoons butter. Heat and stir until mixture thickens. Add sliced beets; heat through.*

# Broccoli

***Brassica oleracea* var. *botrytis***

Broccoli is a member of the mustard family. It and its close relatives are different varieties of *Brassica oleraceae,* commonly called the cole crops. Wild *Brassica oleraceae* grows along the seacoasts of Europe from Denmark to France, and in other locations from Greece to Great Britain. Although it has been cultivated for 5,000 years, broccoli was developed from other cole crops as a specific crop quite late and has been popular in this country only since the 1930s. This vegetable, grown for its compact cluster of flower buds or head, is picked before the flower buds begin to open. Secondary heads that develop in the leaf axils (between the bases of the leaves and the stem) can be harvested for several weeks after the central head is cut.

## When to Plant

This cool-weather crop can stand a freeze. For best results, plant broccoli early and harvest it before hot weather arrives. Sow seed directly in the garden as early as the soil can be worked. For the earliest production, however, start with transplants. Sow seed indoors about 8 weeks before the frost-free date (average date of last frost), and grow the plants under lights or in the greenhouse. Transplant them into the garden about 3 weeks before the frost-free date. Transplants are usually available from garden centers about that time as well. If you choose not to grow your own, make sure that the plants you buy have a good green color, are short and compact, and have no pests on them. A reliable local outlet is the safest source for quality plants. Since the broccoli will be harvested and out of the garden by midsummer, plan to replace it with a second crop. For a fall crop, sow seeds indoors about July 1, then set the seedlings in the garden about August 10. In mild fall weather broccoli may last until Thanksgiving. We have picked broccoli in our garden as late as December.

## Where to Plant

Broccoli prefers full sun (8 to 10 hours will suffice). It will produce well in partial shade (filtered sun all day or shade part of the day), but the heads will be smaller.

## How to Plant

Apply a complete garden fertilizer, such as 10-10-10, at a rate of 11/2 pounds per 100 square feet of garden. Spade or rototill the garden. (See "Soil Preparation" in the introduction to the vegetable garden.) In rows, space the transplants about 18 inches apart, with 36 inches between rows. In a bed, space the plants 16 to 18 inches apart, which will allow 2 or 3 plants across a 48-inch bed. Set the plants at the same depth they were growing. If root maggots have been a problem in the past and your previous crops have suffered damage, cover rows with screening or floating row covers after planting and leave them in place until plants are sizeable, because fly larvae may damage roots or stems.

## Care and Maintenance

Broccoli requires very little care to produce a crop. For the best-quality broccoli, water as necessary to keep the plants vigorous and growing; they need about 1 inch of water per week. Hardened-off plants (those that have been stunted by poor care) will often develop buttons which are useless, tiny heads on the seedling plants. Side-dress them with a complete fertilizer when the plants are about half grown, 10 to 12 inches tall. Pests and diseases may pose a problem. Prevent infestation of cabbage worms with *B.t.* (*Bacillus thuringiensis* Kurstaki). Apply maneb to control leaf spot diseases when the first symptoms appear. Eliminate black rot and blackleg diseases by planting disease-resistant varieties and by rotating the *Brassica* crops (cabbage, collards, Brussels sprouts, broccoli, Chinese cabbage, etc.) to other areas of the garden each year. Use the fungicide PCNB (Terraclor®) in the transplant water to prevent clubroot disease—swollen clublike roots—if it has been troublesome in the past. (See the pest control chart in the introduction to the vegetable garden.) Sometimes birds, especially sparrows, will resort to picking the flowers from broccoli to obtain water in hot, dry weather. Providing an alternative water source or protecting the plants with row covers may be necessary to save your vegetables.

### Additional Information

Harvest the heads with a sharp knife, leaving about 6 inches of stem attached, while they are still compact and before any of the flower buds open. Allow side shoots to develop for continuous production. Eventually, the size of the lateral shoots decreases, and they are not worth harvesting.

Flowers on broccoli heads continue to develop after they are picked, so keep them in the refrigerator and use them as soon as possible because they are unusable after the flowers start to open (they are poor looking and poor tasting, and they have poor texture).

## VARIETIES

| Varieties | Days to Maturity | Comments |
|---|---|---|
| **Hybrids** | | |
| Arcadia | 65 days | Fall. |
| Cruiser | 58 days | Drought tolerant. |
| Green Comet | 55 days | Early producing,heat tolerant, good spring or fall. AAS. |
| Green Goliath | 55 days | 12-inch heads. |
| Packman | 55 days | Summer or fall. |
| Premium Crop | 65 days | Good extended harvest. |
| **Novelty** | | |
| Purple Sprouting | 85 days | Very tender purple heads. |
| Romanesque | 75 days | Spiraling chartreuse heads. |
| **Open Pollinated** | | |
| Waltham 29 | 75 days | Best for fall production. |

# Broccoli Delight

*Sauté 2 chopped onions in 1/3 cup butter in large saucepan. Add 2 cups cooked rice, 1/2 cup grated Cheddar cheese, 1 cup mushroom soup, and 2 pounds chopped broccoli. Pour into a two quart greased casserole dish. Bake uncovered for 40-45 minutes at 350 degrees.*

# Brussels Sprouts

***Brassica oleracea* var. *gemmifera***

Named for the city in Belgium where they first attained popularity, Brussels sprouts have been grown there since the early 1300s. Gardeners usually refer to them as a cole crop. Coles are members of the mustard, or *Cruciferae,* family. They are all varieties in the same genus, *Brassica*. Brussels sprouts are grown for the cabbagelike buds that develop around the stems at the bases of the leaves.

## When to Plant

This cool-weather crop takes a long time to mature. Plants set out in late spring or early summer won't be ready to harvest until fall. Sow seed indoors about 1 month before the frost-free date (average date of last frost), grow the plants under lights or in the greenhouse, and transplant them into the garden in June. Transplants are usually available from garden centers about that time as well. If you choose to buy them rather than grow your own, make sure the transplants are vigorous. Hardened-off transplants that have been in the containers too long will not develop properly.

## Where to Plant

Plant Brussels sprouts in a location that receives full sun (8 to 10 hours will suffice). Plants in shade will be weak and may fall over; the sprouts will be smaller and more widely spaced on the stems. Any well-drained garden soil is satisfactory.

## How to Plant

Apply a complete garden fertilizer, such as 10-10-10, at a rate of $1\frac{1}{2}$ pounds per 100 square feet of garden. Spade or rototill the garden. (See "Soil Preparation" in the introduction to the vegetable garden.) In rows, space the transplants about 18 inches apart, with 36 inches between rows. In beds, space the plants 16 to 18 inches apart, which will allow 2 or 3 plants across the bed. Set the plants at the same depth they were growing. If root maggots have been a problem in the past and your previous crops have suffered damage, cover rows with screening or floating row covers after planting and leave them in place until plants are sizeable, because fly larvae may damage roots or stems.

## Care and Maintenance

With such a lengthy time to maturity, Brussels sprouts require careful attention. Apply sufficient water to keep the plants growing throughout the summer; they require about 1 inch of water per week. Sidedress the plants with a complete fertilizer when they are about 1 foot tall. Sprouts develop in the leaf axils starting at the bottom of the plant, and many growers remove the leaves a few at a time as the sprouts develop. The thought is that the sprouts will have a better chance of developing if there are no leaves to interfere; this may or may not be true. In any case, healthy, full-sized leaves must be left at the top of the stem to provide nutrients for the plant. Without leaves, the plant will cease growing. When the plants have developed sufficient height and enough leaves for a good crop, many growers pinch out the growing tip so that the energy goes into the sprouts instead of leaf production. The height depends on the length of the season: in the southern parts of the Midwest, 4 feet may be the right height; in the northern parts, it may be 2 feet unless they got a good early start. If all the buds have been set that will develop before the season ends, pinch out the tip. Disease and pest control are important parts of care. Prevent infestation of cabbage worms with *B.t.* (*Bacillus thuringiensis* Kurstaki). Apply maneb to control leaf spot diseases when the first symptoms appear. Eliminate black rot and blackleg diseases by planting disease-resistant varieties and by rotating the *Brassica* crops (cabbage, collards, Brussels sprouts, broccoli, Chinese cabbage, etc.) to other areas of the garden each year. Use PCNB (Terraclor) in the transplant water to prevent clubroot. (See the pest control chart in the introduction to the vegetable garden.)

### Additional Information

Harvest the sprouts after the first frost. You may regret harvesting sprouts in hot weather because they may be bitter. Pick or cut the sprouts as they attain full size, 1½ to 2 inches in diameter. There is no need to pick all the sprouts at one time; you can store them on the plants until you need them. These very cold-hardy plants can stand a freeze, and Brussels sprouts can last all winter if the weather is mild or when there is sufficient snow to cover them.

## VARIETIES

| Varieties | Days to Maturity | Comments |
|---|---|---|
| **Novelty** | | |
| Rubine | 105 days | Produces red sprouts, but not as productive as green types. |
| **Standard** | | |
| Jade Cross E | 90 days | Large sprouts, easy to harvest. |
| Long Island Improved | 90 days | Open-pollinated, old-time variety. |
| Oliver | 90 days | Easy picking. |
| Prince Marvel | 90 days | Sweet sprouts. |
| Royal Marvel | 85 days | Productive; tight sprouts. |
| Valiant | 90 days | Sprouts uniform, smooth. |

# Brussels Sprouts Bake

*Preheat oven to 425 degrees. Trim and wash 1½ pounds Brussels sprouts. Bring 6 cups water with 1 teaspoon salt to a boil in a large pot; add the sprouts, cover, and cook for 10 minutes over low heat. Drain and rinse under cold water. Place sprouts in a large, prepared casserole dish; set aside. In a separate bowl, beat 3 eggs with ½ cup milk, a pinch of nutmeg, and salt and pepper to taste. Pour mixture over sprouts. Sprinkle with 4 ounces grated Gouda cheese and 2 tablespoons bacon bits. Cover with aluminum foil and bake for 15 minutes. Remove foil and cook an additional 10 minutes. Serve with crusty bread.*

# Parmesan Brussels Sprouts

*Cook 1 pound fresh Brussels sprouts in boiling water to cover in a saucepan for about 12 minutes or until tender; drain. Sprinkle 2 tablespoons freshly grated Parmesan cheese and salt and pepper to taste over the Brussels sprouts and toss lightly to coat. Serve immediately.*

# Cabbage

***Brassica oleracea* var. *capitata***

Cabbage is a cole crop, a member of the mustard family, *Cruciferae*. It is one of the oldest recorded vegetables, mentioned in literature 3,000 years ago. Cabbage was in general use 2,000 years ago throughout Europe and the Middle East.

## When to Plant

This cool-weather plant produces best in spring. Sow seed indoors under lights about 8 weeks before the frost-free date (average date of last frost), and set the plants into the garden about 6 weeks later. Transplants are often available at garden centers about that time as well; they should have a good green color, be short and compact, and have no pests. For the earliest production, you'll want to start with transplants, whether homegrown or store bought. But if you prefer to sow seed directly in the garden, sow it as early as the soil can be worked. Since the cabbage will be harvested and out of the garden by midsummer, plan to replace it with a second crop. For a fall crop, sow seed indoors about July 1, then set the seedlings in the garden about August 10. Cabbage can tolerate a freeze, and with a mild fall it may last until Thanksgiving.

## Where to Plant

Choose a location in full sun or partial shade (filtered sun all day or shade part of the day); 8 hours of sun would be a minimum. Cabbage prefers well-prepared soil with good drainage.

## How to Plant

Apply a complete garden fertilizer, such as 10-10-10, at a rate of $1^{1}/_{2}$ pounds per 100 square feet of garden. Spade or rototill the garden. (See "Soil Preparation" in the introduction to the vegetable garden.) In rows, space the transplants 12 to 18 inches apart, with 24 inches between rows. In a bed, space the plants 16 to 18 inches apart, which will allow 2 or 3 plants across the bed. Set the plants at the same depth they were growing. Water in the plants with transplant starter fertilizer, such as 10-52-17 or 10-30-10, mixed according to directions on the label, and apply approximately 1 cup per plant. If root maggots have been a problem in the past and your previous crops have suffered damage, cover rows with screening or floating row covers after planting and leave them in place until plants are sizeable, because fly larvae may damage roots or stems. Directly seed fall cabbage in midsummer. Sow seeds 3 inches apart and 1/2 inch deep, then thin seedlings to the proper spacing noted for transplants. (You can recognize cabbage seedlings because they will be in rows and all look the same; weed seedlings will be randomly spaced, and all will look different.) Transplant excess seedlings to another row if you prefer not to dispose of them.

## Care and Maintenance

For the best-quality cabbage, water as necessary to keep the plants vigorous and growing. Plants need about 1 inch of water per week. Hardened-off plants will often crack as they develop, making them useless. Side-dress the plants with a complete fertilizer when they are about half grown. Pests and diseases may pose a problem. Prevent infestation of cabbage worms with *B.t.* (*Bacillus thuringiensis* Kurstaki). Apply maneb to control leaf spot diseases when the first symptoms appear. Eliminate yellows, black rot, and blackleg diseases by planting disease-resistant varieties and by rotating the *Brassica* crops (cabbage, collards, Brussels sprouts, broccoli, Chinese cabbage, etc.) to other areas of the garden each year. Use PCNB (Terraclor) in the transplant water to prevent clubroot. (See the pest control chart in the introduction to the vegetable garden.)

### Additional Information

Harvest the heads when they have achieved full size by cutting just below the heads with a sharp knife. If they are allowed to grow beyond maturity, the heads will crack, especially when the weather has been dry and suddenly becomes wet. Plants of some varieties will make a second crop of smaller heads similar to Brussels sprouts if left in the garden following the first harvest. Homegrown cabbage has a sweet flavor that isn't available in the cabbage at the supermarket. Picking it at the peak of perfection and using it when it is fresh preserve the flavor at its best. Try to make several plantings of cabbages with different maturity dates for a continuous supply. You may store fall-harvested cabbages for months at 40 degrees Fahrenheit in the refrigerator, but be sure to wrap them so they do not dry out.

## VARIETIES

Cabbages may be green or red, smooth or savoy (wrinkled). Heads may be pointed, round, or flat.

| Varieties | Days to Maturity | Comments |
|---|---|---|
| **Red** | | |
| Ruby Ball | 71 days | Resists cracking, early; 4 pounds. |
| Ruby Perfection | 85 days | Slow to crack and stores well; 3 pounds. |
| **Savoy** | | |
| Savoy Ace | 80 days | Cold tolerant; 3 pounds. |
| Savoy Express | 55 days | AAS, earliest savoy; 3 to 4 pounds. |
| Savoy King | 85 days | Uniform dark green; 3 to 4 |
| pounds. | | |
| Savoy Queen | 88 days | Heat tolerant; 5 pounds. |
| **Smooth Green** | | |
| Charmont | 65 days | Early; 3 to 4 pounds. |
| Dynamo | 70 days | Good nearly everywhere; 3 to 4 pounds. AAS. |
| Early Jersey Wakefield | 63 days | Pointed and resists cracking; 4 pounds. |
| Grand Slam | 82 days | Good black rot resistance; 8-inch heads. |
| King Cole | 74 days | Large, firm 8-pound heads. |
| Stonehead | 70 days | Resists cracking; 3 pounds. |
| **Smooth Green, Fall** | | |
| Danish Roundhead | 105 days | Only 4 pounds. |

# Braised Cabbage

*Cook a shredded ½ head green cabbage in a small amount of water in a saucepan over medium heat for 5 minutes or until tender, stirring frequently. Cook 1 chopped yellow onion in a small amount of water in a skillet over medium-high heat for 5 minutes or until the water evaporates. Reduce the heat to medium and stir in 2 to 3 tablespoons vegetable oil. Cook until the onion begins to brown. Add 1 cup tomato sauce, 2 chopped peeled carrots, 2 chopped peeled potatoes and ½ cup water. Simmer for 10 to 15 minutes. Add the cabbage, salt to taste and cayenne pepper to taste and mix well. Simmer, covered, for 10 minutes longer.*

# CARROT

*Daucus carota* var. *sativas*

These vegetables with their bright orange roots may not appeal to the youngest family member as part of a favorite meal—or any meal for that matter. It seems that early peoples may have shared the youngster's sentiment. The ancients probably cultivated carrots but not as a common food plant. Carrots have managed to gain popularity for a lot of folks since those early days. Most of the modern varieties come from those developed in France in the early 1800s.

## When to Plant

Sow seeds as soon as the soil is workable in the spring; a freeze will not harm them. To provide a continuous supply of carrots, sow seeds every 2 to 3 weeks. To produce carrots in the fall, sow seeds in midsummer.

## Where to Plant

These roots require deeply prepared, well-drained soil. (See "Soil Preparation" in the introduction to vegetable gardening.) The long varieties of carrots prefer sandy soils, and the shorter or half-long varieties produce the best quality in most Midwest gardens with heavy soils. Carrots will grow in soils with a wide range of acidity or alkalinity. Do not apply lime or gypsum to garden soils unless you have tested them to make sure the added calcium is needed. A high level of soil potassium is essential for good root development. Give carrots a full-sun location (8 to 10 hours will suffice), and they'll give you a bountiful crop.

## How to Plant

Apply a complete garden fertilizer, such as 10-10-10, at a rate of 1½ pounds per 100 square feet of garden. Work the soil into a fine seedbed (that is, make sure the soil is finely broken up) to promote germination. Poor germination will result when the soil is not well prepared. For rows, sow carrot seeds about 3 per inch, and allow 12 to 15 inches between rows. For a raised bed, sow the rows 8 to 10 inches apart across the bed. For both methods, cover the seeds with 1/4 inch of fine soil. For seeds sown in the summer, place a board over each row to keep the soil from drying or from being compacted by pounding rain. Check the board twice daily to see whether the seedlings have begun to emerge, and remove the board as soon as you notice any of them. When the seedlings are large enough to handle, thin them to 1 plant every 2 inches.

## Care and Maintenance

A little hoeing or pulling of weeds, especially while the seedlings are small, will prevent weeds from competing with the carrots for water and nutrients. If no rain falls for 7 to 10 days, apply 1 inch of water. Carrots that develop in dry weather will be fibrous and woody. As for pests, soil-borne maggots may damage the roots. If they have been a problem in the past, mix Diazinon according to the directions on the label, and apply it to the furrows as you plant the seeds.

### Additional Information

Harvest the carrots when they are at least ½ inch in diameter. Carrots left in the ground will continue to increase in size. Under normal conditions, expect a spring seeding to produce for 3 or 4 weeks. Summer seedings for fall crops may be left in the ground until a killing frost or even later if you mulch them to keep the ground from freezing. Dig late-season carrots and store them in pits of sand or in boxes of sand in a cool place such as a garage. Keep them at just above freezing temperatures; don't let them freeze. To prevent green shoulders that develop when the roots are exposed to light, cultivate a little loose soil over the roots as they begin to swell. Any green portions will be poorly flavored, so cut those portions off the roots before you use them. Poor soil preparation, which may include leaving stones and other debris in the soil, causes forked and twisted roots.

## Carrot Jam

*Combine 4 cups chopped carrots, 3 cups sugar, 3 sliced lemons, 1 teaspoon cinnamon, and ½ teaspoon cloves. Simmer slowly, stirring constantly, until thick.*

## VARIETIES

| Varieties | Days to Maturity | Comments |
|---|---|---|
| **Baby** | | |
| Little Finger | 65 days | ½-inch-diameter roots, 5 inches long, sweet and crisp. |
| Short 'n Sweet | 68 days | 4-inch-long roots, good in poor soils. |
| **Danvers** | | |
| Danvers Half Long | 75 days | 6- to 8-inch-long roots tapered to blunt ends. |
| **Nantes** | | |
| Bolero | 70 days | Hybrid, 7-inch-long roots tapered to blunt ends. |
| Nantes Coreless | 68 days | Red-orange, 6-inch roots. |
| Scarlet Nantes | 70 days | The standard for best quality, 6-inch-long roots, bright orange, sweet. |
| **Regular Chantenay** | | |
| Red-Cored Chantenay | 70 days | Good flavor, short, blunt roots, good in heavy soils. |
| Royal Chantenay | 70 days | Bright orange, broadly tapered, good in heavy soils. |
| **Small Round** | | |
| Thumbelina | 62 days | AAS; excellent for poor or shallow soil and for containers. |

# Gingered Carrots

*Combine ½ cup sugar, ¼ cup fresh orange juice, ¼ cup chicken broth, 1 teaspoon margarine, grated peel of 1 lemon, ½ teaspoon ground ginger and 5 whole cloves in a heavy saucepan. Simmer for 10 minutes, stirring occasionally. Add 1 bunch tiny carrots, trimmed and peeled. Simmer for 10 to 15 minutes or until tender-crisp. Remove the cloves before serving.*

# Cauliflower

***Brassica oleracea*** **var.** ***botrytis***

A member of the mustard family, cauliflower and its close relatives are different varieties of *Brassica oleraceae,* commonly called the cole crops. Wild *Brassica oleraceae* grows along the seacoasts of Europe from Denmark to France, and in other locations from Greece to Great Britain. Although it has been cultivated for 5,000 years, cauliflower was developed from other cole crops quite late and has been popular in this country only since the 1930s. Cauliflower requires the best conditions and most care of all the members of the cabbage family. Some gardeners refer to it as the "college graduate" of the cole crops that will test the amateur gardener's skills. This vegetable, grown for its compact heads of white flower buds or curd, is picked before the flower buds begin to open.

## When to Plant

This cool-season crop is less tolerant of either heat or cold than its close relation, broccoli, and will not grow as well in dry weather either. Grow cauliflower as a spring crop, maturing before the onset of hot weather, or as a fall crop. For the best success, use transplants instead of sowing seeds. Seeds are too slow germinating in the garden, and the crop will tend to be very uneven. In spring, start plants under lights about 8 weeks before the frost-free date (average date of last frost), and set them in the garden about 6 weeks later. Earlier plantings risk cold injury; later plantings may not mature before hot weather. Start seeds for a fall crop indoors about July 1, then set out seedlings in the garden about August 10.

## Where to Plant

Choose a location that is in full sun (8 to 10 hours will suffice) or light shade (a little shade from a distant tree or some shade in the middle of the day). Cauliflower prefers deeply prepared, well-drained soil; good drainage is essential. (See the discussion of soils in the introduction and "Soil Preparation" in the introduction to the vegetable garden.)

## How to Plant

Apply a complete garden fertilizer, such as 10-10-10, at a rate of 1½ pounds per 100 square feet of garden. Spade or rototill the soil. In rows, space the transplants about 18 inches apart, with 36 inches between rows. In a bed, space the plants 16 to 18 inches apart, which will allow 2 or 3 plants across the standard 4-foot bed. Set the plants at the same depth they were growing. Water in the plants with a transplant starter fertilizer that has a very high-soluble phosphorus analysis: 10-52-17, 10-50-10, or 10-30-10. If root maggots have been a problem in the past and your previous crops have suffered damage, cover rows with screening or floating row covers after planting and leave them in place until plants are sizeable, because fly larvae may damage roots or stems.

## Care and Maintenance

Cauliflower must grow vigorously from seeding to harvest. Any disruption will cause the flower to abort and the subsequent failure of the crop. Another problem results from keeping the transplants in the seedling flat too long; tiny buttons, instead of large heads, will form prematurely. Water cauliflower as needed to provide 1 inch per week. When plants are about half grown (8 to 12 inches tall), fertilize them with nitrogen to stimulate continuing vigorous growth. Heads exposed to light will be off-color, and the flavor will be poor. The white, blanched heads desired by gardeners develop in the absence of light. Here is the process to follow to achieve them: when heads are about 3 inches in diameter, lift the leaves over the heads to shade them, and tie them up with twine, rubber bands, or a couple of clothespins. Self-blanching varieties produce upright leaves that shade the heads and require no tying. Pests and diseases may affect plants. Prevent infestation of cabbage worms with *B.t.* (*Bacillus thuringiensis* Kurstaki). Apply maneb to control leaf spot diseases when the first symptoms appear. Eliminate black rot and blackleg diseases by planting disease-resistant varieties and by rotating the *Brassica* crops (cabbage, collards, Brussels sprouts, broccoli, Chinese cabbage, etc.) to other areas of the garden each year. Use PCNB (Terraclor) in the transplant water to prevent clubroot. (See the pest control chart in the introduction to the vegetable garden.)

### Additional Information

The heads will develop quickly under good growing conditions. A week or so following blanching, the heads should be 6 to 8 inches in diameter, firm and white. Harvest them before they start to loosen. Loose, "ricey" heads (those that begin to separate and look like piles of rice instead of being compact and tight) are poor in quality. Cut heads, leaving a few green leaves to protect them. Cauliflower deteriorates quickly after harvest, so use it immediately or freeze it. If you freeze it, you should probably cut it up first. Since cauliflower does not develop usable side shoots, pull the plants immediately following the harvest.

## VARIETIES

| Varieties | Days to Maturity | Comments |
|---|---|---|
| Andes | 68 days | Good self-blanching type. |
| Early White | 52 days | One of the earliest. |
| Green Goddess Hybrid II | 62 days | Lime green, tasty. |
| Self Blanch | 71 days | OP; 7-inch heads, needs no tying, excellent for fall crop. |
| Snowball Y Improved | 68 days | OP; 6-inch heads well protected by leaves. |
| Snow Crown | 60 days | Tolerates heat and cold; yellows resistant. |
| Snow Grace | 65 days | Improved Snowcrown type; grows larger and later. |
| Snow King | 50 days | 9-inch heads, early. |
| Violet Queen Hybrid | 70 days | Purple head turns green when cooked. |

OP = Open Pollinated (versus Hybrid)

# Cauliflower and Broccoli Salad

*Chop 1 head cauliflower, 1 head broccoli, 1 red onion, and 1 green bell pepper into a large bowl. Mix together. Add 1 cup light mayonnaise and 1 cup light sour cream; mix well. Add ½ cup small pieces of fried crisp bacon and 8 ounces Cheddar cheese. Mix well. Chill at least 1 hour until ready to serve.*

# Celery

*Apium graveolens* var. *dulce*

Celery is known for its crisp, flavorful leaf stalks (petioles), growing in a tight, upright bunch. This marsh plant's habitat extends from Sweden to the Mediterranean and India. It has been found growing wild in Tierra del Fuego, California, and New Zealand. More than likely, people used it as a medicinal plant hundreds of years before they started consuming it for food. This relative of carrots, parsley, and parsnips probably originated as a food crop in France and was first mentioned as a cultivated food plant in 1632. Celery is a demanding crop that takes cool weather, lots of water, and even more work. Blanched celery has been grown as a specialty crop in the Chicago area for many years—it is finished in the dark to make it tender and white—and that is still the best way to produce high-quality celery. Regular field celery is inexpensive even in winter, so if you are going to the trouble to grow this crop, make it worth your while by blanching it.

## When to Plant

Celery is a cool-weather crop, but if it is exposed to temperatures below 55 degrees Fahrenheit for an extended period, it will bolt (make a flower stalk). Some varieties will bolt after 1 week of those conditions; others will bolt after almost 2 weeks. You will probably have more success growing it as an autumn crop, which matures during the cool of fall. Start seeds indoors under lights about 8 weeks before the frost-free date. Move transplants to the garden when there is no danger of a freeze.

## Where to Plant

Choose a location that is in full sun (8 to 10 hours will suffice) and has well-drained, deep soil. To grow blanched celery, select beds that can be covered to eliminate the light as the crop matures.

## How to Plant

Apply a complete garden fertilizer, such as 10-10-10, at a rate of $1\frac{1}{2}$ pounds per 100 square feet of garden. Spade or till the soil to produce a fine seedbed (make sure the soil is finely broken up;

see "Soil Preparation" in the introduction to the vegetable garden). In beds, set started plants 12 to 15 inches apart, which will result in 3 or 4 plants across a 4-foot bed. Transplants that are 4 to 6 inches tall are ready for planting; that is the regular size available at a garden center.

## Care and Maintenance

If there is a danger that temperatures will drop below 55 degrees Fahrenheit after planting, be prepared to cover the plants at night. Use old blankets, hot caps (covers available at garden centers or farm supply stores to protect plants during inclement weather), or gallon plastic milk jugs from which the bottoms have been cut out to protect the plants. Water and fertilize to keep the plants growing vigorously. Plants need about 1 inch of water per week. About midseason, after the plants have become well developed, side-dress them with a complete fertilizer at half the recommended rate. If the plants begin to tip over as they grow, hill soil around them to support them, but be careful not to get soil in the crowns or they will rot. Weed control must be ongoing; celery is not a good competitor, and weeds will reduce production. Aphids and earwigs can be troublesome; use insecticidal soap to control aphids when they first appear, and apply Sevin to control earwigs. (See the pest control chart in the introduction to the vegetable garden.) When the weather has cooled in the fall and the plants have achieved full size, about 18 inches in height, prepare to blanch them by building some kind of frames over them to support covers. Commercial growers make the frames from 2-by-2s and cover them with tar paper. Other materials can be used, but they must completely block the light. An alternative to covering the plants to blanch them is to wrap them in brown paper and tie it securely with only the tips of the leaves exposed. Some self-blanching types of celery have been developed that eliminate the need to cover the plants. They are not as tender as properly blanched standard types, however.

### Additional Information

Regularly check the plants. When they have reached a light green color, harvest them. In cool weather, the plants can be kept in the beds under cover until there is danger of freezing. Left too long in the dark, however, celery will begin to rot. Try to harvest the crop in a timely manner because storage is difficult.

## VARIETIES

| Varieties | Days to Maturity | Comments |
|---|---|---|
| Florida | 100 days | Medium green, bushy. |
| Golden Self Blanching | 115 days | Tender without blanching. |
| Hercules | 100 days | Extra heavy plants, high yield. |
| Tall Utah 52-70 R | 98 days | An improved variety that does exceptionally well in home gardens. |

# Celery Casserole

*Cook 4 cups of celery sliced 1 to 2 inches thick in salted water until just tender—still a little crisp—about 8 minutes. Drain and mix with 1 can (5 ounces) drained water chestnuts, 1 can cream of chicken soup, and ¼ cup diced pimientos. Pour into a greased 1-quart casserole dish. Combine ½ cup bread crumbs, ¼ cup slivered toasted almonds, and 2 tablespoons melted butter; sprinkle atop the casserole. Bake at 350 degrees for about 30 minutes, or until hot and bubbly.*

# Celery with Almonds

*Melt 1 tablespoon margarine in a 2-quart saucepan; add 4 cups celery slices, 2 tablespoons minced onion and 1 minced garlic clove. Sauté for 3 to 4 minutes. Add 2 tablespoons chicken stock, 2 tablespoons dry sherry and ½ teaspoon salt. Sauté for 3 to 4 minutes longer; drain. Add ½ cup toasted slivered almonds. Serve immediately.*

# Chard, Swiss

***Beta vulgaris* var. *cicla***

Chard, more commonly called Swiss chard, is actually a beet that has been bred for leaves at the expense of the bulbous roots. Grown as a summer green, it is prepared like spinach. The attractive colorful stalks of red and yellow also can be prepared and used like asparagus, eaten raw or cooked, adding interest to summer dishes. Chard is becoming more common in grocery stores and can be bought at community and farm markets. But growing it yourself is the best way to obtain it. Swiss chard isn't readily available in the stores, and when it is available, the quality is not as good as your homegrown vegetables. And you may grow more varieties, including the multi-colored 'Rainbow' and 'Bright Lights' kinds.

## When to Plant

Start seeds indoors under lights about 6 weeks before the frost-free date (average date of last frost). Sow seeds directly in the garden or set out transplants at the frost-free date. A spring planting will produce all summer if it is kept picked.

## Where to Plant

Chard does best in a location with full sun (8 to 10 hours will suffice). Good drainage and well-prepared soil will assure a quick start and bountiful production. (See "Soil Preparation" in the introduction to the vegetable garden.)

## How to Plant

Apply a complete garden fertilizer, such as 10-10-10, at a rate of 1½ pounds per 100 square feet of garden. Work the soil into a fine seedbed (make sure that the soil is finely broken up) to promote seed germination. In rows, sow chard seeds 1 inch apart, allowing 12 to 15 inches between rows. In a raised bed, sow the rows 8 to 10 inches apart across a standard 3- to 4-foot bed. In rows or beds, cover the seeds with ½ inch of fine soil. For summer seedings, place a board over each row to keep the soil from drying or from being compacted by pounding rain. Check twice a day to see whether the seedlings have begun to emerge, and remove the board as soon as you notice any seedlings. Swiss chard seeds are actually dried-up fruits containing 2 or more seeds, so don't plant them too close together. As soon as the seedlings are large enough to handle, thin them to 4 to 6 inches apart. (You can recognize chard seedlings because they will be in rows and all look the same; weed seedlings will be randomly spaced, and all will be different.) After you have thinned them several times to obtain the correct spacing, the final spacing should be 8 to 10 inches apart. If you wait until the seedlings are about 6 inches tall, you can cook the thinned seedlings as greens. In beds, set seedlings 8 to 10 inches apart; and in rows, about 10 inches apart, with 18 inches between rows.

## Care and Maintenance

Chard needs 1 inch of water per week to develop tender leaves. These plants are very susceptible to leaf miner damage. The insects lay eggs just under the surface of the leaves. Then the larvae hatch and mine their way in the leaves, making dead brown trails. Covering the planting with cheesecloth or commercial row covers is the only way to protect the plants. Beet leaf spot disease affects chard as well. Apply a copper fungicide such as Bordeaux to prevent this disease, being sure to read and follow the label directions before you use it. Try to keep the foliage dry, and do not go in the garden when leaves are wet in order to avoid spreading diseases. (See the pest control chart in the introduction to the vegetable garden.)

### Additional Information

Harvest leaves when they are young and tender, about 12 inches long. Cut individual leaves 1 inch above the ground, being careful not to injure the remaining leaves. Or cut the entire bunch just below the ground.

## VARIETIES

| Varieties | Days to Maturity | Comments |
|---|---|---|
| **Mixed** | | |
| Bright Lights | 40 days | Stems red, white, orange, pink, violet, and yellow mixed. AAS. |
| **Red** (Rainbow) | | |
| Burgundy | 40 days | Dark-green leaves with burgundy stems. |
| Rhubarb | 40 days | Red stems, deep green leaves with red veins. |
| Ruby | 45 days | Ruby-red stems, reddish-green leaves, red veins. |
| **White** (Rainbow) | | |
| Fordhook | 42 days | Dark-green, savoyed leaves, light green stalks. |
| Lucullus | 40 days | Dark-green leaves, white stalks. |
| Winter King | 40 days | Dig in fall, keep cool and moist for winter harvest indoors. |

# Swiss Surprise

*Cook 1 pound young, tender Swiss chard; drain and chop. Add 2 tablespoons butter, ¼ cup light cream, and ½ tablespoon horseradish. Heat; garnish with sliced hard-boiled eggs dusted with paprika.*

# Scalloped Chard

*Cook 10 ounces chopped Swiss chard; drain. Add 2 tablespoons chopped onion, 2 beaten eggs, ½ cup milk, ½ cup shredded sharp processed cheese, dash of pepper, and ½ teaspoon salt, and turn into loaf pan. Top with ½ cup soft buttered bread crumbs. Bake at 350 degrees until knife comes out clean, about 20 minutes.*

# Chinese Cabbage

***Brassica rapa* var. *pekinensis***
***Brassica rapa* var. *chinensis***

Chinese cabbage is another of the cole crops. Although it was not very well known in this country until recently, this vegetable has been cultivated in China for 1,500 years. With the popularity of stir-frying, Chinese cabbage has "arrived" here, and the demand for it has increased. It has a mild taste and is excellent whether eaten fresh or steamed. There are two types, pe-tsai and bok choi. Pe-tsai (*Brassica rapa* var. *pekinensis*) is commonly used for cole slaw; pe-tsai napa has short, broad heads, and pe-tsai michihili has elongated, upright heads. Bok choi (*Brassica rapa* var. *chinensis*), which grows more like Swiss chard, is a part of nearly every vegetable offering in Chinese restaurants.

## When to Plant

This cool-weather crop can be grown for a spring or a fall crop. For a spring crop, sow seeds indoors under lights about 8 weeks before the frost-free date (average date of last frost); transplant the seedlings into the garden 10 days before the frost-free date. For a fall crop, start seeds indoors under lights in July, and transplant the seedlings into the garden about mid-August. Be careful to avoid injuring the roots of these plants or they will stop growing. Seed them in peat pots so you can plant them directly into their permanent location without disturbing the roots. If you prefer, seed the fall crop directly into the garden in midsummer. (Note: transplants are rarely available from commercial sources.)

## Where to Plant

This crop requires full sun (8 to 10 hours will suffice) and good drainage. (See the discussion of soils in the introduction.)

## How to Plant

Apply a complete garden fertilizer, such as 10-10-10, at a rate of $1\frac{1}{2}$ pounds per 100 square feet of garden. Spade or rototill the garden. (See "Soil Preparation" in the introduction to the vegetable garden.) In rows, space the transplants 12 to 18 inches apart, with 24 inches between rows. In a bed, space the plants 16 to 18 inches apart, which will allow 2 or 3 plants across the bed. Set the plants at the same depth they were growing. Water in the plants with transplant starter fertilizer, such as 10-52-17 or 10-30-10, mixed according to directions on the label, and apply approximately 1 cup per plant. If root maggots have been a problem in the past and your previous crops have suffered damage, also use Diazinon in the water, mixed according to label directions, as transplants are watered in. For fall Chinese cabbage, sow seed directly in the garden 3 to 4 inches apart. Then thin seedlings to the proper spacing noted for transplants.

## Care and Maintenance

Chinese cabbage produces a crop with very little care. For the best quality, water as necessary to keep the plants vigorous and growing; they require about 1 inch of water per week. Water them when they begin to wilt or when there has been no rain for 7 to 10 days. Side-dress the plants with a complete fertilizer at half the recommended rate when the plants are about half grown (10 to 12 inches high), then water in thoroughly after application to wash fertilizer off the plants and to activate the fertilizer. Pests and diseases may need attention. When you see white butterflies in the garden or notice any damage, prevent infestation of cabbage worms with *B.t.* (*Bacillus thuringiensis* Kurstaki). Apply maneb to prevent leaf spot diseases when the first symptoms appear. Eliminate yellows and black rot and blackleg diseases by planting disease-resistant varieties and by rotating the *Brassica* crops (cabbage, collards, Brussels sprouts, broccoli, etc.) to other areas of the garden each year. Use PCNB (Terraclor) in the transplant water to prevent clubroot. (See the pest control chart in the introduction to the vegetable garden.)

### Additional Information

Harvest the heads with a sharp knife, cutting just below the heads, as soon as they have achieved full size (12 to 18 inches tall) and become solid. If they are allowed to grow beyond maturity, the heads will form seed stalks and will be useless, especially if the weather has been hot and dry.

## VARIETIES

| Varieties | Days to Maturity | Comments |
|---|---|---|
| **Bok Choi** | | |
| Joi Choi | 45 days | Good for fall. |
| Mei Quing Choi | 45 days | Withstands heat; good for warm-season crop. |
| Mi Choi | 45 days | Good warm-season production. |
| **Pe-tsai Michihili** | | |
| Green Rocket | 65 days | Tall, firm heads. |
| Michihili | 75 days | Dark green, good in cool seasons. |
| Monument | 80 days | Tall, good disease resistance. |
| **Pe-tsai Napa** | | |
| Blues | 65 days | Good for spring. |
| China Flash | 55 days | Extra early, good in spring or fall. |
| Orient Express | 43 days | Very early, small heads; try in spring. |

# Pe-tsai Chinese Cabbage Coleslaw

*Pe-tsai Chinese cabbage makes a fine-tasting coleslaw. To make this tasty dish, finely chop (into ¼-inch-size pieces) 1 head of Pe-tsai cabbage and 1 medium carrot. Combine ½ cup sugar, ½ cup milk, ¼ cup buttermilk, 1½ tablespoon vinegar, 2½ tablespoons lemon juice, ½ teaspoon salt and ⅛ teaspoon pepper in a large bowl and beat until smooth. Add the chopped carrots and cabbage and mix well. Refrigerate for at least 3 to 4 hours to blend the flavors.*

# Collard

***Brassica oleracea* var. *acephala***

A cool-season leafy vegetable, collard is a member of the cabbage family. Collards tolerate both warm and cold temperatures better than cabbage does. It is an important vegetable in the South where it is used as a leafy table green, one of the constituents of traditional southern cooking. And since the middle of the twentieth century, collards have become increasingly popular in the Midwest because it can tolerate frost.

## When to Plant

Plant collards in early spring for a summer harvest. For the earliest production, start with transplants, either homegrown or store bought. To grow your own, sow seed indoors under lights about 8 weeks before the frost-free date (average date of last frost), and set plants into the garden 6 weeks later. Transplants are often available at garden centers about that time as well; buy ones that have a good green color, are short and compact, and are free of pests. Or if you prefer, sow seed directly in the garden as early as the soil can be worked. Since the collards will be harvested and out of the garden by midsummer, plan to replace them with a second crop. For a fall crop, sow seed indoors about July 1, and set the seedlings in the garden about August 10; or direct seed in midsummer. With mild fall weather collards may last until Thanksgiving.

## Where to Plant

Collards need a full-sun (8 to 10 hours will suffice) location with well-drained soil. (See the discussion on soils in the introduction.) They will produce in partial shade (lightly filtered sunlight or full sun for only part of the day), but the quality will be different. The leaves will be larger and floppier, and the flavor will be milder.

## How to Plant

Apply a complete garden fertilizer, such as 10-10-10, at a rate of 1½ pounds per 100 square feet of garden. Spade or rototill the soil. (See "Soil Preparation" in the introduction to the vegetable garden.) In rows, space the transplants 12 to 18 inches apart, with 30 inches between rows. In beds, space the plants 16 to 18 inches apart, which will allow 2 or 3 plants across each bed. Set the plants at the same depth they were growing. Water in the plants with transplant starter fertilizer, such as 10-52-17 or 10-30-10, mixed according to directions on the label, and apply approximately 1 cup per plant. If root maggots have been a problem in the past and your previous crops have suffered damage, cover rows with screening or floating row covers after planting and leave them in place until plants are sizeable, because fly larvae may damage roots or stems. For plants that were direct seeded, thin seedlings to the proper spacing noted for transplants. (You can recognize collard seedlings because they will be in rows and all look the same; weed seedlings will be randomly spaced, and all will look different.) Move excess seedlings to another row if you prefer not to dispose of them.

## Care and Maintenance

These plants need adequate water, especially in hot weather, so you should provide 1 inch per week if insufficient rain falls. Pests and diseases may affect the plantings. Prevent infestation of cabbage worms with *B.t.* (*Bacillus thuringiensis* Kurstaki). Apply maneb to prevent leaf spot diseases when first symptoms appear. Eliminate black rot and blackleg diseases by planting disease-resistant varieties and by rotating the *Brassica* crops (cabbage, collards, Brussels sprouts, broccoli, Chinese cabbage, etc.) to other areas of the garden each year. Use PCNB (Terraclor) in the water for the transplants or spade it into the soil to prevent clubroot. (See the pest control chart in the introduction to the vegetable garden.)

### Additional Information

If seedlings from a planting are thinned to about 6 inches apart and allowed to grow to 12 inches tall, Harvest them, leaving 1 plant every 18 inches. Allow these remaining plants to mature. Harvest collards either by cutting outer leaves as they reach full size or by cutting the entire plant at the soil line. Some gardeners who prefer the young, tender inner leaves blanch them, which makes them tender for use in salads; blanching involves tying up the outer leaves to block the light. Commercial growers cut the plants when they are about half grown (12 to 15 inches tall) and tie them in bunches for sale. Home gardeners may choose to follow that practice and cut plants at the half-grown stage.

## VARIETIES

New hybrid varieties are more vigorous and better adapted to midwestern gardens, but some gardeners still prefer open-pollinated varieties.

| Varieties | Days to Maturity | Comments |
|---|---|---|
| **Hybrid** | | |
| Blue Max | 68 days | Heavy yields. |
| HiCrop | 75 days | Maintains excellent flavor in hot weather. |
| Top Bunch | 67 days | Heavy yields on a small plant. |
| **Open Pollinated** | | |
| Champion Long Standing | 60 days | Tolerates frost. |
| Morris Heading | 80 days | Savoy type. |
| Vates | 67 days | Old standard. |

# Collards

*Many Midwesterners have never learned to appreciate collards. Perhaps they just don't know what to do with them. Here is an easy way to enjoy collards.*

*Wash leaves well, shake dry, and place in a kettle. Add 2 or 3 cups of canned chicken broth and simmer until tender. Add some bacon drippings, salt and pepper to taste, and a dash or so of Tabasco. Serve with ham hocks, pork chops, or even roast beef. Collards add character to any meal.*

# Collards and Rice

*Bring 2 cups chicken or meat stock to a boil in a 2-quart saucepan. Add 1 cup of long-grain rice, 1 tablespoon butter or margarine, and ½ teaspoon salt; stir. Add 3 cups chopped loosely packed collard greens, a handful at a time, stirring after each addition. Bring back to a boil; cover and reduce heat. Cook approximately 15 to 20 minutes, or until rice is tender. Season with pepper before serving.*

# Corn, Sweet

### *Zea mays* var. *rugosa*

Nearly everyone loves sweet corn. Who can resist a steaming hot ear of corn on the cob? It is as American as apple pie. Sweet corn was developed from common field corn. Field corn is harvested after it has matured, and it is used for innumerable products from cereals to livestock feed to chemicals and sweeteners. Sweet corn is harvested before it matures while it is tender and the sugar content is at its highest. Dr. C. J. Arnold of the University of Illinois, a developer of many improved sweet corn varieties, always taught that to have the "sweetest" sweet corn, plant the patch just 50 feet outside the kitchen door. When the corn is ready for harvest, start the pot of water boiling. As it reaches a full boil, pick the corn. Husk it as you run to the kitchen and then pop it into the pot. He figured that you could run about 50 feet in the time it takes to shuck a couple of ears of sweet corn, thus the distance from the back door.

The original sweet corn varieties were open pollinated, and very few can be found anymore. Some open-pollinated examples include 'Golden Bantam', 'Country Gentleman', and 'Double Standard'. Today, almost all named varieties of sweet corn are hybrids and do not come true from saved seed. Three types are currently available: standard, sugary enhancer, and supersweet. Standard (SU) varieties of sweet corn contain a "sugary gene" making them sweet and creamy, but they quickly lose their sweetness after harvest. Unless the corn is rapidly cooled, the sugars are converted to starch. The newer hybrids have been developed to reduce this tendency. Sugary enhancer (SE) types are the ones of choice for the home gardener. They have superior texture and flavor, and they do not need to be separated from other kinds of corn to prevent cross-pollination. They have a higher sugar content and stay sweeter longer. Supersweet (Sh2) hybrids were developed at the University of Illinois; 'Illini Xtra Sweet' was the first of this type. Supersweet hybrids have a higher sugar content than the other 2 types, and they hold their sugar longer. The kernels have a tougher skin and lack the creamy texture of the standard and sugary enhancer varieties. Growing supersweet varieties is a challenge because the seeds do not germinate well, and the supersweet varieties need to be isolated from other types of corn to prevent cross-pollination.

## When to Plant

Begin planting the earliest varieties during the first week of May or about the frost-free date (average date of last frost) in your area. Make additional seedings until the first week of July if you desire.

## Where to Plant

Sweet corn needs full sun (8 to 10 hours will suffice), good drainage, and lots of room. Unless your garden is large (100 by 200 feet or so), you may want to secure space in a community garden for your sweet corn. Quite a few plants are needed to provide enough corn at one time for a meal. Most varieties produce only 1 ear per plant, so you will need at least 12 plants that mature simultaneously to provide 12 ears for your family.

## How to Plant

Apply a complete garden fertilizer, such as 10-10-10, at a rate of $1\frac{1}{2}$ pounds per 100 square feet of garden. Spade or rototill the soil. (See "Soil Preparation" in the introduction to the vegetable garden.) Sow seeds $\frac{1}{2}$ inch deep in cool soils or $1\frac{1}{2}$ inches deep in warm soils. Space the seeds 9 inches apart in the rows, with 24 to 36 inches between rows. Plant 2 or more rows of each variety side by side to assure pollination. Try to prevent cross-pollination by field corn or popcorn by planting upwind or more than 500 feet downwind from either type. Cross-pollination between white and yellow sweet corn will affect color but not sweetness. Make successive plantings of early, midseason, and main crop varieties to provide a continuous supply of sweet corn all summer. Make the first planting of SU or SE varieties about the frost-free date with an extra-early variety such as 'Earlivee'. Make a second planting of a later variety such as 'Spring Treat'. For the main crop, plant a favorite kind such as 'Kandy Korn'. Make additional plantings of your favorite varieties when seedlings of the previous planting have 3 leaves. Plant until about July 4.

## Care and Maintenance

Control weeds by hoeing the rows. Once the corn is tall enough, it will shade out weed seedlings. When the plants are about $1\frac{1}{2}$ feet tall, side-dress them with a complete fertilizer, such as 10-10-10, at the rate of 1 pound per 100 square feet of garden. Water is important as the plants are tasseling and making silk. Pollination takes place then and will be poor if the plants are wilted. Kernel development takes water too. Once the silks begin to dry, be sure to keep the plants from wilting by providing about 1 inch of water per week. When the plants reach head height, overhead watering by using sprinklers will be difficult. Flooding or soaking will be necessary at that point, and you can use soaker hoses if you have a small plot. Some pests and diseases may pose a problem. The most common pest is corn earworm, which affects later-developing plantings; apply Sevin insecticide to the silks as the pollen is being shed (you'll be able to see it on everything) to reduce numbers of the pest. Sevin controls corn borers, too; apply it to the leaf whorls and ears 4 times if feeding damage appears. Smut disease develops a mass of sooty stuff where the ear should be. To prevent it, plant resistant varieties.

## Additional Information

Harvest sweet corn as soon as the ears are filled out and the kernels are milky inside, usually about 16 days after silks appear.

### VARIETIES

| Varieties | Days to Maturity | Comments |
|---|---|---|
| **Open Pollinated** | | |
| Country Gentleman | 96 days | White. |
| Double Standard | 73 days | Bicolor. |
| Golden Bantam | 82 days | Rich corn flavor. |
| **Bicolor** | | |
| Bi Queen | 92 days | Similar to Silver Queen; SW, NCLB. |
| Butter and Sugar | 75 days | Adapted to home gardens. |
| Honey and Cream | 80 days | Commonly grown for sale at roadside stands and community markets. |
| Honey and Frost | 80 days | SW, S, R, NCLB, SCLB. |
| Quickie | 64 days | Earliest bicolor. |
| Sugar and Gold | 67 days | Better in cooler climates. |
| **Standard White** | | |
| Pearl White | 75 days | Cold soil tolerant. |
| Platinum Lady | 86 days | Tender. |
| Silver Queen | 92 days | Top-quality white, good disease resistance; SW, NCLB. |

## VARIETIES

| Varieties | Days to Maturity | Comments |
|---|---|---|
| **Standard Yellow** | | |
| Earlivee | 58 days | Extra early. |
| Golden Cross Bantam | 85 days | Old-time favorite. |
| Jubilee | 82 days | Midseason; S. |
| Lochief | 86 days | Midseason. |
| NK-199 | 84 days | Extra-deep kernels, a personal favorite. |
| Sundance | 69 days | Good early. |
| **Sugary Enhancer Bicolor** | | |
| Ambrosia | 75 days | Large, tasty; SW. |
| Calico Belle | 79 days | Delicious; SW, R. |
| Peaches & Cream | 83 days | Popular garden variety, glitzy name. |
| Seneca Dawn | 69 days | Early, vigorous plants, quality eating. |
| **Sugary Enhancer White** | | |
| Cotton Candy | 72 days | Fancy name, extended harvest. |
| Divinity | 78 days | All-around excellent variety; SW. |
| Pristine | 76 days | Top quality; SW. |
| Seneca Starshine | 71 days | Tender, flavorful. |
| Spring Snow | 65 days | Very early, tender. |
| Sugar Snow | 71 days | Very sweet, good in early cool weather. |
| **Sugary Enhancer Yellow** | | |
| Bodacious | 72 days | Superior quality, needs warm soil for good start. |
| Champ | 68 days | Excellent, early. |
| For Heaven's Sake | variable maturity | Bred specifically for home gardens; ears mature at different times to spread harvest. |
| Kandy Korn | 89 days | Top quality, keeps well. |
| Miracle | 84 days | Large, tasty ears; SW, S, R, NCLB. |
| Precocious | 66 days | Excellent, very early. |
| Spring Treat | 67 days | Nice straight rows of kernels, very early. |
| Terminator | 83 days | Large ears. |
| Tuxedo | 75 days | Vigorous, excellent quality, try this one; SW, S, R, NCLB, SCLB. |

## VARIETIES

| Varieties | Days to Maturity | Comments |
|---|---|---|
| **Supersweet Bicolor** | | |
| Candy Corner | 76 days | Popular at community markets. |
| Honey 'N Pearl | 78 days | AAS. |
| Serendipity | 82 days | So-called TripleSweet™, with enhanced flavor and shelf life. |
| **Supersweet Multicolor** | | |
| Indian Summer | 79 days | Red, white, yellow, and purple kernels. AAS. |
| **Supersweet White** | | |
| How Sweet It Is | 85 days | AAS, does not tolerate cold soil; SW, NCLB. |
| **Supersweet Yellow** | | |
| Challenger | 76 days | Excellent early; SW, NCLB. |
| Early Xtra Sweet | 70 days | Similar to original. |
| Illini Xtra Sweet | 85 days | The first supersweet hybrid. |
| Jubilee Super Sweet | 83 days | Best for home gardens; S. |
| Legend | 68 days | New, early. |
| **TripleSweet™** | | |
| Honey Select | 79 days | AAS. This is a new type that combines SE and SH2 characteristics in one variety. Designed for home gardens. |
| **3-Gene Hybrids** | | |
| Mirai | 75 days | Series of hybrids combining best of SU+SE+Sh2 types. |

Abbreviations for disease resistance:
NCLB=Northern corn leaf blight, R=Common rust, S=Corn smut, SCLB=Southern corn leaf blight, SW=Stewarts Wilt. (MDM=Maize dwarf mosaic virus is just becoming a problem in garden-grown sweet corn; resistance will be added to some current varieties as they are improved.)

# Roasted Sweet Corn on the Cob

*Soak 8 ears of sweet corn for approximately 30 minutes in cold water. Remove from water and shuck corn husks without separating from cob, remove the silks, and brush the corn with 4 tablespoons melted butter and sprinkle with salt and pepper. Replace the husks over the corn and grill over medium heat for 20 to 30 minutes.*

# Cress

***Lepedium sativum***

Sometimes called peppercress or garden cress, this member of the cabbage family is grown as a salad green or condiment. It has a pungency that adds character to plain lettuce salads. Water cress is similar, but needs to be grown in flowing water, so it is not a good candidate for planting in a regular garden. Winter or upland cress is another species grown for fall harvest.

## When to Plant

Sow seeds directly in the garden as soon as the soil can be worked to have plants ready to be harvested before hot weather. The heat causes the plants to become bitter. Make repeated sowings every few days until June for a continuous supply of fresh cress. For a fall crop, sow cress after the weather cools, usually in September.

## Where to Plant

Cress is a quick crop that will grow in nearly any good, well-drained garden soil. It needs adequate moisture, about 1 inch of water per week, and should not be allowed to wilt excessively. Cress accepts locations in full sun (8 to 10 hours will suffice) or partial shade (filtered sun all day or shade part of the day). A crop in shade will be cooled and may be harvested later than a crop in full sun.

## How to Plant

Planting cress in beds is the preferred method. Apply a complete garden fertilizer, such as 10-10-10, at a rate of 1½ pounds per 100 square feet of bed. Prepare the bed by tilling or spading, then rake out a smooth seedbed. (See "Soil Preparation" in the introduction to the vegetable garden.) Sow seeds about 1 inch apart in rows 8 inches apart across the bed. The seeds germinate rapidly, often in 3 or 4 days; do not thin the seedlings.

## Care and Maintenance

Flea beetles may be very troublesome, making lace of the cress leaves. Covering the planting with cheesecloth or commercial row covers is the best means of preventing this damage. (See the pest control chart in the introduction to the vegetable garden.) Cress will tolerate some frost, and you can grow it in a cold frame for winter production if you protect it from the coldest temperatures. Or you can grow it in pots indoors under lights, but you must keep the temperatures cool, from 50 to 60 degrees Fahrenheit. If mites become a problem indoors, treat infested plants with insecticidal soap, or isolate the infested plants and discard them immediately before the rest of the plants are attacked.

### Additional Information

Cress matures within 14 to 21 days. Harvest leaves when they attain full size, or cut the whole plants when they reach usable size (for instance, big enough to use in a salad).

### VARIETIES

Only one named variety, 'Curleycress', is offered in garden catalogs. Winter cress, **Barbarea verna**, can be sown in late summer for a fall crop, but it is not of the same quality as garden cress; it matures in 55 days. Water cress, **Radicula nasturtium-aquatica**, can be grown in backyard water features where there is swiftly flowing clear water. Since it is a bit aggressive, regular harvests are necessary to prevent it from taking over.

## Tasty Cress Sandwiches

*Our friend Irene from Liverpool often revives our memories of cress sandwiches. We enjoyed these when we were little, during the time World War II had put a damper on the meat supply.*

*Spread cream cheese on two slices of dark brown pumpernickel bread. Thinly slice a fresh, chilled cucumber and layer slices on one piece of the bread. Cover generously with sprigs of cress, and top with the other slice of bread. Serve with chips and tea.*

# CUCUMBER

*Cucumis sativus*

Cucumbers are vine crops that are closely related to squashes, pumpkins, and melons. They are warm-season plants known for their refreshingly mild fruits. Many kinds of cucumbers have been developed to satisfy the demands of different cuisines. Some are short, and others are long and curved. Burpless types, often grown in greenhouses, are never bitter and are more typical of European tastes. As is the case with most vine crops, cucumbers can take up a lot of room, which makes them unsuitable for some gardens. The space required is about 50 square feet per plant on the ground; less space is required if they are grown on a trellis. In the last 12 to 15 years, bush types have been developed that take much less space and can even be grown in pots.

## When to Plant

These plants need warm weather to develop and may rot off if the weather is cool and wet, so don't be in a hurry to plant cucumbers in the garden. Sow seeds in peat pots indoors under lights on the frost-free date (average date of last frost). Because vine crops do not tolerate root injuries common to transplanting, be careful when setting transplants in the garden to avoid disturbing the tiny roots. Set out started plants or sow seed directly in the garden on the latest date of last frost, after the danger of frost has passed.

## Where to Plant

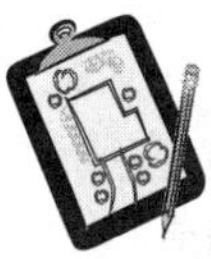

Soil with good drainage is important for cucumbers. (See the discussion on soils in the introduction.) They prefer a full-sun (8 to 10 hours will suffice) location, but they will grow and produce in light shade (a little shade from a distant tree or a honeylocust tree, or some shade in the middle of the day). Grow vining types on supports to save space and to make harvesting easier; grow bush types in beds or containers.

## How to Plant

Apply a complete garden fertilizer, such as 10-10-10, at a rate of $1\frac{1}{2}$ pounds per 100 square feet of garden. Spade or rototill the soil. (See "Soil Preparation" in the introduction to the vegetable garden.) After danger of frost has passed, sow 6 seeds or set 2 or 3 transplant seedlings in hills about 36 inches apart. In beds, space the plants 36 inches apart down the middle of each bed. Set the plants at the same depth they were growing. Thin the seedlings to 2 or 3 per hill when they are big enough to handle. If there is danger of disturbing the other seedlings, pinch off the extras instead of pulling them. Plants at this spacing can be left to vine or can be grown on supports. Vining cucumbers can grow vertically on a trellis, on a fence, or up strings; whatever the support, it must be sturdy enough to bear the weight of a vine that may have as many as 6 or 8 cukes developing at one time.

## Care and Maintenance

Water as needed to make sure that plants get about 1 inch of water per week. Cucumber beetles are serious threats that not only eat the plants but also infect them with bacterial wilt that will kill the plants about the time they begin to produce fruit. As soon as cucumber seedlings are planted or germinate in the garden, protect them from these pests. Apply Sevin insecticide, or use row covers over the plants, being sure to tuck in the edges and ends, to keep the beetles out. After the plants begin to vine, feel free to remove the covers or stop applying the insecticide. A virus disease, cucumber mosaic, may cause misshapen, lumpy cucumbers. To prevent this disease, which aphids carry from infected weeds, grow resistant varieties, and control aphids with Malathion or insecticidal soap. (See beetles and aphids on the pest control chart in the introduction to the vegetable garden.)

### Additional Information

Harvest cukes when they reach a mature size, before they turn yellow. Cucumbers, like all vine crops, have both male and female flowers. The male flowers, which usually appear first, are smaller than the females. Many times new gardeners are dismayed that the flowers fall off without any cucumbers. That usually happens because the flowers are all males. Female flowers have tiny cucumbers below the flowers themselves; male flowers have only slender stems (see page 54). New gynoecious hybrids produce only female flowers. They produce a lot more cucumbers per plant, but need pollen from male flowers. A few seeds of a standard variety that produces both male and female flowers are included in each seed packet. Unless you intend to plant the entire packet of seeds, plant a few seeds of the standard types. (They are usually larger than the gynoecious ones.) Bees that feed on the male flowers and then on the females carry pollen from one to the other. Without bees, there will be no cucumbers.

## VARIETIES

Standard cucumbers are 6 to 8 inches long, borne on vines or bush-type plants. Burpless types, European or Asian cucumbers, are often 1 foot or more—sometimes up to 3 feet—long and are never bitter; they grow on either vines or bush-type plants. Pickling types are 2 to 6 inches long; most are vining types, although a few bush kinds are beginning to appear on the home garden market. Generally, the vining types are much more productive than the bush-types.

| Variety | Days to Maturity | Comments |
|---|---|---|
| **Pickling** | | |
| Bush Pickle | 48 days | Good for pots. |
| Calypso | 52 days | Gynoecious, dark green with white spines, vining. |
| National Pickling | 54 days | Black spines. |
| **Slicing (Bush)** | | |
| Bush Crop | 55 days | Delicious cukes on dwarf bushes. |
| Fanfare | 63 days | Great taste, disease resistant; AAS. |
| Salad Bush | 57 days | Excellent disease resistance, 8-inch cukes on compact plant; AAS. |
| **Slicing (Vine)** | | |
| Burpless | 62 days | The original burpless, no bitterness. |
| Marketmore 76 | 68 days | Good disease resistance. |
| Marketmore 86 | 56 days | Early. |
| Slice Master | 58 days | Gynoecious, good disease resistance. |
| Straight 8 | 58 days | Longtime favorite in home gardens; AAS. |
| Sweet Success | 54 days | European-type, long slicing cuke; AAS. |

# EGGPLANT

***Solanum melongena* var. *esculentum***

Most people recognize eggplants with their dark purple fruits and wonder how they got the name. Actually, there are varieties with small white fruits that look very much like eggs hanging on the plants. These are often available as potted plants for decorations rather than for food. Eggplant is a member of the same family as tomatoes, potatoes, and peppers. Culture of eggplant is very similar to that of bell peppers. Neither plant requires support, although eggplants are bigger than peppers. These warm-weather crops thrive where the summer is long and hot. Eggplant is probably a native of India and has been cultivated for more than 1,500 years. It is of great importance as a crop in the Far East and is more common than tomatoes in India, China, and the Philippines.

## When to Plant

There is no need to plant eggplants into the garden very early. They need warm weather to develop and may rot off when the weather is cool and wet. Eggplants are much more sensitive to cold than tomatoes are. They will not grow until the soil is warm. Sow seeds indoors under lights about 2 weeks before the frost-free date (average date of last frost). The plants are slow to start, taking at least 6 to 8 weeks to reach a transplanting size. Set out started plants after the latest date of last frost, or sow seed directly in the garden after any danger of frost has passed.

## Where to Plant

The sun provides the warmth needed by these plants to thrive. Plant them in a full-sun (8 to 10 hours will suffice) location with good drainage. Well-drained soils warm up more quickly than other soils.

## How to Plant

Prepare the soil by spading or tilling. (See "Soil Preparation" in the introduction to the vegetable garden.) Incorporate organic matter and fertilizer at half the normal rate ($1/2$ pound of 10-10-10 or a similar proportion) per 100 square feet of garden. To seed directly in the garden in rows, sow seeds in hills 12 inches apart, with 24 to

30 inches between rows or even closer for smaller-fruited varieties. After seedlings are up, thin them to 1 per hill. (You can recognize eggplant seedlings because they will be in rows and all look the same; weed seedlings will be randomly spaced, and all will look different.) In a bed, space the hills 12 to 18 inches apart in each direction, which will allow 2 or 3 plants across the bed.

Transplants started indoors or bought from greenhouses or garden centers should have 3 to 4 sets of leaves with a healthy green color. Check plants carefully for signs of insects because aphids and whiteflies often gain entrance to the garden on infested transplants. Remove the plants from the containers, and set the plants at the same depth they were growing in the containers. Firm the soil gently around the plants, and water in with 1 cup of transplant starter fertilizer, mixed according to directions on the package, per plant. In rows, space the plants 12 inches apart, with 24 to 30 inches between rows. In a bed, space the hills 12 to 18 inches apart in each direction. Homegrown transplants tend to become weak and leggy, but even leggy ones will make decent plants in the garden with proper handling. Do not plant them deeper to compensate, or the roots will suffocate. Plant them on their sides, and cover the long stems lightly with soil. The tips of the stems will quickly turn upward, and the buried stems will sprout new roots.

## Care and Maintenance

After they are established, eggplants can stand dry weather. For best production, however, water them as needed to provide 1 inch per week. When the plants are half grown (about 12 inches high, but size depends on the variety; check the seed packet for size), side-dress them with a high-nitrogen fertilizer. Pests and diseases may pose problems with eggplants. Flea beetles will make small holes in the leaves, and a severe infestation can reduce yield; control the pests with Sevin insecticide. Verticillium wilt is a serious disease that causes the plants to dry up about the time they start to produce fruit; plant resistant varieties, and rotate the planting from one part of the garden to another each year. (See the pest control chart in the introduction to the vegetable garden.)

### Additional Information

Harvest the fruit when it reaches full size and is still glossy. Overly mature fruit will be spongy, seedy, and bitter. Cut the stem with shears or a sharp knife instead of trying to tear the fruit off. Watch out! The stems may be thorny.

| Varieties | Days to Maturity | Comments |
|---|---|---|
| **Long-Fruited** | | |
| Ichiban | 70 days | Long, slim fruit. |
| Little Fingers | 68 days | Fruit in clusters. |
| Slim Jim | 70 days | Lavender. |
| **Novelty** | | |
| Easter Egg | 52 days | White, egg-sized, egg-shaped, ornamental and edible. |
| **Oval-Fruited** | | |
| Black Beauty | 80 days | Deep purple heirloom, but still popular. |
| Black Magic | 72 days | Classic shape. |
| Burpee Hybrid | 80 days | Improved production. |
| Cloud Nine | 75 days | Pure white, bitter-free. |
| Dusky | 60 days | Early. |
| Ghostbuster | 80 days | White and sweeter than purple varieties. |

# Eggplant Parmigiana

FROM RALPH COLUCCI'S KITCHEN

*My next door neighbor, Ralph the Chef, picked all of my eggplants just as they were ready to harvest. Before I could get angry with him, they were returned as eggplant parmigiana in little, single-serving trays for freezing.*

*Pare and cut eggplant into ½-inch thick slices. Dip slices in butter and bread crumbs. Place in greased baking pan (or single-serving trays), salt to taste, and cover with spaghetti sauce with mushrooms. Sprinkle with crushed fresh oregano, and top with shredded or sliced Parmesan cheese. Bake at 450 for 10 to 12 minutes or until done.*

# ENDIVE-ESCAROLE

*Chicorium endivia*

These cool-season crops are closely related. The main difference is that endive has finely cut, curly leaves, while escarole leaves are broad and flat or cupped. For production purposes, they are virtually the same, grown like leaf lettuce in the spring or fall. The bitter flavor is an acquired taste, and the leaves are used sparingly in salads with lettuce and other greens or as garnish. These plants are often blanched, which reduces the bitterness a bit. A little in the garden will go a long way. We grow only 2 or 3 plants of each to meet the needs of 2 of us.

## When to Plant

Sow seeds indoors under lights 8 weeks before the frost-free date (average date of last frost), and set transplants into the garden as soon as they are large enough to handle. Seed directly into the garden in late March when the soil can be worked. For a fall crop, start seeds about July 15, and set plants in the garden when they are transplant size, usually August 15 to 20. Fall production can last well into winter as the plants can stand a hard freeze. The flavor improves with freezing.

## Where to Plant

Endive and escarole need well-drained soils that dry quickly for planting early in spring, and good drainage promotes their root development. A location in full sun (8 to 10 hours will suffice) will produce large, vigorous plants that experience fewer problems with diseases, slugs, and earwigs; a location in partial shade (filtered sun all day or shade part of the day) will reduce production, but will make the plants less bitter.

## How to Plant

Apply a complete garden fertilizer, such as 10-10-10, at a rate of $1\frac{1}{2}$ pounds per 100 square feet of garden. Spade or rototill the soil. (See "Soil Preparation" in the introduction to the vegetable garden.) Sow seeds 8 to 10 per foot in rows 18 inches apart. In a bed, sow seeds in rows 10 inches apart across the bed. Thin seedlings to 1 plant every 10 inches. (You can recognize endive or escarole seedlings

## VARIETIES

Harvesting of endive and escarole can begin within 80 to 100 days in normal seasons, that is, seasons that are not unusually hot or cold.

| Varieties | Comments |
|---|---|
| **Endive** | |
| Frisian | Good in fall. |
| Green Curled Ruffec | Attractive as a garnish. |
| Neos | Frilly and self-blanching. |
| Nina | Early, deeply cut foliage. |
| Salad King | Large leaves to 2 feet. |
| Traviata | Self-blanching. |
| **Escarole** | |
| Broad-Leaved/ Batavian | Large, smooth. |
| Full Heart | Crumpled leaves. |
| Nuvol | Self-blanching. |
| Sinco | Best for cool weather, fall. |

because they will be in rows and all look the same; weed seedlings will be randomly spaced, and all will look different.) In rows, space the transplants 9 to 12 inches apart, with 18 inches between rows. In a bed, space the plants 9 to 12 inches apart, which will allow 4 or 5 plants across the bed. Set the plants at the same depth they were growing. For summer seeding directly in the garden, sow the seed, moisten it, and cover the rows with boards to keep them from drying out. Lift the boards every morning and evening to see whether the seedlings have emerged. As soon as the first seedlings appear, remove the boards.

## Care and Maintenance

You won't have to spend a lot of time caring for these plants. Keep the soil slightly on the dry side, but do not let the plants wilt. They require about 1 inch of water or less per week. Control weeds until the plants spread enough to shade them out. Earwigs and slugs can be troublesome because they will get into the heads as they develop. Control these pests while the plants are small. For slugs, use bait; for earwigs, use Sevin insecticide, but do not harvest within 14 days of using Sevin on these plants. (See the pest control chart in the introduction to the vegetable garden.)

### Additional Information

These greens have better flavor when they are blanched before harvest. Leaves that develop in full sun will be dark green, tough, and bitter. When the plants have spread enough to touch each other, tie up the outer leaves over the developing heads. Harvest them 2 or 3 weeks later, and discard the outer leaves. For continuing production, tie up a few plants each week. As daytime temperatures begin to exceed 75 degrees Fahrenheit, the plants will bolt (send up flower stalks) and quality will deteriorate.

# GARLIC

***Allium sativum***

Garlic is a hardy perennial bulb that is grown as an annual. The bulb actually consists of a cluster of small bulblets called cloves or toes, covered in a papery wrapper. Garlic is an ancient vegetable, native to the Mediterranean. The Romans fed it to their slaves and soldiers because they thought it would impart extra strength to the hardworking people. The Romans themselves despised it because of its objectionable odor. Health benefits are attributed to garlic today, and it is a common item in health food stores. Garlic is used primarily as a flavoring in European and Asian dishes, although more people are using it more often in all kinds of cooking. Roasted garlic, which loses much of its pungency, is a tasty appetizer, especially with Italian or Greek cuisine.

## When to Plant

Plant garlic in late summer or fall; it requires a long growing season to develop large bulbs. In parts of the Midwest with a long growing season, garlic can be planted in early spring as soon as the soil can be worked. The garlic will make a crop that summer, although the bulbs will be small.

## Where to Plant

Garlic prefers a location in full sun (8 to 10 hours will suffice) with well-prepared, well-drained soil. Planting in compacted soil will result in small, misshapen bulbs. (See "Soil Preparation" in the introduction to the vegetable garden.)

## How to Plant

Apply a complete garden fertilizer, such as 10-10-10, at a rate of 3 pounds per 100 square feet of garden. Then work the soil into a fine seedbed (make sure that the soil is finely broken up). Start garlic from the cloves (sometimes called toes) which you have separated from the bulbs. Plant individual cloves 2 inches deep and 4 inches apart in rows 1 foot apart. In beds, plant in rows 4 inches apart. To have straight necks on the bulbs, keep the pointed ends up. If onion maggots have plagued your plants in the past, mix Diazinon in the water according to label directions, and use it as you water in the bulbs.

**VARIETIES**

Elephant garlic, which is actually a leek that forms a large bulb, smells and tastes like garlic, and it is grown the same way as common garlic. Some gourmet seed catalogs list several kinds of garlic. For example, topset garlic develops bulbs on the tops of the leaves. These tiny bulbs can be planted closely in rows and grown like green onions. The entire small plants are harvested and chopped for use in soups, spaghetti sauces, or wherever garlic would typically be added.

## Care and Maintenance

Make sure the garlic has plenty of water if the weather turns dry; it requires about 1 inch of water per week. Keeping weeds under control is an ongoing task. Since the garlic does not provide complete cover, weeds will germinate all season. If thrips become troublesome, treat them with insecticidal soap. (See the pest control chart in the introduction to the vegetable garden.)

### Additional Information

Garlic begins to bulb when the days are longest in June. The larger the plants at that time, the larger the bulbs will be, so it is important to keep the plants growing. Harvest the garlic as soon as most of the leaves have turned yellow, usually in midsummer. Do not wait for all the leaves to turn yellow. You can begin harvesting when 5 to 6 green leaves still remain. If the plants are allowed to stay in the ground too long, the papery covering may begin to deteriorate. The ideal situation is to dig in the morning during dry weather. Let the bulbs dry where they are in the garden until afternoon, then collect them and spread them on screens or slats where they can cure for 2 to 3 weeks. After they are cured, brush off as much soil as possible, and cut off the tops. Or braid them together, and hang them in a dry place. Do not peel the bulbs, and do not wash them. Use damaged ones immediately. Dry garlic keeps much better than onions. Save some of the very best bulbs for planting the next season.

# HORSERADISH

*Armoracia rusticana*

The pungent roots of horseradish are unforgettable. This easily produced crop can be grown as a perennial and pieces of root harvested as needed, but the best roots are produced when the plant is grown as an annual, replanted every spring. Horseradish is a member of the cabbage family, related to mustard, turnips, cauliflower, cress, and broccoli. A native of Eastern Europe, it has been under cultivation since the Middle Ages, and it is a favorite of people of European origin. Horseradish has been grown commercially for markets in this country where these immigrants settled. The sharpness of horseradish adds character to roast prime rib and corned beef; it is an essential with oysters along the eastern seaboard of the U.S. Although it is readily available in jars at the supermarket, there is nothing like freshly ground horseradish mixed with a little vinegar or maybe cut with a little fresh beet to calm it down a tad.

## When to Plant

Horseradish is a completely hardy plant that will tolerate freezing. It is propagated from root cuttings planted as early in the spring as the ground can be prepared.

## Where to Plant

Deeply prepared, well-drained soil in full sun (8 to 10 hours will suffice) produces large, tasty roots. (See "Soil Preparation" in the introduction to the vegetable garden.) Plant them at the side of the garden where they will not be disturbed if you plan to leave them in the ground all winter.

## How to Plant

Apply a low-nitrogen garden fertilizer, such as 5-20-20, at a rate of 2 pounds per 100 square feet of garden. Work the soil deeply and well so that long, straight roots will develop. Shallow or difficult soils will result in crooked, branched roots. The plant is propagated from root cuttings (small, thin roots) trimmed from the large roots as they are harvested. The cuttings should be 8 to 10 inches long and the diameter of a pencil. As the cuttings are collected, they are cut off squarely at the top end and on an angle at the bottom. Doing this assures that the roots are planted right side up. Planted upside down, the roots will not grow. During the winter, root cuttings are stored by tying them in bundles and healing in moist sand. In the spring plant the cuttings in a furrow 6 inches deep, or dibble them into holes spaced about 18 inches apart in rows 3 feet apart. Set each cutting on an angle with the pointed end down and the top about 2 inches below the surface; place the cuttings so that they are parallel to the furrow. Make sure all the cuttings are pointing the same direction. Cover them to make a ridge of soil about 4 inches high, and firm the soil over the cuttings. Water to settle the soil. Usually, 3 or 4 plants are sufficient for a family garden.

## Care and Maintenance

Horseradish grows slowly until late summer. Keep weeds under control so they do not compete with the crop. Water as needed to keep the plants from wilting, about 1 inch of water per week. To produce large, compact roots like those in commercial operations, lifting the plants is necessary. Here is how to do it: 4 to 6 weeks after the tops begin to grow, carefully dig under the roots from the top end, lifting each one without loosening the lower tip. Do you remember which way you planted it? If you lift the wrong end, you will sever the last remaining roots at the lower tip, and the plant will not develop. You must lift the top end, so keep track of which way you planted the roots. Brush away the soil and strip off the small rootlets that have begun to grow along the sides. Do not damage the lower part where it is still hooked in the soil. Set the stripped root back in the ground, cover it carefully, and soak thoroughly to settle the soil. The best production of horseradish occurs when it is replanted each season. Dig the last of it before growth begins in the spring and the bed is prepared. Make sure to remove all the small roots or they will grow into small, inferior plants. Or you may prefer to leave horseradish in the ground from year to year. Although the roots will be small, they will grow very nicely and have good flavor and pungency. Few pests affect horseradish in the garden. Flea beetles may make holes in the leaves; if they seem to be a threat, apply Sevin insecticide to prevent damage. Root maggots may be troublesome, but seldom do much damage to large roots. (See the pest control chart in the introduction to the vegetable garden.)

### Additional Information

Harvest horseradish in the fall after a good freeze. The freeze stops the growth of the plant, and the sugars that impart the sharpness accumulate. Dig only as much as you need at one time because the roots deteriorate if they're not used quickly after harvesting. Save small side roots for planting the next year. Kept in tightly closed jars in the refrigerator, prepared horseradish will last about 6 weeks. Frozen in small containers, it can be used year-round. Horseradish is always best used freshly ground.

## VARIETIES

Most catalogs list either of these 2 varieties, but some may list only horseradish. Properly grown, either is excellent.

| Varieties | Days to Maturity | Comments |
|---|---|---|
| Bohemian | 180 to 200 days | Smooth, pointed leaves. |
| Maliner Kren | 180 to 200 days | Crinkled, round leaves. |

## Horseradish

*I like horseradish on just about any kind of meat, especially bratwurst and roast beef. Freshly prepared horseradish is the best.*

*Peel and cut up about 2 cups of horseradish chunks. In a food processor, combine the chunks with about ¾ cup white vinegar and 1 teaspoon salt. Grind until it is the texture you like. (I prefer it medium fine.) Be careful when you taste freshly ground horseradish. It may be hotter than you think! If it is too hot, try grinding about ¼ cup of freshly harvested and peeled beets cut into chunks with 1¾ cups horseradish chunks. This will cut the heat a bit. You can vary the amount of beets to suit your palate.*

# KALE

***Brassica oleracea* var. *acephala***

Kale is a member of the cabbage family and is grown as a cool-weather crop. It is a blue, leafy cabbage used as a garnish or in salads, or it may be cooked just as you would cook cabbage. Ornamental flowering kale, with red, white, pink, or purple foliage, has become popular as a garnish or as decoration for salad bars. Ornamental kale is edible but not tasty.

## When to Plant

This plant produces well in spring, but may be better grown for a fall crop because frost improves the flavor by taking out some of the bitterness. For the earliest spring production, start with transplants, either homegrown or store bought. If you prefer to grow your own, sow seed indoors under lights about 8 weeks before the frost-free date (average date of last frost), and set plants into the garden about 6 weeks later. Transplants are often available at garden centers about that time as well; buy plants that have a good green color, are short and compact, and have no pests. If you choose to sow seed, sow it directly in the garden as early as the soil can be worked. Since the kale will be harvested and out of the garden in midsummer, plan to replace it with a second crop. For a fall crop, sow seed indoors about July 1, then set the seedlings in the garden about August 10. Kale can stand a freeze, and mild fall weather may last well into December some seasons. With protection (for example, snow cover or light straw mulch), the plants can survive a mild winter and produce the following spring before they bolt.

## Where to Plant

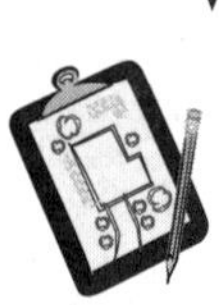

Plant kale in a location with full sun (8 to 10 hours will suffice) or partial shade (filtered sun all day or shade part of the day) and good drainage.

## How to Plant

Apply a complete garden fertilizer, such as 10-10-10, at a rate of $1\frac{1}{2}$ pounds per 100 square feet of garden. Spade or rototill the soil. (See "Soil Preparation" in the introduction to the vegetable garden.) In rows, space the transplants 12 inches apart, with 18

to 24 inches between rows. In a bed, space the plants 12 inches apart in each direction, which will allow 3 or 4 plants across the bed. Set the plants at the same depth they were growing. Water in the plants with a transplant starter fertilizer, such as 10-52-17 or 10-30-10, mixed according to directions on the label, and apply approximately 1 cup per plant. If root maggots have been a problem in the past and your previous crops have suffered damage, cover rows with screening or floating row covers after planting and leave them in place until plants are sizeable, because fly larvae may damage roots or stems. Or sow seeds in rows 1/4 inch deep and 1 inch apart; then when the seedlings appear, thin them to 9 to 12 inches apart. Sow seeds in beds 1/4 inch deep and 1 inch apart in rows 12 inches apart across the beds, and when the seedlings appear, thin them to 12 inches in each direction. To have kale in the fall, sow seed directly in the garden in midsummer; thin the seedlings to the proper spacing, and move excess seedlings to another row. Cover the rows with screens after sowing seed, and leave them in place until the seedlings are sizable because fly larvae may damage stems or roots.

## Care and Maintenance

Kale is a low-maintenance crop. For the best quality, water to keep the plants vigorous and growing; they require about 1 inch of water per week. Prevent infestation of cabbage worms with *B.t.* (*Bacillus thuringiensis* Kurstaki). Apply maneb to prevent leaf spot diseases when the first symptoms appear. Eliminate yellows and black rot and blackleg diseases by planting disease-resistant varieties and by rotating the *Brassica* crops (cabbage, collards, Brussels sprouts, broccoli, Chinese cabbage, etc.) to other areas of the garden each year. Use PCNB (Terraclor) in the transplant water to prevent clubroot.

### Additional Information

Harvest leaves when they have achieved full size (8 or 10 inches long) or cut the heads. If possible in the fall, wait until a frost before harvest. The flavor is much better after the leaves have been frosted.

**VARIETIES**

| Varieties | Days to Maturity | Comments |
|---|---|---|
| Dwarf Blue Curled Scotch | 70 days | Tightly curled, blue. |
| Dwarf Curled Vates | 60 days | Highly curled, blue-green. |
| Winterbor | 65 days | New hybrid, worth a try. |

# KOHLRABI

*Brassica oleracea* var. *gongylodes*

This member of the cabbage family is often called stem turnip because of the large swelling that develops just above the soil line. The leaves of kohlrabi grow out from the turniplike swelling, which is the edible part of the plant; some cooks also use the leaves like cabbage. Kohlrabi tastes like mild white turnips.

## When to Plant

Kohlrabi is a cool-weather plant that is most productive in spring, but may be grown for a fall crop. For the earliest production, start with transplants, either homegrown or store bought. To have a continuous supply of kohlrabi, plan on starting seedlings every 2 weeks or so. Begin sowing seed indoors under lights about 8 weeks before the frost-free date (average date of last frost), and set plants into the garden about 6 weeks later. Transplants are often available at garden centers about that time as well; buy plants that have a good green color, are short and compact, and are free of pests. If you choose to sow seed, sow it directly in the garden as early as the soil can be worked. Since the kohlrabi will be harvested and out of the garden in midsummer, plan to replace it with a second crop. For a fall crop, sow seed indoors about July 1, and set the seedlings in the garden about August 10. Kohlrabi can tolerate a freeze and may last until Thanksgiving with mild fall weather.

## Where to Plant

Plant kohlrabi in well-prepared, well-drained soil in a location with full sun (8 to 10 hours will suffice) or partial shade (filtered sun all day or shade part of the day).

## How to Plant

Apply a complete garden fertilizer, such as 10-10-10, at a rate of $1\frac{1}{2}$ pounds per 100 square feet of garden. Spade or rototill the soil. (See "Soil Preparation" in the introduction to the vegetable garden.) In rows, space the transplants 6 inches apart, with 24 inches between rows. In a bed, space the plants 6 inches apart in each direction, which will allow 7 or 8 plants across the bed. Set the plants at the same depth they were growing. Water in the plants with a transplant starter fertilizer, such as 10-52-17 or 10-30-10, mixed according to directions on the label, and apply approximately 1 cup per plant. If root maggots have been a problem in the past and your previous crops have suffered damage, cover rows with screening or floating row covers after planting and leave them in place until plants are sizeable, because fly larvae may damage roots or stems. To have a fall crop, sow seed directly in the garden in midsummer; thin seedlings to the proper spacing noted for transplants, and move excess seedlings to another row if you prefer not to dispose of them.

**VARIETIES**

| Varieties | Days to Maturity | Comments |
|---|---|---|
| **Purple** | | |
| Early Purple Vienna | 62 days | The standard purple. |
| Rapid | 45 days | Earliest purple type. |
| **White** | | |
| Early White Vienna | 55 days | The favorite early white. |
| Eder | 38 days | Very early. |
| Grand Duke | 50 days | Hybrid, good quality, early. |

## Care and Maintenance

This is not a labor-intensive plant. Rapid growth results in the best quality, so water kohlrabi as necessary—it requires about 1 inch per week—to keep it vigorous and growing. Slowly growing plants are tough and woody. Some pests and diseases may affect the plantings. Prevent infestation of cabbage worms with *B.t.* (*Bacillus thuringiensis* Kurstaki). Apply maneb to prevent leaf spot diseases when the first symptoms appear. Eliminate yellows and black rot and blackleg diseases by planting disease-resistant varieties and by rotating the *Brassica* crops (cabbage, collards, Brussels sprouts, broccoli, Chinese cabbage, etc.) to other areas of the garden each year. Use PCNB (Terraclor) in the transplant water to prevent clubroot. (See the pest control chart in the introduction to the vegetable garden.)

### Additional Information

Harvest kohlrabi when it is about 3 inches in size by cutting just below the head with a sharp knife. Allowed to grow beyond maturity, the plant will be tough, woody, and poorly flavored. Use the small, tender leaves like other greens.

# LEEK

***Allium ampeloprasum***

Leeks are relatives of onions and chives. They have a milder, smoother flavor than the sharp, pungent taste that many people find objectionable in onions. The edible portion is the cylindrical base of the leaves instead of a bulb like an onion. Native to the Mediterranean, leeks have been cultivated since prehistoric times. Old Testament accounts of Moses mention them along with cucumbers, melons, onions, and garlic.

## When to Plant

For the earliest production, start with transplants, either homegrown or store bought. If you grow your own, sow seed indoors under lights about February 15, and set plants into the garden 3 weeks before the average date of last frost or as early as the soil is workable. Transplants are often available at garden centers about that time as well; buy ones that have a good green color, are short and compact, and have no pests. If you prefer to sow seed, sow it directly in the garden as early as the soil can be worked.

## Where to Plant

Leeks require deeply prepared, well-drained soil. (See "Soil Preparation" in the introduction to the vegetable garden.) The plants prefer full sun (8 to 10 hours will suffice) for maximum production. This long-term crop usually requires 100 or more days to mature.

## How to Plant

Apply a complete garden fertilizer, such as 10-10-10, at a rate of 1½ pounds per 100 square feet of garden. Spade or rototill the soil to a depth of at least 6 inches; double-digging beds is even better. In rows, space transplants 4 inches apart, with 12 to 18 inches between rows. In a bed, space the plants 4 inches apart in rows 12 inches apart, which will allow 10 to 12 plants across the bed. Set the plants somewhat deeper than they were growing. Water in the plants with a transplant starter fertilizer, such as 10-52-17 or 10-30-10, mixed according to directions on the label, and apply approximately 1 cup per plant. If onion maggots have been a problem in the past and your previous crops have suffered damage, cover rows with screening or floating row covers after planting and leave them in place until plants are sizeable, because fly larvae may damage roots or stems. To direct seed, sow 10 to 15 seeds per 1 foot of row, and thin to the proper spacing noted for transplants when the seedlings are about 4 inches tall.

### VARIETIES

Many new varieties are coming from Europe where leeks are more popular than here in the United States. Check garden catalogs for the latest available varieties that suit your purposes.

| Varieties | Days to Maturity | Comments |
|---|---|---|
| Alaska | 105 days | Winter hardy. |
| Broad London | 100 days | An old standby. |
| Titan | 70 days | For summer use. |

## Care and Maintenance

As the plants begin to grow, blanch the lower parts of the stems. Cultivate lightly, hilling soil up on the plants. Be careful not to bury the plants too deeply or too soon, or they will rot. When the plants approach full size, bank them with several inches of soil. An alternative to banking with soil is to wrap the bases of the plants with brown wrapping paper. This system is probably a good choice if you are growing just a few plants. Leeks are heavy feeders, so side-dress them with nitrogen 6 weeks after transplanting. Water the plants adequately to keep them growing; they require about 1 inch of water per week. Leeks are susceptible to damage by thrips and by onion maggots. Control thrips with Malathion or insecticidal soap; control maggots with Diazinon in the transplant water. (See the pest control chart in the introduction to the vegetable garden.)

### Additional Information

Harvest leeks when the bases of the stems are about 1 inch in diameter. Dig only what you need because the plants store well in the ground and continue to increase in size. Some varieties will reach 3 inches in diameter in a good season. Carefully dig under the leek, and sever the roots. Make sure to dig deeply enough to miss the buried stem. Then wiggle the leek out of the ground without breaking it off. Trim off the rest of the roots and the tops, leaving about 2 inches of leaves. For leeks that remain by winter, mulch them in, and continue the harvest all winter (as long as the ground is not frozen) and in spring until the end of March. After that they start to send up seed stalks, and the quality deteriorates.

# Lettuce

***Lactuca sativa***

No other salad crop is grown or used in such large quantities as lettuce, which has become an essential part of salads. Lettuce is a cool-weather crop that can be grown in spring or fall. Hot weather causes it to become bitter and to develop a tall seed stalk. The iceberg lettuce commonly found in grocery stores is head lettuce grown in the South in the winter and in the cooler parts of the country during the summer. Leaf, romaine, and butterhead or Bibb lettuce often are grown in greenhouses and are more common in home gardens.

## When to Plant

Lettuce can stand a freeze. Plant it early and harvest it before hot weather arrives. For the earliest production, start with transplants, either homegrown or from garden centers. To grow your own, sow the earliest seed for head lettuce indoors about 8 weeks before the frost-free date (average date of last frost), and sow seed for leaf lettuce indoors 2 weeks later. Grow the plants under lights or in the greenhouse, and transplant them into the garden when they are large enough to handle—about 3 or 4 weeks before the frost-free date. Transplants are usually available from garden centers about that time as well; buy plants that have a good green color, are short and compact, and have no pests. Unless you want lots of lettuce at one time, make several seedings to spread out the harvest. Lettuce seed needs light to germinate, so do not cover it. Sow seed of leaf lettuce varieties directly in the garden as early as the soil can be worked. Since the lettuce will be harvested and out of the garden by midsummer, plan to replace it with a second crop. Sow seed directly in the garden or indoors about July 15. Set the seedlings in the garden about August 10. With a mild fall, lettuce may last until Thanksgiving. We have picked lettuce in our garden as late as December.

## Where to Plant

Lettuce prefers full sun (8 to 10 hours will suffice), but to have extended production during the hot summer months, plant it in partial shade (filtered sun all day or shade part of the day). Excellent drainage is beneficial for these plants need lots of water for vigorous growth. The roots cannot stand soggy soils, however; plants in soggy soils will be susceptible to diseases, and leaves may scald (dry out and become papery) at the edges.

## How to Plant

Apply a complete garden fertilizer, such as 10-10-10, at a rate of $1\frac{1}{2}$ pounds per 100 square feet of garden. Spade or rototill the soil. (See "Soil Preparation" in the introduction to the vegetable garden.) In rows, space the transplants of head lettuce about 12 inches apart, with 12 to 18 inches between rows. In a bed, space the plants of head lettuce 12 inches apart, which will allow 3 or 4 heads across the bed. Set transplants at 4 by 6 inches for leaf types, or 6 by 6 inches for Bibb or romaine types. Set the plants at the same depth they were growing. Seed leaf lettuce in triple rows (3 closely spaced rows in a row) 12 inches apart. Thin leaf lettuce to 4 inches and Bibb or romaine types to 6 inches. In beds, sow rows 6 inches apart, then thin to 4 to 6 inches between plants.

## Care and Maintenance

To keep the plants growing, water them as needed, about 1 inch of water per week. Control weeds while the plants are small by careful hoeing or pulling. Be careful; lettuce plants are shallowly rooted and easily uprooted. Pests may affect the plantings. Control earwigs by keeping the plants well spaced and harvested as they mature. Sevin insecticide may be used up to two weeks before harvest. Control aphids by spraying them with insecticidal soap, then rinse the foliage to remove the residue. (See the pest control chart in the introduction to the vegetable garden.)

### Additional Information

Harvest leaf lettuce by snipping off the outer leaves as soon as they are large enough for your use. When plants are large enough, harvest every other one, leaving more room for the others. Harvest head, Bibb, and romaine lettuce when the heads are full size. Mesclun is a mixture of many kinds of leaf lettuce and some other salad greens (such as escarole, arugula, cress, and endive) broadcast-sown together and harvested by snipping leaves of each kind as they mature. It makes an interesting salad. A problem with lettuce picked in hot weather is that it will be bitter. Wash it and store it in the refrigerator for a couple of days, and it will lose the bitterness.

## VARIETIES

Four types of lettuce are grown in gardens. **Bibb lettuce** forms small, loose heads and has a mild, buttery flavor. **Head lettuce** is the kind available year-round in supermarkets; it is not heat tolerant. **Leaf lettuce** may be either green or red. Various leaf forms are grown; some are smooth and round, and others are deeply cut, wrinkled, serrated, or curled. **Romaine lettuce** forms loose, upright bunches; outer leaves are green while the interior leaves are blanched and white.

| Varieties | Days to Maturity | Comments |
|---|---|---|
| **Bibb Lettuce** | | |
| Buttercrunch | 50 to 60 days | Tolerates high temperatures. AAS. |
| Dark Green Boston | 50 to 60 days | Large heads, grown commercially. |
| Summer Bibb | 50 to 60 days | Holds well in heat; does not bolt. |
| Tom Thumb | 50 to 60 days | Tender, miniature heads. |
| **Head Lettuce** | | |
| Great Lakes | 90 days | Tolerates warm weather. |
| Iceberg | 90 days | Standard head lettuce type commonly available in food stores. |
| Ithaca | 90 days | Resists bitterness. |
| Summertime | 90 days | Slow to bolt. |
| **Leaf Lettuce, Green** | | |
| Black-Seeded Simpson | 50 days | Early. |
| Early Curled Simpson | 50 days | Curled leaves. |
| Grand Rapids | 50 days | For fall crop. |
| Oak Leaf | 50 days | Good in hot weather. |
| Salad Bowl | 50 days | Finely cut. |
| **Leaf Lettuce, Red** | | |
| Red Sails | 50 days | Slow bolting. AAS. |
| Red Salad Bowl | 50 days | Deeply cut burgundy. |
| Ruby | 50 days | Darkest red. |
| **Romaine Lettuce** | | |
| Green Towers | 60 days | Early. |
| Parris Island Cos | 60 days | Slow to bolt. |
| Sangria | 60 days | Rose-tinged. |

# MUSKMELON

***Cucumis melo* var. *reticulatus***

Muskmelons are vine crops, closely related to cucumbers, squashes, and pumpkins. These hot-weather plants with sweet, juicy fruit are commonly called cantaloupes, especially the small, smooth, and round ones shipped from the South and available in grocery stores year-round. Actually, cantaloupes are small, hard, and warty fruits common in Europe but rarely seen here in the U.S. Muskmelons, as well as honeydews and Crenshaws—2 other summer melons—need a long, hot season to develop. Crenshaws are rarely grown in the North because the season is so short. Like most vine crops, muskmelons can occupy a lot of room, which may make you reconsider planting them if yours is a small garden. A way to use less space is to grow them on trellises.

## When to Plant

Don't be in a hurry to get muskmelons into the garden very early. They need warm soil (about 70 degrees Fahrenheit or higher) to develop and may rot off if weather is cool and wet. Sow seeds in peat pots indoors under lights a week before the frost-free date (average date of last frost), then set out started plants or sow seed directly in the garden after the latest date of last frost.

## Where to Plant

Muskmelons need a full-sun (8 to 10 hours will suffice) location with well-drained soil and plenty of space. The minimum area required is 25 to 30 square feet per hill. There are alternatives if you have only a small space, however. You may train the vines on a trellis, making sure the structure is strong enough to support the plants; each melon may weigh 2 pounds, and several may develop on a vine. Or you may choose to grow bush types in beds or containers.

## How to Plant

Apply a complete garden fertilizer, such as 10-10-10, at a rate of 1½ pounds per 100 square feet of garden. Spade or rototill the soil. (See "Soil Preparation" in the introduction to the vegetable garden.) Sow seeds 1 inch deep in hills about 36 inches apart. In a bed, space them 36 inches apart down the middle. Careful handling is necessary with vine crop transplants because they do not tolerate root injuries common to transplanting. Indoors under lights, sow seeds in peat pots that can be planted without disturbing the roots. Start them about 4 weeks before the latest date of last frost to have large enough plants for setting out. After danger of frost has passed, carefully set 2 or 3 transplant seedlings in hills about 36 inches apart. In a bed, space the plants 36 inches apart down the middle. Set the plants at the same depth they were growing. Melon transplants in peat pots are sometimes available in garden centers at the correct planting time; if you choose to buy them rather than grow your own, be sure that they have a good green color and are free of pests.

## Care and Maintenance

Water the plants as necessary; they require about 1 inch of water per week. Pests and diseases may affect the plantings. As soon as muskmelon seedlings are planted in the garden, protect them from cucumber beetles. Cucumber beetles not only eat the plants but also infect them with bacterial wilt that will kill the plants about the time they begin to produce fruit. Apply Sevin insecticide, or use row covers on the plants, being sure to tuck in the edges and ends, to keep the beetles out. After the plants begin to vine, remove the covers, and stop the application of Sevin. Protect the foliage from diseases with maneb or an all-purpose garden fungicide. Rotate vine crops to a different part of the garden each year to reduce chances of disease. (See the pest control chart in the introduction to the vegetable garden.)

### Additional Information

Growing melons vertically on a trellis or on a fence requires sturdy supports to bear the weight of the plants with fruits on them. To provide additional support for the heavy fruits, use a little net or a cloth parachute under each melon, tied securely to the trellis or fence. Muskmelons, like all vine crops, have both male and female flowers. (See page 78.) The male flowers, which usually appear first, are smaller than the females. Many times new gardeners are dismayed that the flowers fall off without any melons. That usually happens because the flowers are all males. Female flowers have tiny melons below the flowers themselves; male flowers have only slender stems. The flowers are pollinated by bees that feed on the male flowers and then on the females, carrying the pollen from one to the other. Without bees, there will be no melons. If the weather is unfavorable for bees (cold, dark, and wet weather), pollinate the melons by hand by clipping a male flower and dusting pollen from it on the pistils of the female flowers. For the best quality and sweetness, harvest melons when they are ripe. How can you tell when they are ripe? The rind changes from green to tan between the netting, and a ripe melon will smell sweet. Also a small crack will appear next to where the stem is attached when the melon is ready to be picked. Muskmelons do not continue to ripen once they are picked. They will become softer, but not sweeter.

## VARIETIES

| Varieties | Days to Maturity | Comments |
|---|---|---|
| **Bush** | | |
| Honeybush | 80 days | Sweet bush hybrid. |
| **Green** | | |
| Jenny Lind | 75 days | Heirloom. |
| Sweet Dream | 79 days | Sweet. |
| **Honeydew** | | |
| Limelight | 96 days | Sweet. |
| Venus | 88 days | Aromatic. |
| **Orange** | | |
| Ambrosia | 86 days | Too soft to ship, the sweetest of the muskmelons. |
| Earlisweet | 68 days | Better where season is short. |
| Harper Hybrid | 86 days | Excellent disease resistance; AFPM. |
| Magnifisweet | 85 days | Rivals Ambrosia; FF2. |
| Saticoy | 86 days | FPM. |
| Supersun | 85 days | Large, good flavor. |

Abbreviations for disease resistance:
A = Alternaria, F = Fusarium wilt,
F2 = Fusarium wilt, Race 2,
PM = Powdery mildew.

# Mustard

*Brassica juncea*

This leafy relative of cabbage and collards is grown early in the season and also as a fall crop. Mustard is an important green vegetable in southern gardens and is used as a leafy table green, one of the constituents of traditional southern cooking. Since the middle of the twentieth century, mustard has become increasingly popular in the Midwest. Even midwestern gardeners can add it to their list of plantings because it will withstand frost.

## When to Plant

Seed directly in the garden about 21 days before the frost-free date (average date of last frost). For continuous production, sow seed every 3 weeks until warm weather arrives. Sow again starting in August for a fall crop.

## Where to Plant

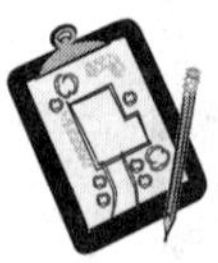

Mustard prefers full sun (8 to 10 hours will suffice), although it is often grown in partial shade (filtered sun all day or shade part of the day) with good results. The leaves will be larger and thinner in shade. Providing a location with good drainage will reduce disease problems.

## How to Plant

Apply a complete garden fertilizer, such as 10-10-10, at a rate of 1½ pounds per 100 square feet of garden. Spade or rototill the soil. (See "Soil Preparation" in the introduction to the vegetable garden.) In rows, sow seed 15 to 20 inches apart. In a bed, sow seed in rows 10 to 12 inches apart across the bed. Thin the seedlings to 6 inches apart. Many old-time gardeners broadcast-sow mustard in beds and thin the seedlings as they develop. They don't waste the ones they pull out because they put them in the soup pot. If root maggots have been a problem in the past and your previous crops have suffered damage, cover rows with screening or floating row covers after planting and leave them in place until plants are sizeable, because fly larvae may damage roots or stems.

## Care and Maintenance

Mustard that is well-watered can be very productive; provide 1 inch of water per week if insufficient rain falls. Control weeds by careful hoeing or pulling. Pests and diseases may affect the plantings. Prevent infestation of cabbage worms with *B.t.* (*Bacillus thuringiensis* Kurstaki). Apply maneb to prevent leaf spot diseases when the first symptoms appear. Eliminate black rot and blackleg diseases by planting disease-resistant varieties and by rotating the *Brassica* crops (cabbage, collards, Brussels sprouts, broccoli, Chinese cabbage, etc.) to other areas of the garden each year. (See the pest control chart in the introduction to the vegetable garden.)

**VARIETIES**

| Varieties | Days to Maturity | Comments |
|---|---|---|
| Green Wave | 45 days | Curled leaves, slow to bolt. |
| Savannah | 35 days | Vigorous, slow to bolt. |
| Southern Giant Curled | 50 days | Brightly colored curly leaves, slow to bolt. |

### Additional Information

Harvest individual leaves when they are large enough for your use, or harvest the entire plant when leaves are full size. Warm weather will cause the plants to bolt (send up flower stalks). Pull out the plants when this happens, then work the soil and prepare to sow another crop for fall.

## Cooked Mustard Greens with Bacon and Onion

*Wash 1 pound of mustard greens carefully; about 5 times (like spinach, they can hide an incredible amount of grit). First soak, then swish in the water, then shake out above the water and check for dirt in the water. Repeat several times until there has been no grit twice. Slice a handful at a time into thin (½ inch wide) strips.*

*Cook ½ pound bacon in a deep dish to render the fat. Remove the bacon and sauté 1 sliced yellow onion until the slices just begin to turn brown. Add the sliced greens and stir over medium heat until they wilt, then add the reserved bacon and cover the dish. When cooked, add ½ teaspoon pepper and 2 tablespoons vinegar. Serve warm.*

# Okra

***Abelmoschus esculentus***

Okra is a relative of hollyhock and hibiscus. Gardeners grow it for the immature fruit pods or seed pods that they use to thicken soups and stews and to cook as vegetables. Okra is what makes gumbo . . . gumbo!

## When to Plant

A warm-weather crop, okra should be planted after soils have warmed up (70 degrees Fahrenheit or higher). There is no need to get an early start because seeds will not germinate in cool soils. Sow seed directly in the garden a week or so after the latest date of last frost. Usually, the first week of June is a good time to plant. Or start okra indoors under lights about May 1, and set out seedlings when soils have warmed.

## Where to Plant

Plant okra in full sun (8 to 10 hours will suffice) in a well-drained part of the garden. Locate these large, tall plants in an area where they will not shade out smaller plants.

## How to Plant

Apply a complete garden fertilizer, such as 10-10-10, at a rate of 1½ pounds per 100 square feet of garden. Spade or rototill the soil. (See "Soil Preparation" in the introduction to the vegetable garden.) Sow seeds in rows 36 inches apart, then thin to 1 plant every 12 inches. In a bed, sow seeds in hills 24 inches apart, then thin to 1 plant per hill. Usually, 2 plants across the bed is enough. To prepare transplants indoors, sow 3 seeds in each peat pot, thin to 1 seedling, and set the plant into the garden at the spacing noted above after soils have warmed. Set the plants at the same depth they were growing while being careful not to damage the roots. Water in the plants with a transplant starter fertilizer mixed according to label directions. This complete fertilizer has a very high-soluble phosphorus analysis, such as 10-52-17, 10-50-10, or 10-30-10.

## Care and Maintenance

Okra needs little care to produce a good crop. Provide 1 inch of water per week, and remove the weeds by hoeing or pulling.

### Additional Information

Harvest the pods when they are about 3 inches long and still tender. Use a knife or shears, and cut them every 2 days so they won't become woody. Okra plants have irritating hairs that cause some people to break out in a rash, so wear gloves and long sleeves when working with them. Be sure to remove any overripe pods to stimulate continuing production. The plants will produce until damaged by the cold.

**VARIETIES**

| Varieties | Days to Maturity | Comments |
|---|---|---|
| Burgundy | 60 days | Red pods. AAS. |
| Cajun Delight | 50 days | Early, attractive plants fit in flower garden. AAS. |
| Clemson Spineless | 56 days | Nearly spine-free. AAS. |
| Dwarf Green Long Pod | 52 days | Small plants, ribbed pods. |

# Gumbo

*Here's a recipe for chicken gumbo from Grandma June in East Tennessee: In 6 quarts of water, simmer 1½ pounds chicken legs and thighs cut into serving portions, 1 cup lima beans, 2 teaspoons salt, ½ teaspoon pepper, and 1 bay leaf. In separate pan, fry 1½ pounds sliced okra, 1 medium sliced onion, and 1 cup corn in 2 tablespoons butter. When light brown, add one #10 can tomatoes. After about an hour, add the vegetables and ¼ cup uncooked rice to the chicken and lima beans. Continue to simmer about 30 more minutes.*

# Okra and Rice

*For a tasty, quick dish, fry 3 slices chopped bacon in a skillet until crisp. Remove the bacon to a bowl. Add 2 cups cooked rice and 1 cup cooked bite-size pieces okra to the bacon drippings and mix well. Simmer for several minutes, stirring occasionally. Stir in the bacon just before serving.*

# Onion

***Allium cepa***

Gardeners grow these members of the lily family for the immature green bunching onions, often called scallions, or for the mature dry bulbs. Onions seem to have originated in the eastern Mediterranean from Palestine to India. The Old Testament describes them as one of the items the Israelites longed for during their long sojourn in the desert. Onions are so easy to grow and so useful in the kitchen that they should be part of every garden.

## When to Plant

Onions are completely hardy; put them out as soon as the soil can be worked in spring. Start them from seed sown directly in the garden, from seedling transplants (called stick-outs), or from onion sets (sets are most often available commercially). Sets which are tiny onion bulbs grown the previous season are the easiest way to start onions in the home garden. Sow seed for stick-outs indoors under lights about mid-January.

## Where to Plant

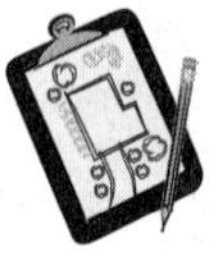

Plant onions in full sun (8 to 10 hours will suffice) in well-prepared, well-drained soil. (See "Soil Preparation" in the introduction to the vegetable garden.)

## How to Plant

Apply a complete garden fertilizer, such as 10-10-10, at a rate of 1½ pounds per 100 square feet of garden. Work the soil until it is finely broken up. In rows, space stick-outs 3 inches apart, with 12 to 15 inches between rows. In beds, space the plants 3 inches apart in rows 12 inches apart across the beds, which will allow 12 to 15 plants across the beds. Set the plants somewhat deeper than they were growing, about 1 inch. Water in the plants with a transplant starter fertilizer, such as 10-52-17 or 10-30-10, mixed according to directions on the label. If onion maggots have been a problem in the past and your previous crops have suffered damage, cover rows with screening or floating row covers after planting and leave them in place until plants are sizeable, because fly larvae may damage roots or stems. Space onion sets 1 inch apart for green onions and 3 inches apart for dry onions. For dry onions, push the sets into the soil surface. For green onions, plant the sets 2 or 3 inches deep to develop the long, white stems. Direct seed 12 to 15 seeds per foot of row, and thin to the proper spacing when they are about 4 inches tall. Thin to 1 per inch for green bunching onions, and eventually to 1 every 3 inches for dry onions. Use the green onions as you remove them for thinning.

## Care and Maintenance

Onions are shallowly rooted, so be careful as you hoe or pull weeds. Try to get as much top growth as possible by the first day of summer. Bulbs begin to form when the days reach about 15 hours in length, and the size of the dry onions is determined by the size of the tops. Apply 1 inch of water each week if the weather is dry. Side-dress onions with 10-10-10 fertilizer when the plants are about 12 inches tall. If thrips become troublesome, treat the plants with Malathion or insecticidal soap. (See pest control chart in the introduction to the vegetable garden.)

### Additional Information

Harvest green onions when the stems are pencil-sized. Pull any dry onions that form flower stalks, and use them immediately because they will not store well as dry onions. When the tops begin to yellow and fall over, pull them to one side with the back of a rake. Do not walk the tops down or the development of the bulbs will stop. (Walking the tops down refers to an old-fashioned idea that you needed to crush the tops to get the bulbs to form.) Pull the dry onions when all the tops have gone down, preferably in the morning during dry weather. Let them dry there in the garden where you pulled them until afternoon, then collect them and spread them on screens or slats so that they can cure for 2 to 3 weeks. After they are cured, knock off as much soil as possible, and cut the dry tops to about $1\frac{1}{2}$ inches long. Do not peel the bulbs, and do not wash them. Use damaged onions immediately. Store the onions in mesh bags or wire baskets in a dry, cool place, and they will last all winter.

## VARIETIES

Some onions form bulbs when days are short, others when days are long. Short-day varieties are grown in the winter in the South; for example, the Vidalia onions grown in Georgia are short-day varieties. Use only long-day varieties for midwestern gardens. Short-day varieties will not form bulbs in the long days of midwestern summers. Home gardeners have little choice when buying sets: onions are yellow, white, or red, and they can be round or flat. There are more choices when buying seed for stick-outs or direct seeding. The following are suitable for the Midwest; use the varieties that are the easiest to obtain.

| Varieties | Days to Maturity | Comments |
|---|---|---|
| **Red** | | |
| Red Barron | 85 days | Colorful in salads. |
| Southport Red Globe | 85 days | Good on hamburgers and attractive in salads. |
| **White** | | |
| Southport White Globe | 85 days | Globe, good slices. |
| Sugar Star | 90 days | Mild, sweet flavor; Spanish type. AAS. |
| White Portugal | 85 days | A good white for home garden. |
| White Sweet Spanish | 85 days | Globe. |
| **Yellow** | | |
| Early Yellow Globe | 85 days | Good keeper. |
| Ebenezer | 85 days | Slightly flat. |
| Stuttgarter | 85 days | Popular. |
| Sweet Spanish Hybrid | 85 days | Sweet. |
| Walla Walla Sweet | 85 days | Mild. |
| Yellow Globe Danvers | 85 days | Globe. |
| Yellow Sweet Spanish | 85 days | Globe. |

# Caramelized Onion Pizza

*Preheat oven to 450 degrees. Heat 1 tablespoon olive oil in skillet over medium heat. Add 2 sliced jumbo onions, ½ teaspoon salt, and 2 teaspoons sugar, and cook until onions are soft and golden, stirring occasionally, for about 25 minutes. Remove from heat and stir in ¼ teaspoon dried basil, a pinch of garlic powder, and a pinch of seasoned salt to taste. Place 1 large or 2 small pre-cooked pizza shells on cookie sheet, heap onion mixture on top, and top with 6-8 ounces grated Swiss or mozzarella cheese. Bake 10 to 12 minutes, until cheese is melted and golden.*

# PARSNIP

*Pastinaca sativa*

Parsnips are long-season vegetables grown for their carrotlike roots. They are native to Europe and Asia and have been cultivated in this country since the first colonists arrived, as early as 1609 in Virginia and the 1620s in Massachusetts. Colonists from the *Mayflower* may have brought parsnips with them and used them for food and seed during those first difficult years.

## When to Plant

Sow seed as soon as the soil can be worked in the early spring. Members of the parsley family, parsnips take very little effort to grow once the seed germinates.

## Where to Plant

This crop will be in the ground for nearly a year, so grow it where it will not be disturbed by other garden activities. Because parsnips develop long, deep roots, they need deeply prepared, well-drained soil in full sun (8 to 10 hours will suffice).

## How to Plant

Apply a complete garden fertilizer, such as 10-10-10, at a rate of 1½ pounds per 100 square feet of garden. Spade the soil over deeply, at least 1 full spade deep or deeper if possible. Make sure that any organic matter is well incorporated or the roots will be crooked or forked. Work the soil surface into a fine seedbed; improperly prepared soil will cause poor germination. Check the date on the seed pack to assure the freshness of parsnip seed, which is very short-lived. In rows, sow seeds 2 inches apart, with 12 inches between rows. In a raised bed, sow the rows 8 to 10 inches apart across the bed. Cover the seed with ½ inch of fine soil. Thin the seedlings to 3 or 4 inches. Parsnip seed takes forever to germinate. One method of seeding in a raised bed is to sow 3 or 4 parsnip seeds in hills every 6 or 7 inches in the row, and to sow radish seeds in between. The radishes will mark the rows and will help prevent crusting of the soil over the seeds. Harvest the radishes shortly after the parsnip seedlings are up, then thin the parsnip seedlings to 1 per hill.

## VARIETIES

| Varieties | Days to Maturity | Comments |
|---|---|---|
| All American | 150-180 days | Good flavor, favorite of commercial growers. |
| Cobham Improved Marrow | 150-180 days | Sweet, half-long, and best for shallow soils. |
| Hollow Crown | 150-180 days | An old standard, fine-grained and sweet. |

# Care and Maintenance

To prevent weeds from overtaking parsnip seedlings, carefully cultivate or hand weed until the plants are large enough to shade out the weeds. See that soil moisture is consistent—about 1 inch per week—to encourage even development of the roots. When the plants are about half grown (tops are 8 to 10 inches tall), side-dress them with a complete fertilizer, 10-10-10, at the rate of $\frac{1}{2}$ to 1 pound per 100 square feet of garden.

## ADDITIONAL INFORMATION

To grow show-quality parsnips, or to grow parsnips in heavy or stony soil, plant them in individual holes in the garden. Use a post hole digger, an auger, or a crowbar to make holes 3 feet deep, 6 inches wide at the top, and about 12 inches apart. Fill the holes with a prepared soil of $\frac{1}{3}$ coarse sand, $\frac{1}{3}$ brown peat moss, and $\frac{1}{3}$ fine garden soil. With a broom handle, a 2-by-2, or something similar, compact the soil as the holes are filled to 1 inch or so from the surface. Sow 6 seeds at the center of each hole, and cover them with $\frac{1}{2}$ inch of the prepared soil. Thin the seedlings to the one nearest the center of the hole. Since these holes will dry out faster than the surrounding soil, check them and be prepared to water them; they need about 1 inch per week. Harvest parsnips after they have been exposed to freezing temperatures. The cold changes the starch in the roots to sugar. People who don't like parsnips have probably never tasted them when they were properly grown. Store parsnips in the ground all winter, and dig them as needed. Place heavy mulch, 6 to 12 inches, over them to keep the ground from freezing. Dig the roots carefully with a deep spade or fork, being careful to get completely to the bottoms of the roots. Harvested roots may be stored in plastic bags in the refrigerator for several weeks.

# PEA

***Pisum sativum* var. *sativum* (English and Snap)**
***Pisum sativum* var. *macrocarpon* (Sugar)**

Peas are decidedly cool-weather plants, intolerant of hot weather. As soon as the weather warms up, production ceases, much to the dismay of many pea-loving gardeners. Peas lose their flavor quickly after harvest. That explains why peas from the market are never as flavorful as those picked fresh. "Picking the vines" as the peas develop in your garden is a sure way to have the best-tasting vegetables on your kitchen table. Gardeners grow peas for the immature, edible pods (sugar or snow peas); for the edible pods with immature seeds (snap peas); or for the mature seeds (English or garden peas), which are shelled out for use.

## When to Plant

Sow peas in the garden as soon as the soil can be worked in spring. St. Patrick's Day is none too early most years. I have planted on Valentine's Day in a few unusual years and picked a reasonable crop. The seeds germinate when soil temperatures reach about 45 degrees Fahrenheit. To produce a fall crop, use heat-tolerant varieties, and sow them in midsummer so they mature in the cool weather of fall.

## Where to Plant

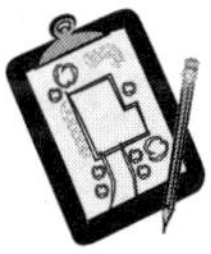

Peas need full sun (8 to 10 hours will suffice) for full production. Since they will be planted very early, a soil in a part of the garden that drains well and dries out early in the spring is an advantage. For late production, partial shade (filtered sun all day or shade part of the day) shields the plants from intense heat and may prolong the season.

## How to Plant

By preparing the soil in the fall, you can sow the seeds at the earliest opportunity in the spring without having to wait to till the soil. Peas are legumes; they derive their nitrogen from the air and do not need nitrogen fertilizers. Whether preparing the soil in spring or fall, apply a garden fertilizer, such as 5-20-20, at a rate of 1½ pounds per 100 square feet of garden. Spade or rototill the soil. (See "Soil Preparation"

in the introduction to the vegetable garden.) Rake out the seedbed and leave it over winter if you till in the fall. Peas may be either bush or vining types. Sow seeds 1 inch apart and 1 inch deep in rows 12 to 18 inches apart. Thin seedlings to 8 to 10 inches apart. (You can recognize pea seedlings because they will be in rows and all look the same; weed seedlings will be randomly spaced, and all will look different.) In a bed, sow seeds in rows across the bed, or plant double rows, 6 inches apart along each side of the bed, and set supports between them.

## Care and Maintenance

Bush peas are self-supporting. Placing vining types on a support of some kind conserves space, makes picking easier, and keeps the peas from getting muddy every time it rains. Many gardeners use "pea sticks" to support both bush and vining plants. "Pea sticks" are small branches, 2 to 4 feet long, stuck in the ground along the rows to support the plants as they grow. Some enterprising garden centers collect such branches and offer them for sale each spring. Sugar and snap peas are nearly all vining types. Gardeners grow them on various kinds of trellises, fences, or poles, and biodegradable netting supported on stakes is a popular system too. After harvest is completed, the netting and vines are removed for composting. Peas need to be watered only during a dry spring; they require about 1 inch of water every 10 days. Since fall is often dry, fall crops usually need to be watered to get them to germinate and to achieve full production.

### Additional Information

Harvest English or garden peas when they are full sized and before the seeds begin to dry. Pods should be green, not yet turning tan. Harvest snap peas when the pods are full sized for the variety and before the seeds are mature. Harvest sugar peas when the pods are fully formed, but before the seeds begin to develop.

## VARIETIES

Early, midseason, and late varieties of peas are available. Since the season is usually too short anyway, and plants have not finished producing by the time hot weather arrives, plant the earliest varieties. The wrinkled-seeded varieties listed here tolerate cold, wet soils better than smooth-seeded varieties.

| Varieties | Days to Maturity | Comments |
|---|---|---|
| **English Peas** | | |
| Alaska | 57 days | Early. |
| Little Marvel | 63 days | Old standard. |
| Mr. Big | 58-60 days | Sweet flavor, needs no support. AAS. |
| Sparkle | 60 days | Freezes well. |
| **Snap Peas** | | |
| Early Snap | 60 days | Thick pods. |
| Sugar Daddy | 72 days | Stringless. |
| Sugar Lace | 65 days | Sweet, good producer. |
| Sugar Snap | 74 days | The original snap type, needs support. AAS. |
| **Sugar Peas** | | |
| Dwarf Gray Sugar | 65 days | Tall. |
| Snowbird | 58 days | Pods in clusters. |

# Creamed Peas with Mushrooms

*Steam 2½ cups of fresh peas until just tender; set aside. In a large frying pan, over medium low heat sauté 2 chopped green onions and ½ pound fresh sliced mushrooms in ¼ cup of butter until just soft, about 5 minutes.*

*Sprinkle 2 tablespoons flour into the pan; stir. Gradually add in ¾ cup milk, stirring constantly to make a smooth sauce. Add 1 teaspoon sugar, ⅛ teaspoon thyme, ⅛ teaspoon nutmeg, ½ teaspoon savory, 1 teaspoon salt, and pepper to taste and continue stirring until sauce is thickened and smooth. Add peas to sauce in pan, and heat through.*

# PEPPER

***Capsicum annuum, Capsicum chinense***
***Capsicum frutescens***

Peppers are available in so many types and varieties that most gardeners stick to a few types that they will use in their recipes. The most familiar peppers are the bells: green-red, yellow, purple-lilac, and orange. These are generally mild and can be used as green peppers or allowed to ripen. All green peppers eventually turn one of the other colors. Sweet peppers are usually *C. annuum* whereas hot peppers can be any of the 3 species noted. Hot peppers are usually called chilies, and the intensity of the heat and the flavor vary tremendously. The heat, measured in Scoville units, can be as tolerable as jalapenos at a respectable 3000 to 5000 Scoville units, to the frighteningly hot habaneros at a staggering 285,000 Scoville units. Peppers and chilies can be bell-shaped, round, pointed, or slender, but most chilies are long and slim.

## When to Plant

Peppers are warm-weather plants. There is no sense getting them in the garden before soils warm up because the plants will just sit there. Start seed indoors under lights about 2 weeks before the frost-free date (average date of last frost). Set the plants in the garden when all danger of frost has passed, usually about the first of June.

## Where to Plant

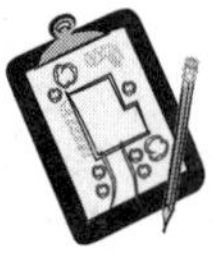

Plant peppers in a well-drained part of the garden that receives full sun (8 to 10 hours will suffice).

## How to Plant

Apply a complete garden fertilizer, such as 10-10-10, at a rate of ¾ pound per 100 square feet of garden. Spade or rototill the soil. (See "Soil Preparation" in the introduction to the vegetable garden.) Use your homegrown pepper transplants, or buy transplants from greenhouses or garden centers. Transplants should have 3 to 4 sets of leaves that are a healthy green color. Purple- or yellow-tinged plants will have difficulty getting started; the color indicates that they are weak or hungry and will need time to begin growing after being damaged. Check plants carefully for signs of insects because aphids and whiteflies often gain entrance to the garden on infested transplants. In rows, space the plants 10 inches apart, with 18 to 24 inches between rows. In beds, space the plants 15 inches apart in each direction, setting 2 or 3 plants across a bed. Remove the plants from the containers, and set the plants at the same depth they were growing in the containers. Firm the soil gently around each plant, and water in with 1 cup of transplant starter fertilizer mixed according to directions on the package. Homegrown transplants may become weak and leggy. Do not plant them deeper to compensate, or the roots will suffocate. Plant them on their sides, and cover the long stems lightly with soil. The tips of the stems will quickly turn upward, and the buried stems will sprout new roots.

## Care and Maintenance

Peppers are easy to grow, but diseases and pests may become problems if you are not alert to them. Eliminate verticillium and fusarium wilts, and yellows, by planting disease-resistant varieties. Control foliar diseases with maneb fungicide. These plants are very susceptible to a virus disease, tobacco mosaic, carried from infected weeds by aphids. There are some reports that the disease maybe transferred to the plants by working with them after handling tobacco products. Some researchers think curing the tobacco destroys the virus. Be safe. Wash your hands. Use insecticidal soap to combat aphids and mites; apply Sevin to cope with caterpillars and beetles. (See pest and disease control chart in the introduction to the vegetable garden.) Other troubles include blossom-end rot and lack of fruit set. Blossom-end rot appears as a leathery-brown spot on the bottom of a pepper. Poor growing conditions, such as cold or wet weather—not disease—cause blossom-end rot. Usually, only the first few peppers show this problem, and the rest of the fruits are fine. Catfacing (malformed fruit) is due to poor pollination. Peppers are sensitive to weather conditions while flowers are being pollinated. Too hot, too cold, or too calm and the flowers abort and fail to set fruit. Certain varieties are less susceptible to aborting, so try several until you find ones that do well in your garden's conditions. To promote pollination, tap flower clusters in early morning to shake pollen from the flowers onto the pistil. I usually use a pencil to tap the flowers. Peppers need 1 inch of water per week; water them if nature does not cooperate. Side-dress the plants with a complete fertilizer when they have set fruit.

## Additional Information

Handle all hot peppers with care! This point cannot be overemphasized. Wear rubber gloves if there are any cuts on your hands. Do not touch your face or eyes after touching hot peppers or serious eye damage can result. Harvest sweet peppers at any size. Pick bell peppers while they are green, before they turn color. Pick the new brightly colored bell peppers as they mature. After ripening, the flavors improve. Harvest hot peppers when they are red-ripe unless the recipe calls for green chilies. Cutting the peppers with a sharp knife or shears is a better method than pulling them off, which may break the plants.

## VARIETIES

There are more and more choices for good quality peppers turning various colors at maturity. The following are worth trying:

| Varieties | Days to Maturity | Comments |
|---|---|---|
| **HOT PEPPERS** | | |
| Big Chili | 68 days | Classic Anaheim type, large. |
| Cherry Bomb | 65 days | Not as hot as others. |
| Habanero | 90 days | Blistering, watch out! |
| Hungarian Wax | 70 days | Really hot. |
| Jalapeno | 75 days | Familiar in Tex-Mex cuisine. |
| Large Red Thick Cayenne | 75 days | These are really hot. |
| Long Red Slim Cayenne | 75 days | Hot enough! |
| Red Chili | 85 days | The familiar chili. |
| Tam Jalapeno | 65 days | Not quite as hot as a regular jalapeno. |
| **SWEET PEPPERS** | | |
| **BELL TYPES** | | |
| **Chocolate** | | |
| Chocolate Beauty | 85 days | Late, slow to set. |
| Chocolate Belle | 75 days | Earlier, maybe smaller. |
| **Green/Orange** | | |
| Orange Sun | 80 days | Late but good fall color. |
| Valencia | 90 days | Very late, good color in salads. |
| **Green/Red** | | |
| Bell Boy Hybrid | 70 days | 4-lobed, excellent for stuffing; TMV. AAS. |
| Better Belle Improved | 65 days | Better than the original; TMV. |

## VARIETIES

| Varieties | Days to Maturity | Comments |
|---|---|---|
| **Green/Red** (continued) | | |
| Giant Marconi | 70 days | Excellent for grilling; not bitter; TMV, PVY. AAS. |
| King Arthur | 72 days | Large fruit, very productive. |
| Lady Bell | 72 days | Sets well in cooler areas. |
| Vidi | 64 days | Sets well under stress; TMV. |
| **Green/Yellow** | | |
| Canary | 72 days | Fresh color, early. |
| Ori | 74 days | Sets well under stress. |
| Orobelle | 76 days | Blocky, colorful. |
| **Ivory/Red** | | |
| Blushing Beauty | 75 days | Ivory to blush-pink to red. AAS. |
| **Purple** | | |
| Lilac | 70 days | Lavender, turning red at maturity. |
| Purple Belle | 70 days | Nearly black, turning red at maturity. |
| **FRYING TYPES** | | |
| Biscayne | 65 days | Pale green to red at maturity. |
| Gypsy | 65 days | Pale yellow to orange to red. AAS. |
| Key Largo | 66 days | Pale green, red at maturity. |
| Sweet Banana | 70 days | Pale yellow, waxy. |
| **PIMENTO TYPES** | | |
| Pimiento Elite | 85 days | Red at maturity. |
| Super Red | 70 days | Good, early. |

Abbreviation: TMV = Tobacco mosaic disease resistance.
PVY = Potato virus Y

# Green Pepper Chutney

*Grind 5 green peppers, 4 jalapeños, 2 teaspoons tamarind paste, 2 teaspoons sugar, ½ teaspoon salt, 1 teaspoon mustard, and ½ teaspoon turmeric with a little water. In a medium saucepan, season a little mustard in 2 tablespoons of oil. After it sputters, add the ground items and cook till it separates from the sides. Tastes great with sandwiches.*

# Potato

***Solanum tuberosum***

The potato ranks with rice and wheat as one of the world's leading food crops. It is the number one vegetable crop, grown in nearly every country of the world. The potato is actually a shortened stem called a tuber. It contains dormant buds (eyes), which sprout to start new plants. Potatoes originated in the high country of South America and were cultivated by the Incas. They made their way to Europe with the early Spanish explorers in the sixteenth century. After achieving wide acceptance in Europe, they reached North America in the 1700s and had become a staple by the end of that century. People in some parts of the world have relied heavily on potatoes. Their importance to Ireland was evident when early blight ruined the crop, causing the potato famines of 1845 to 1847. The results were starvation and mass immigration to this country. Potatoes continue to be essential to the well-being of people in some parts of the world, particularly Eastern Europe where they are the main source of carbohydrate. Potatoes are less important as staples in this country, but are very popular as snacks, chips, fries, double-baked potatoes, and side dishes. Health-conscious Americans equate potatoes with high calories, but the vegetables are not at fault. The butter and sour cream that are mounded on the spuds cause the problems. Potatoes are actually low in calories and fat, and high in vitamins, complex carbohydrates, potassium, and fiber.

## When to Plant

Although potatoes can stand a frost, a freeze will kill them. (With a frost, temperatures do not go below 32 degrees Fahrenheit, but water vapor crystallizes on surfaces. A freeze is colder than 32 degrees Fahrenheit, and water freezes.) Don't be in a rush to plant them. If the soil is too wet and cold, the plants will not grow, and the seed pieces may begin to rot. If the weather is moderate and the soils are workable, plant seed about 3 weeks before the average date of last frost.

## Where to Plant

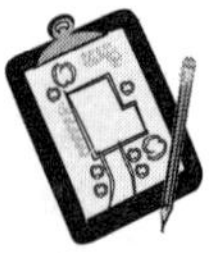

Plant potatoes in a full-sun (8 to 10 hours will suffice) location that has well-drained and well-tilled soil. Hard, lumpy soil will result in poorly formed potatoes. If the soil is heavy or puddled (hard, compacted condition of heavier soil with a high clay content), incorporate organic matter and till the soil during the preceding fall. Allow it to remain rough over the winter to mellow it.

## How to Plant

Potatoes are started from seed pieces, not from actual seeds. The seed pieces are sections of tuber $1\frac{1}{2}$ to 2 ounces in size to give the sprout enough energy for a good start. Do not save potatoes for seed because they may carry diseases. And do not try to grow plants from store-bought potatoes, which have been treated with sprouting inhibitors. Eventually, the treatment wears out and store-bought potatoes will sprout, but they will be delayed and are not certified disease free. To get the best start with your plants, buy certified seed potatoes from a reliable outlet. Seed that has already sprouted will develop faster and produce a bigger crop. Some gardeners intentionally sprout the seed potatoes before cutting them for planting. To follow that practice, spread out the seed potatoes in a bright, warm, humid place for 3 or 4 weeks. Cut the seed pieces a couple of days before planting, and spread them out to dry. Each piece should have at least 1 good sprout, and having 2 or 3 sprouts is even better. Be careful not to break the sprouts in planting. Apply a complete garden fertilizer, such as 10-10-10, at a rate of $1\frac{1}{2}$ pounds per 100 square feet of garden. Spade or rototill the soil.(See "Soil Preparation" in the introduction to the vegetable garden.) In rows, space the seed pieces 12 to 15 inches apart, with 24 inches between rows. In a bed, space the seed pieces 12 by 18 to 24 inches apart, which will allow 2 plants across the bed. Plant them 2 to 3 inches deep with the eyes up, then cover them gently to avoid breaking off any sprouts. In soil that is very heavy, shallow, full of rocks, or poorly drained, grow potatoes above ground (called straw potatoes). Set the seed pieces at the correct spacing but gently firmed into the soil surface, then cover them loosely with 6 inches of clean straw. The potatoes will root into the soil, but the tubers will form at the soil surface.

## Care and Maintenance

When the sprouts are about 6 inches high, begin hilling soil around them. With a hoe, pull soil from the spaces between the rows, being careful not to dig too deeply and injure roots. The hills eventually should be about 6 inches high and 1 foot wide. Potatoes that develop in light will be green and inedible. Hilling covers them and also cultivates the soil to loosen and aerate it while eliminating weeds. Fluff up straw over the straw potatoes, and as it thins out, add more straw to cover the developing tubers. Potatoes develop better in moist, cool soil. Water to provide 1 inch a week if nature does not cooperate because drought seriously reduces production, and uneven moisture causes knobby tubers. Soil temperatures of 60 to 70 degrees Fahrenheit are optimum for tuber production. (You may want to purchase a soil thermometer from a garden supplier or a garden catalog.) Pests and diseases may affect the plantings. Protect the plants from leaf hoppers, potato beetles, or flea beetles by applying Sevin insecticide or using floating row covers. Avoid planting potatoes and other solanaceous crops (peppers, tomatoes, eggplants, etc.) in the same place in the garden 2 years in a row because these plants are susceptible to the same diseases. Scab is a common potato disease that causes a rough surface to the tuber. Buying resistant varieties is the best prevention. The disease does not develop in acidic soils, but most Midwest soils are alkaline, and attempts to lower the alkalinity are usually less than successful. (See the pest control chart in the introduction to the vegetable garden.)

## Additional Information

Harvest new potatoes about 10 weeks after planting. When the first flowers on the potatoes appear, small tubers are usually ready. If you dig to remove a few, be very careful not to damage the others. New potatoes are easy to find under straw; simply lift the straw and steal a few. Be sure to replace the straw, and try to avoid damaging the roots or other tubers. When vines begin to yellow, dig the potatoes as soon as possible because potatoes left in the ground after they are ready for harvest may be harmed by insects or diseases. Cut off yellowing, old vines. The potatoes are usually 4 to 6 inches below ground, so carefully lift them with a fork or spade. Start far enough from the row to avoid cutting into any of the potatoes. Harvest straw potatoes by collecting them from the soil surface. If the soil is in good condition beneath the straw, some tubers may develop in the ground; be sure to dig after them too. Spread the potatoes on the ground for a couple of hours to dry off before collecting them. Do not wash them or they will not keep. Store them in the dark in a warm place to cure for a week or so, then store them at about 40 degrees Fahrenheit for the winter. Always keep them in the dark to prevent them from turning green.

## VARIETIES

The most commonly grown potatoes are either white or red skinned with white flesh. Less common are the potatoes with yellow, pink, blue, or purple flesh. Yellow potato varieties are gaining popularity because they are moist and seem to have better flavor than the more typical commercially grown varieties. While most commercial varieties are dry and tasteless as dust, home garden varieties are moist and flavorful.

| Varieties | Days to Maturity | Comments |
|---|---|---|
| **Blue** | | |
| All Blue | 100 days | Blue through and through. |
| **Red** | | |
| Norland | 110 days | Scab resistant. |
| Red Pontiac | 120 days | Does well in heavy soil. |
| Viking | 120 days | Unusually productive. |
| **White** | | |
| Green Mountain | 120 days | Heirloom, many misshapen tubers, but the best-tasting baking potato ever. |
| Katahdin | 130 days | Good looking, but marginal quality. |
| Kennebec | 130 days | Our favorite for excellent quality and production, large tubers. |
| Irish Cobbler | 110 days | Irregularly shaped. |
| Russet Burbank | 110 days | The most common commercial variety, needs cool soil, marginal quality. |
| **Yellow** | | |
| Yukon Gold | 100 days | Good flavor, moist. |

# Colorful Potato Salad

*For a colorful addition to any picnic, use different colored potatoes in your potato salad! Peel, boil and chill 3 large or 4 medium white, yellow, and purple potatoes. Cut into coarse chunks so the colors show. Mix 2½ cups potatoes with 1 teaspoon each of sugar and vinegar. Add ½ cup chopped celery for green color, ½ cup chopped onion, and salt to taste. Fold in ¾ cup mayonnaise and ¼ cup mustard; top with sliced hard boiled eggs, salad tomatoes, and parsley.*

# PUMPKIN

***Cucurbita pepo, Cucurbita maxima***
***Cucurbita moschata, Cucurbita mixta***

Pumpkins are much-loved decorations for the fall, but many people grow these warm-season vine crops for their flavorful flesh and for their seeds too. Actually, pumpkins are winter squashes, picked when they are fully colored and mature. The classification of the many varieties is thoroughly mixed up with 4 species represented. Varieties can have 2 or more species in their parentage; thus, it cannot be said that certain pumpkins are 1 species. As is the case for most vine crops, pumpkins can take a lot of room, which may cause some gardeners with restricted space to avoid growing them. In recent years, however, bush types have been developed that require much less space and can be grown in pots.

## When to Plant

There is no need to get pumpkins into the garden very early. They need warm weather to develop and may rot off if the weather is cool and wet. Sow seeds indoors under lights 1 month before the frost-free date (average date of last frost). Set out started plants or sow seeds directly in the garden after any danger of frost has passed.

## Where to Plant

Pumpkins prefer full sun (8 to 10 hours will suffice), although they will grow and produce in light shade (a little shade from a distant tree or some shade in the middle of the day). They need a location with well-drained soil. Expect the pumpkins to make huge vines, so allow them plenty of room to spread. If your garden has restricted space, grow smaller-fruited vining types on supports, or grow bush types in beds or containers.

## How to Plant

Apply a complete garden fertilizer, such as 10-10-10, at a rate of 1½ pounds per 100 square feet of garden. Spade or rototill the soil. (See "Soil Preparation" in the introduction to the vegetable garden.) Vine crops do not tolerate root injuries common to transplanting. To alleviate this problem, sow seeds indoors under lights in peat pots that can be planted without disturbing the tiny roots. After danger of frost has passed, sow 6 seeds or carefully set 2 or 3 transplant seedlings in hills about 5 feet apart, with rows 10 feet apart. Or space the plants 10 feet apart down the middle of a bed. Set the plants at the same depth they were growing. Thin the seedlings to 2 or 3 per hill when they are big enough to handle. If there is danger of disturbing the other seedlings, pinch off the extras instead of pulling them. Space bush types, which are well suited for a bed, 3 feet apart down the middle of the bed. Sow or plant dwarf bush types, 1 per container, in a commercial potting mix used in 5-gallon buckets or half barrels. Make sure they drain. Set plants at the same depth that they were growing.

## Care and Maintenance

After they set fruit, pumpkins need lots of water and fertilizer. Apply 1 inch of water per week when nature does not cooperate. Side-dress with nitrogen at half the normal rate when the vines have almost covered the ground, being careful to rinse with a hose if fertilizer gets on the leaves. Pumpkins produce both male and female flowers on the same plant. Usually, male flowers are produced first. Many gardeners are dismayed when these flowers fall off without making any pumpkins. Female flowers have tiny pumpkins just below the petals; male flowers have straight stems. (See page 54.) Bees are necessary for pollination as they carry the pollen from the male flowers to the female flowers while they feed. Pests may affect the plantings, requiring application of insecticides. Apply these products carefully in the evening—sometime after the sun sets but before it is too dark to see—to avoid harming the bees. All squashes are susceptible to attack by squash vine borers, which are the larvae of red beelike moths that lay eggs on the bases of the plants. The eggs hatch into grubs that burrow into the vines, turning them to frass and eventually killing them. Control these insects by applying Sevin insecticide to the stems of the plants every 2 weeks during the season. Start when the plants begin to vine. If stems have been invaded, try to save them by slitting them lengthwise (where the damage is evident) to kill the grubs inside. Then bury the damaged stem so it can form new roots. Control cucumber beetles with Sevin insecticide and control squash bugs with sabidilla dust. Squash bugs will damage the pumpkins so they rot in storage. (See pest control chart in the introduction to the vegetable garden.)

### Additional Information

Harvest pumpkins when they have developed full color (no green on them). Cut the handles 3 to 4 inches long using a pair of shears to avoid breaking them. Pumpkins without handles do not keep well. Wear gloves during the harvest because the stems may have sharp spines on them. Keep the pumpkins in a warm place (about 80 degrees Fahrenheit if possible) after harvest to harden them off, then store them in a dry place at 50 to 60 degrees Fahrenheit. Well-grown pumpkins, those that are fully ripe and have no diseases or insect damage, can be stored all winter. Growing giant pumpkins is an art in itself. Most growers select seed from their biggest pumpkins, start the seed indoors very early, and set out the plants after the soil is warm. Some growers set a temporary greenhouse over the pumpkin patch to keep it as warm as possible. Secret methods are used as well, but since they're secret, well, how can I describe them? It is known that some gardeners manure the plants heavily, some set up heat lamps, and most limit the hills to 1 plant every 150 square feet. When a pumpkin is set (at least 1 flower has started developing into a pumpkin), growers remove all the other flowers on that vine. They water, fertilize, and pamper the vine to get the biggest pumpkin possible. When the day for the weigh-in arrives, the pumpkins are loaded with forklifts for the trip to the site. Both ripe and immature pumpkins are eligible. The orange ones are considered pumpkins; the green ones are squashes.

## VARIETIES

Cushaws (**C. mixta** types) are 'Green-Striped Cushaw' and 'White Cushaw'. A **C. moschata** type is 'Golden Cushaw'. Cushaws are usually used for pies and custard. Jack-o'-lantern-sized pumpkins weigh from 6 to 10 pounds. They are just right for carving, but can be used for cooking too. Jumbo pumpkins are grown strictly for their size. The Biggest Pumpkin weigh-in each year features these giants, some years approaching 1000 pounds for the largest. All in this list are **Cucurbita maxima**. Large-sized pumpkins weigh up to 25 pounds and are used almost exclusively for carving. These **Cucurbita pepo** types require about 100 days from planting to harvest. Miniatures (**C. pepo**) are used for decorations and sometimes painted. Naked seeded varieties (**C. pepo**) have seeds without the tough skin and need no hulling before roasting and eating. Pie pumpkins weigh about 5 pounds and are used for cooking and carving; 1 pumpkin is the right size for 1 pie. Commercial canning pumpkins, **Cucurbita moschata**, don't look like the picture on the can. They are referred to as processing pumpkins and are buckskin-colored and shaped like watermelons; they require 110 days to maturity. They include 'Buckskin'; 'Dickinson Field'; and 'Kentucky Field'. For all practical purposes, these are the same, so grow the variety for which you can get seed. The varieties of white painting pumpkins have white skin suitable for painting. 'Lumina', 'Casper', and 'Snowball' are **C. maxima**; 'Little Boo' is a **C. pepo**. The days to maturity are 100 to 110.

## VARIETIES

| Varieties | Days to Maturity | Comments |
|---|---|---|
| **Jack-O'-Lantern** | | |
| Bushkin | 100–110 days | Semibush. |
| Funny Face | 100–110 days | Hybrid. |
| Harvest Moon | 100–110 days | Hybrid. |
| Mystic | 100–110 days | Large stem, uniform. |
| Spirit | 100–110 days | Semibush. |
| **Jumbo** | | |
| Atlantic Giant | 110–140 days | Most winners from this variety. |
| Big Max | 110–140 days | 50-100 pounds. |
| Prizewinner | 110–140 days | Not the biggest, but best looking. |
| **Large** | | |
| Connecticut Field | 100–120 days | The old standard, continually improved. |
| Happy Jack | 100–120 days | Dark orange. |
| Howden Biggie | 100–120 days | Extra-large jack-o'-lantern. |
| Howden Field | 100–120 days | Best commercial pumpkin for the last 25 years. |
| Rouge Vif d'Etamps | 100–120 days | The original "Cinderella's carriage" pumpkin, deep orange, flat, pronounced lobes. |
| **Miniature** | | |
| Ironsides | 90–100 days | Smooth sides, globular, nice stem. |
| Jack Be Little | 90–100 days | 3 inches. |
| Munchkin | 90–100 days | Attractive orange. |
| Sweetie Pie | 90–100 days | Small, scalloped. |
| **Naked Seeded** | | |
| Snack Jack | 90–110 days | 1 to 2 pounds, bush type, bred for seeds. AAS. |
| Trick or Treat | 90–110 days | 10 to 12 pounds, semibush, great for carving. |
| Triple Treat | 90–110 days | 6 to 8 pounds, good for carving and cooking. |
| **Pie** | | |
| Baby Bear | 100 days | Flattened shape. AAS. |
| New England Pie | 100 days | The standard. |
| Small Sugar | 100 days | Same as New England Pie. |
| Sugar Treat | 100 days | Semibush. |
| Oz | 100 days | Semibush. |
| Winter Luxury | 100 days | Old-time favorite. |

# RADISH

***Raphanus sativus***

Radishes are fast-growing, cool-weather vegetables. They grow any place they can have some sun and moist, fertile soil. They do well in gardens, pots, planters, flower beds, and cold frames. Some people grow them in boxes of sand on high-rise balconies. Fresh radishes make tasty garnishes, hors d'oeuvres, or additions to salads. Because they are some of the first things to plant in spring and develop so quickly, radishes are great vegetables to use to introduce children to gardening. The kids don't get bored waiting for something to happen.

## When to Plant

Sow seeds as soon as the soil is dry enough to work for a spring crop. You can tell when you can squeeze a handful of soil into a ball and it crumbles. Sow seeds in late summer or fall for a fall or winter crop.

## Where to Plant

Plant radishes in full sun (8 to 10 hours will suffice) or partial shade (filtered sun all day or shade part of the day). Choose a well-drained part of the garden, which will dry out more quickly and allow an early start.

## How to Plant

Apply a complete garden fertilizer, such as 10-10-10, at a rate of 1½ pounds per 100 square feet of garden. Work the soil into a fine seedbed (make sure the soil is finely broken up). Poor germination will result from improperly prepared soil. (See "Soil Preparation" in the introduction to the vegetable garden.) Sow seeds about 3 per inch in rows 8 to 10 inches apart, and cover them with ¼ inch of fine soil. Thin spring radishes to 1 inch; thin winter radishes to 3 or 4 inches. In beds, broadcast the seed, and thin to 2 or 3 inches in each direction. Make sowings every week to have a continuous supply of radishes all spring. For summer seedings, place a board over each row to keep the soil from drying or from being compacted by pounding rain. Check twice a day to see whether the seedlings have begun to emerge, and remove the boards as soon as any appear. Because the fall crop will take longer to mature, sow more seeds every 10 days or so. Fall radishes are larger and crisper—and hotter—and they can be stored in the ground longer since they do not bolt.

## Care and Maintenance

Radishes are not labor-intensive plants. Hoe or pull the weeds, especially while the seedlings are small, so they don't compete with the radishes for water and nutrients. Keep the plants growing because radishes that develop slowly will be hot and pithy (soft and mealy). Apply 1 inch of water when there has been no rain for a week or so. Soil-borne maggots may damage the roots. If they pose a problem, apply Diazinon according to label directions to the furrows as the seeds are planted.

### Additional Information

Harvest spring radishes at about 1 inch in size and winter radishes at 3 inches. Radishes stop developing in hot weather and send up seed stalks.

**VARIETIES**

| Varieties | Days to Maturity | Comments |
|---|---|---|
| **Spring (Other)** | | |
| Easter Egg | 25 days | Various colors. |
| Plum Purple | 25 days | Deep magenta. |
| **Spring (Red)** | | |
| Champion | 28 days | Large, round. |
| Cherry Belle | 22 days | Round, bright red. |
| Early Scarlet Globe | 23 days | Bright red. |
| **Spring (White)** | | |
| Burpee White | 25 days | Smooth. |
| Snow Belle | 30 days | Round. |
| **Spring/Summer** | | |
| French Breakfast | 23 days | Slow to bolt, red with white tip. |
| French Dressing | 25 days | Red with white top. |
| Icicle | 25 days | Long, slim, white. |
| **Winter** | | |
| Black Spanish | 55 days | White with black skin. |
| Chinese White | 60 days | Blunt. |
| Tama | 70 days | White daikon type, 18 inches long. |

# RHUBARB

***Rheum rhabarbarum***

Although rhubarb is a vegetable, cooks use it in pies, sauces, custards, and tarts because it produces in spring when few fresh fruits are ready to be harvested. They often combine it with strawberries, which are available at the same time. Grown for its leaf stalks or petioles, rhubarb is a perennial, which seems to have originated from a Siberian species. It was introduced into European gardens in the seventeenth century.

## When to Plant

Plant root divisions as early in the spring as the ground can be worked. Plant container-grown transplants nearly anytime.

## Where to Plant

Rhubarb will stay in the same place for several years. Plant it where it will not be disturbed and where it will not interfere with working the rest of the garden, such as one end or along the side. For maximum production, rhubarb prefers full sun (8 to 10 hours will suffice), but it accepts partial shade (filtered sun all day or shade part of the day). Well-drained soil is so essential that if it is not available in your garden, consider raising the grade or planting in raised beds.

## How to Plant

Apply a 10-10-10 fertilizer, at a rate of 1½ pounds per 100 square feet of garden. Deeply prepare the soil. Work in the fertilizer and large amounts of organic matter, digging the bed at least 1 spade depth (6 inches). In a raised bed, double-dig the bed to a depth of 2 spades (12 to 18 inches), adding compost to both layers. Rototilling will not prepare the soil to a sufficient depth. Select plump root sections with at least 1 strong bud each. Set the roots with the buds about 1 inch below the soil surface, and space them 36 inches apart in rows 48 inches apart. Set containerized plants at the same spacings, even though they will take longer to develop into large plants.

## Care and Maintenance

Keep weeds under control as the plants develop. Once the plants have become established, they take little care other than watering for maximum growth and production. Apply 1 inch per week if nature doesn't cooperate. Fertilize each spring with 10-10-10, at a rate of 1 pound per 100 square feet of bed.

### Additional Information

*Do not harvest the first season after planting.* In the second season, harvest in spring when the leaves reach full size, for 1 or 2 weeks, or until the stalks become noticeably smaller. Harvest 6 weeks each spring after that, or until the stalks decrease in size. Do not harvest in the fall unless the bed is to be discarded the next year. Leave the plants enough foliage to sustain themselves for the winter. Harvest the leaves when they reach full size. Pull them with a twist to release them from the crown, but remove only about 1/3 of the leaves on a plant at any one time. Trim the leaf blade from the stalk; the leaf blade is not edible and contains harmful calcium oxalate crystals. The oxalic acid crystals may move into the leaf stalks after a freeze, too, so it is better not to harvest frozen stalks. After a week or so, the oxalic acid moves out of the stalks, and they are again safe to harvest. As seed stalks appear, pull them out because they steal nutrients that should go to the leaves. After the plants die down in fall, mulch them heavily with compost, being careful not to cover the crowns (center parts of the plants). After several years, rhubarb plants begin to crowd themselves out. The stalks become smaller and seed stalks are more abundant. It is time to renew the beds when this starts to happen. In early spring, lift a few of the oldest plants, remove damaged or rotted portions, and cut the crowns into sections, each with a healthy piece of fleshy root and at least 1 good bud. Set these pieces back in the bed after thoroughly preparing the soil. If only part of the planting is renewed each year, leave the remainder to produce while the new planting is becoming established. Rhubarb can be forced for winter use. Three-year-old plants are best; older plants scheduled for replacement can be used, but they will make smaller stalks. Lift the plants in the fall, and leave them on top of the ground where they will freeze. Hill them with soil to protect them from sub-zero cold. After 60 days, move the roots into an area with a temperature of 55 to 60 degrees Fahrenheit where they may be kept in the dark, and cover them with peat, sawdust, or soil. Stack the roots tightly together and keep them moist. Harvest the stalks when they are about 1 foot long and before the leaves expand. Roots for forcing will last about 1 month. After forcing them, discard them, or put them into a nurse bed (a temporary nursery with plants spaced close together to grow until they are strong enough to set in the production garden).

## VARIETIES

| Varieties | Comments |
|---|---|
| Canada Red | Long, red, extra sweet. |
| Cherry Red | Red inside and out. |
| MacDonald | Tender, brilliant red. |
| Valentine | Large red stalks with good flavor. |
| Victoria | Green stalks tinted with red. |

# Aunt Jane's Strawberry-Rhubarb Streusel Cobbler

*Streusel: Mix 1 cup flour, 1 tablespoon sugar, 1½ teaspoons baking powder, ¼ teaspoon salt, 2 teaspoons grated lemon peel, 1 teaspoon vanilla and ½ stick butter and coarsely cut in a bowl. Add 1 beaten egg and ¼ cup milk to flour mixture, stirring just to moisten.*

*Rhubarb: Mix 1½ cups sugar and 2 tablespoons cornstarch in a large saucepan. Stir in 4 cups of 1-inch sliced rhubarb and 2 cups quartered strawberries. Let rest for 10 minutes; stir. Heat to a full boil; continue stirring for an additional minute. Pour into a greased 9-inch-square pan. Spinkle with cinnamon to taste. Drop the streusel by spoonfuls onto the top of the HOT strawberries and rhubarb. Sprinkle with a mixture of cinnamon and sugar. Bake at 400 degrees for 20 minutes. Serve warm with whipped cream or over ice-cream.*

# RUTABAGA

***Brassica napus*** **var.** ***napobrassica***

Rutabaga is a cool-weather crop producing a large root used as a substitute for potatoes in the diet. This crop seems to have originated in the Middle Ages from a cross between the turnip and cabbage. It is related to collards, kohlrabi, and Brussels sprouts, and it is another of the many members of the mustard family, *Cruciferae*.

## When to Plant

Since the best rutabagas develop their roots in cooler weather, gardeners usually grow them as a fall crop. In the cooler parts of the Midwest, they can be grown as a spring or a fall crop. Sow seeds directly in the garden in March or early April for a spring crop; sow seeds in June for a fall crop.

## Where to Plant

Plant rutabagas in a location with full sun (8 to 10 hours will suffice) and well-prepared, well-drained, fertile soil.

## How to Plant

Apply a complete garden fertilizer, such as 10-10-10, at a rate of $1\frac{1}{2}$ pounds per 100 square feet of garden. Spade or rototill the soil. (See "Soil Preparation" in the introduction to the vegetable garden.) In rows, sow seeds $\frac{1}{2}$ inch deep, 3 to 5 per foot, with 18 to 24 inches between rows. In beds, sow seeds in rows 12 to 15 inches apart across the beds. If root maggots have been a problem in the past and your previous crops have suffered damage, cover rows with screening or floating row covers after planting and leave them in place until plants are sizeable, because fly larvae may damage roots or stems. When the seedlings are 2 to 3 inches tall, thin them to about 6 inches apart, and use the extra ones for greens.

## Care and Maintenance

Rapid growth results in the best-quality rutabagas, so water as necessary to keep the plants vigorous. They need about 1 inch of water per week.

## VARIETIES

| Varieties | Days to Maturity | Comments |
|---|---|---|
| American Purple Top | 90 days | Light yellow flesh. |
| Laurentian | 90 days | Smooth, uniform. |
| Pike | 100 days | Holds well late in fall. |

### Additional Information

Harvest the roots when they are about 5 inches in size. Allowed to grow beyond maturity, they will be tough, woody, and poorly flavored. Rutabagas are quite hardy and will stand a freeze. Late crops stored in the ground will become sweeter with the cold. Protect them with heavy straw mulch to prolong the harvest into the early part of the winter, but dig the remaining roots before they are exposed to a hard freeze. Although rutabagas store well in refrigeration, they may shrivel. You can protect them from shriveling by dipping them in warm paraffin wax or storing them in plastic bags.

# Mashed Rutabaga (or Turnip) Potatoes

*Rutabaga or turnip roots are sweet and tasty additions to mashed or double-baked potatoes.*

*Bake four large potatoes. Cut in half lengthwise and scoop out the flesh into a large bowl. Add 2 cups cooked, mashed rutabaga or turnip, 3 table-spooons butter, ½ teaspoon salt, ¼ teaspoon pepper and ¼ cup hot milk. Beat until light and fluffy. Pile lightly into the potato shells. Bake in 400 degree oven 5 minutes to brown. Garnish with grated cheese and chives.*

# Rutabaga and Mushrooms

*Cook 1 medium peeled and sliced rutabaga in water with ¼ teaspoon salt until soft. Drain, mash, and stir in 3 tablespoons butter. Sauté 1 cup chopped mushrooms in 3 tablespoons butter until brown, and add the rutabaga. Season with ½ teaspoon freshly ground pepper and serve.*

# Shallot

***Allium cepa* var. *aggregatum***

Shallots are related to onions, but have a milder, more delicate flavor. In some parts of the country people call any green onion a shallot. The difference is that onion bulbs develop only 1 sprout per bulb, while shallots develop 6 to 10 sprouts per bulb. The shallots can be pulled when they are the size of green bunching onions and used as green onions would be, for example, in salads or as garnishes for soups. Gardeners grow shallots for the dry bulbs as well. Having originated in western Asia, probably Syria, shallots have been mentioned in literature for centuries.

## When to Plant

Shallots are hardy. Plant them in early spring as soon as the soil can be worked.

## Where to Plant

Plant shallots in a full-sun location with well-prepared, well-drained soil. (8 to 10 hours will suffice. See "Soil Preparation" in the introduction to the vegetable garden.)

## How to Plant

Apply a complete garden fertilizer, such as 10-10-10, at a rate of 1½ pounds per 100 square feet of garden. Work the soil into a fine seedbed (the soil should be finely broken up). Start shallots from clumps of bulbs. Separate the clumps into individual bulbs, and plant them 2 inches deep, 4 inches apart, in rows 1 foot apart, or plant them in rows across a bed. Keep the pointed ends up to have straight shallots. If onion maggots have been a problem in the past and your previous crops have suffered damage, cover rows with screening or floating row covers after planting and leave them in place until plants are sizeable, because fly larvae may damage roots or stems.

## VARIETIES

Most catalogs list only shallots and no varieties. There are some varieties, however, and occasionally, catalogs of exotic garden plants list them. Once you get a supply, try to keep them going. If diseases affect the planting, however, buy new bulbs to obtain a fresh start. Some varieties I have seen include 'Frog Legs', 'Dutch Yellow', 'Prince de Bretagne', and 'French Epicurean'.

# Care and Maintenance

Provide plenty of water for shallots during dry weather; they need about 1 inch per week. Be vigilant in controlling weeds; since the shallots do not provide complete cover, weeds will germinate all season. Pests and diseases may affect plantings. If thrips become troublesome, treat them with insecticidal soap. (See the pest control chart in the introduction to the vegetable garden.) The same diseases that affect onions affect shallots, so don't plant them in the same part of the garden each year, and don't replant bulbs from plants that are stunted or off-color. To have green shallots with long, blanched stems, hill them up with 2 inches of soil when the shoots are about 4 inches tall, 4 to 5 weeks before harvest.

## ADDITIONAL INFORMATION

Harvest green shallots when they are 6 to 8 inches tall, 10 to 12 weeks after planting. As I noted earlier, each bulb produces many sprouts, so pull the individual sprouts and leave the rest to develop later. You may prefer to grow shallots for dry bulbs, which mature in mid- to late summer. Allow the tops to dry down naturally, then pull the dry shallots when all the tops have gone down, preferably in the morning during dry weather. Let them dry where you pull them in the garden until afternoon, collect them, and spread them on screens or slats so that they can cure for 2 to 3 weeks. After they are cured, knock off as much soil as possible, braid them together, and hang them in a dry place. Do not peel the bulbs, and do not wash them. Use damaged ones immediately. The dry shallots keep much better than onions. Save some of the very best bulbs for planting the next season.

# Spinach

*Spinacia oleracea*

Spinach is probably native to southwest Asia. Gardeners have cultivated it for centuries as a salad green and cooked vegetable. Even though many youngsters are dissuaded by early experiences with boiled spinach, most adults eventually appreciate its diversity in such treats as salads, quiches, pizzas, crepes, and omelets. Spinach is a cool-weather crop that can produce in spring or fall. It matures when little else is coming from the garden, and some gardeners grow it indoors under lights as well.

## When to Plant

These plants can stand a freeze. They must be planted early and harvested before hot weather arrives. In hot weather, spinach sends up a seed stalk (bolts), and the quality quickly deteriorates. Unless you want lots of spinach at one time, however, make several seedings to spread out the harvest. If you prefer to direct-seed, sow seed in the garden as early as the soil can be worked. Some gardeners prepare the soil in the fall and broadcast the seed over the frozen ground. If you want the earliest production, start with transplants, either homegrown or from garden centers. To grow your own, sow the earliest seed for spinach indoors about 2 months before the frost-free date (average date of last frost). Grow the plants under lights or in the greenhouse, and transplant them into the garden when they are large enough to handle, 3 or 4 weeks before the frost-free date. Transplants may be available from garden centers about that time; buy plants that have a good green color, are short and compact, and have no pests. Since the spinach will be harvested and out of the garden by midsummer, plan to replace it with a fall crop. Sow seed directly in the garden or indoors about August 10, then set the seedlings in the garden about August 31. For fall seeding, chilling the seeds in the refrigerator for 2 weeks before sowing them will hasten germination. Mild fall weather may last until Thanksgiving, and in the milder parts of the Midwest, spinach may be sown in late fall. The small seedlings will survive the winter if they are carefully mulched and will produce a crop very early the next spring.

## Where to Plant

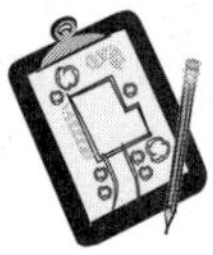

Spinach prefers full sun (8 to 10 hours will suffice), but to extend its production into the hot summer months, plant it in partial shade (filtered sun all day or shade part of the day) to keep it cooler. A well-drained location can provide healthier plants. The plants need lots of water for vigorous growth, but the roots cannot stand soggy soils. Plants in soggy soils will be susceptible to diseases, and leaves may scald at the edges.

## How to Plant

Apply a complete garden fertilizer, such as 10-10-10, at a rate of $1\frac{1}{2}$ pounds per 100 square feet of garden. Spade or rototill the soil. (See "Soil Preparation" in the introduction to the vegetable garden.) In rows, space transplants 6 to 8 inches apart, with 12 inches between rows. In a bed, space the plants 6 inches apart in each direction, which will allow 6 to 8 plants across the bed. Set the plants at the same depth they were growing. To seed directly in the garden, sow spinach seed in rows 12 inches apart, and thin to 1 plant every 6 inches. In a bed, seed in rows 6 inches apart across the bed, or broadcast the seed; thin seedlings to 4 to 6 inches in each direction. For a continuous supply of spinach, make additional plantings every 7 to 10 days.

## Care and Maintenance

Keep the plants growing, and water as needed to provide about 1 inch per week. Spinach plants are shallowly rooted and easily uprooted, so weed by careful hoeing or pulling while the plants are small. Pests and diseases may affect plantings. Control aphids with insecticidal soap. Leaf miners lay eggs just under the surface of the leaves, then the larvae hatch and mine their way around inside the leaves, making dead brown trails. Covering the plants with cheesecloth or using commercial row covers is the only way to protect them. Plant resistant varieties to avoid disease problems. (See the pest control chart in the introduction to the vegetable garden.)

### Additional Information

Harvest spinach by snipping off outer leaves as soon as they are large enough to use. When plants are large enough to harvest, cut every other one, leaving more room for the others. As soon as the plants begin to bolt (send up seed stalks), harvest all that remain before they are spoiled.

## VARIETIES

Spinach varieties are either savoyed or smooth-leafed. Savoyed spinach has puckered or cupped leaves that can catch grit splashed by rains or watering. Sometimes the grit does not wash out completely despite repeated attempts, and a gritty salad is the result. Commercial growers often avoid the problem by growing spinach on muck soils (black organic soils, often called peat) that have no grit. If your spinach has tended to be gritty, grow a smooth-leafed variety. New Zealand spinach, **Tetragonia tetragonioides**, is a summer substitute for spinach; there is only 1 variety. It is not a true spinach, but has a similar taste and is heat resistant. Plant New Zealand spinach after danger of frost has passed.

| Varieties | Days to Maturity | Comments |
|---|---|---|
| **Savoy** | | |
| Avon | 42 days | Good heat tolerance. |
| Bloomsdale Long Standing | 46 days | An old favorite. |
| Melody | 42 days | Spring or fall. AAS. |
| Winter Bloomsdale | 45 days | Slow to bolt, good for overwintering. |
| **Smooth Leaf** | | |
| Catalina | 45 days | Upright, long-standing, slow to bolt. |
| Giant Noble | 43 days | Slow to bolt. |
| Olympia | 46 days | Long-standing. |

# Crustless Spinach Quiche

*In skillet, sauté 1 chopped onion and 1 cup sliced fresh mushrooms in 1 tablespoon vegetable oil until tender. Add 1 bunch washed and drained spinach and ⅔ cup finely chopped cooked ham. Stir while cooking until the excess moisture is evaporated. Cool slightly. Beat 5 eggs in a large bowl; add 3 cups shredded Monterey Jack cheese; mix well. Stir in spinach mixture and ⅛ teaspoon pepper; blend well. Spread evenly into a greased 9-inch pie pan. Bake at 350 degrees for 40 to 45 minutes or until a knife inserted in the center comes out clean.*

# SQUASH

***Cucurbita pepo, Cucurbita moschata***
***Cucurbita maxima, Cucurbita mixta***

Squashes are warm-season vine crops with flavorful flesh. The many types are divided into summer squash, grown for the immature fruit, and winter squash, which is harvested mature. Squash can take a lot of room, so be prepared. Vining types will spread 10 feet or more, but can be grown on trellises with adequate support for the heavy fruits. In recent years, bush types have been developed that take much less space and can even be grown in pots.

## When to Plant

Don't hurry to get squash into the garden very early. The plants need warm weather to develop and may rot off if weather is cool and wet. Sow seeds indoors under lights about 1 week before the frost-free date (average date of last frost). Set out started plants or sow seeds directly in the garden after any danger of frost has passed.

## Where to Plant

To have the best harvest, plant squashes in well-drained soil in an area with full sun (8 to 10 hours will suffice), although they will grow and produce in light shade (a little shade from a distant tree or some shade in the middle of the day). Grow bush types in beds or containers.

## How to Plant

Apply a complete garden fertilizer, such as 10-10-10, at a rate of 1½ pounds per 100 square feet of garden. Spade or rototill the soil. (See "Soil Preparation" in the vegetable garden introduction.) Because vine crops do not tolerate root injuries common to transplanting, indoors under lights sow squash seeds in peat pots that can be planted without disturbing the tiny roots. After danger of frost has passed, sow 6 seeds or set 2 or 3 transplant seedlings in hills about 5 feet apart, with rows 10 feet apart. Or space the plants 10 feet apart down the middles of beds. Set the plants at the same depth they were growing. Thin the seedlings to 2 or 3 per hill when they are big enough to handle. If there is danger of disturbing the other seedlings, pinch off the extras instead of pulling them. Bush types are well suited for beds, spaced 3 feet apart down the middles of the beds. Dwarf bush types flourish in 5-gallon buckets, half barrels, or similar-sized containers, but you must make sure they drain. Sow or plant dwarf bush types, 1 per container, in a commercial potting mix.

## Care and Maintenance

Squashes require lots of water and fertilizer after they set fruit. Apply 1 inch of water per week if nature does not cooperate. Fertilize with nitrogen when the vines have almost covered the ground, but be sure to rinse the fertilizer off the leaves. (See instructions for sidedressing in "Understanding Fertilizers" in the introduction.) All vine crops produce both male and female flowers on the same plant. (See page 54.) Usually, male flowers are produced first. Many gardeners are dismayed when these flowers fall off without making any squashes. Female flowers have tiny squashes just below the petals; male flowers have straight stems. Bees play an important role in pollination by carrying the pollen from the male flowers to the female flowers as they feed. Use insecticides carefully in the evening—sometime after the sun sets but before it is too dark to see—to avoid harming the bees. Pay even closer attention to plants in containers than plants in the garden. Water them as often as necessary to prevent wilting, and apply a complete liquid fertilizer every week or so, according to directions on the package. All squashes are susceptible to attack by squash vine borers. These larvae of red beelike moths lay eggs on the bases of the plants, and the eggs hatch into grubs that burrow into the vines, turning them to frass (a mass of shredded plant parts and often insect parts) and eventually killing them. Control these insects by applying Sevin insecticide to the stems of the plants when the plants begin to vine and then every 2 weeks during the season. Stems that have been invaded may be saved by slitting them lengthwise where the damage is evident to kill the grubs inside, then burying the damaged stem so it can form new roots. Control cucumber beetles with Sevin insecticide, and squash bugs with sabidilla dust. Squash bugs will damage the fruits of winter squash so they rot in storage. (See the pest control chart in the introduction to the vegetable garden.)

### Additional Information

Harvest summer squashes while they are still immature, at the proper size for the type. Pick elongated types when they are 6 to 8 inches long and less than 2 inches in diameter. Pick patty pan (scalloped) types when they reach about 4 inches in diameter. Plan to harvest every day when the plants are producing heavily to stimulate continued production and to make sure fruits are not allowed to become overly large. Some people like larger, straight types, which they hollow out and fill with stuffings, or which they grind for baking in breads. Harvest winter squashes when they have developed full color and when the rinds are hardened sufficiently that you cannot cut into them with your fingernail. Cut the handles 3 to 4 inches long using a pair of shears to avoid breaking them. Winter squashes without handles do not keep well. Wear gloves during the harvest because the stems may have sharp spines on them. Keep the winter squashes in a warm place after harvest to harden them off, then store them in a dry place at 50 to 60 degrees Fahrenheit. Well-grown winter squashes can be stored all winter.

## VARIETIES

Just a few varieties are listed here. There are many more, and new ones are developed each year. Check seed catalogs for additional kinds. Summer squash matures in 50 to 60 days, and winter squash matures in 80 to 120 days.

| **Varieties** | **Comments** |
|---|---|
| **Summer Squash** (C. pepo and C. maxima) | |
| **Golden Zucchini** | |
| Gold Rush | Deep gold, superior fruit. AAS. |
| **Green Zucchini** | |
| Aristocrat | Productive. AAS. |
| Black Zucchini | Best known and most common summer squash. |
| Chefini | Excellent quality, productive. AAS. |
| Spineless Beauty | No spines on stem. |
| **Scallop (Patty Pan shaped)** | |
| Peter Pan | Light green. AAS. |
| Scallopini | Productive. Good fresh or cooked. AAS. |
| Sunburst | Yellow. |
| White Bush Scallop | Traditional scalloped type. |
| **Yellow Crookneck** | |
| Early Yellow Summer Crookneck | Familiar warty fruit. |
| Sundance | Smooth skin. |
| **Yellow Straightneck** | |
| Early Prolific Straightneck | The standard, light cream color. |
| Goldbar | Golden yellow. |

## VARIETIES

| Varieties | Comments |
|---|---|
| **Winter Squash** | |
| **Acorn** (C. pepo) | |
| Cream of the Crop | White acorn type. AAS. |
| Table Ace | Dark green, low fiber, |
| Table Gold | Bush. |
| Table King | Bush. |
| Table Queen | Standard, dark-green acorn. |
| **Buttercup** (C. maxima) | |
| Buttercup | Fine-grained, sweet 3 pounds. |
| Emerald Bush Buttercup | Bush. |
| Sweet Mama | Semivining, sweet, 3 to 4 pounds. AAS. |
| **Butternut** (C. moschata) | |
| Butterbush | Bush. |
| Butternut Supreme | Early, sweet. |
| Early Butternut | Flavorful and early. AAS. |
| Waltham | Uniform, 12-inch fruits. |
| **Hubbard** (C. maxima; all 10 to 25 pounds) | |
| Baby Hubbard | Smaller. |
| Blue Hubbard | Blue skin. |
| Chicago Hubbard | Midwest favorite. |
| Green Hubbard | Green skin. |
| Warted Hubbard | Exceptionally warty. |
| **Others** (C. maxima) | |
| Banana | 24 inches long, gray-blue or pink, 25 pounds. |
| Cushaw | 30 inches long. |
| Turks Turban | Turban shaped, orange and green. |
| **Spaghetti** (C. pepo) | |
| High Beta Gold | High in beta-carotene. |
| Stripetti | Great taste, stores well. |
| Tivoli | Bush. AAS. |
| Vegetable Spaghetti | Light yellow, good keeper. |
| **Sweet Potato** (C. pepo) | |
| Delicata | Long, cream colored with green stripes. |
| Honey Boat | Very sweet. |
| Sugar Loaf | Dark-green stripes, very sweet. |
| Sweet Dumpling | Flattened, round, fluted white with green stripes. |

# TOMATO

## *Lycopersicon lycopersicum*

Tomatoes are unquestionably the most popular garden vegetables in the United States. The flavor of a newly picked red tomato from your garden easily surpasses that of premium, greenhouse-grown fruit and no other vegetable comes close to producing as much in a limited space. Native to the Americas, tomatoes were introduced into the gardens of Europe in the 1500s, but people considered them poisonous and grew them only as ornamentals. Tomatoes were reintroduced into American gardens in the late 1700s but did not become popular as edible vegetables until about 1850. Gardeners immigrating from overseas often bring a few seeds of precious varieties grown by their families in the Old Country. Even gardeners visiting Italy or Greece are tempted to remove a few seeds from a salad tomato and secret them away to be planted when they arrive home. (This isn't a good idea, however, because they may introduce a disease or insect that could destroy tomatoes here.)

Tomatoes are tender, warm-weather plants. You set them out after danger of frost has passed, and they will grow until frost arrives in the fall. Hundreds of tomato varieties are available to home gardeners. Newer varieties have eliminated many of the problems associated with these plants. More predictable habit, better fruit set in inclement weather, and disease resistance have been bred into modern tomatoes to make growing them as easy as possible. People with an interest in heirloom plants have preserved inbred lines for gardeners who remember and appreciate the characteristics of traditional varieties. Researchers have improved many of these older, standby varieties so that they are more disease resistant.

Selecting varieties to grow in your garden can be quite a challenge. Tomatoes are offered in a wide range of sizes, shapes, colors, growth habits, and maturity dates. Seed catalogs present tantalizing selections of varieties, each with a glowing description and luscious photo. But not all of them may be suited to your growing conditions. Local garden centers, especially those affiliated with greenhouses that grow their own plants, usually limit choices to plants that do well in their locality. Garden departments of some larger chains import plants grown elsewhere, but offer good varieties if you know what to look for.

Two distinct growth habits of tomato plants determine how you handle them in the garden. **Determinate plants** form low bushes. A cluster of flowers is set at the ends of stems, stopping the growth on the plant so that all of the fruit forms about the same time. These varieties are good for processing. You can pick and can all of the fruit in a few days. After 1 or 2 pickings, all the fruit is harvested, and you can pull out the plants. Some determinate varieties produce fruit very early in the season, especially when you start them indoors. You will want to make successive plantings and choose varieties of different maturity dates if you want to use determinate varieties to produce fruit for picking throughout the entire season.

**Indeterminate varieties** set fruit clusters along a vining stem, which continues to grow all season. They never set a terminal flower cluster, so they grow indefinitely. They produce fruit throughout the season until killed off by frost. These varieties are excellent for growing on trellises or stakes. Tomato greenhouses, once common throughout the Midwest, produced indeterminate varieties that grew up to 10 feet tall on strings attached to the rafters of the structures.

Recently, some intermediate varieties have been developed and classified as semideterminate. These varieties are suitable for growing in cages because they stay short and produce all season.

Dwarf varieties have been developed for growing in containers, hanging baskets, planters, or areas with limited space. Some produce small salad tomatoes, but other varieties have large, slicing-sized fruit.

## When to Plant

Tomatoes are tender plants. A light frost may not kill them but will set them back. Sow seed at the frost-free date (average date of last frost), or set out plants in the garden at the frost-free date if some protection is available. Row covers could be used, but old bed sheets, comforters, and blankets will do. Since the plants do not grow much until soils warm up, plants set at the latest date of last frost will usually develop as fast as those set earlier. For continuous production, make successive plantings of early-, mid-season-, and late-maturing varieties. (The seed packs usually indicate when varieties mature, but the listings in the Varieties chart are better guides.)

## Where to Plant

These plants prefer well-prepared, well-drained soil in full sun (8 to 10 hours will suffice). Plant indeterminate varieties or those in cages or on stakes to the north side of the garden to avoid shading lower-growing plants.

## How to Plant

Prepare the soil by spading or tilling. (See "Soil Preparation" in the introduction to the vegetable garden.) Incorporate organic matter and fertilizer such as 1 pound of 5-20-20 or ½ pound of 10-10-10 per 100 square feet. To plant tomato seeds directly in the garden, sow seeds in hills spaced 2 feet apart for smaller determinate varieties and staked plants; sow seeds 36 to 42 inches apart for caged or larger indeterminate plants on the ground. After seedlings have sprouted, thin to 1 plant per hill. Start tomato transplants indoors, or buy plants from greenhouses or garden centers. Transplants should have 3 to 4 sets of leaves with a healthy green color. Purple or yellow plants will have difficulty getting started. Check plants carefully for signs of insects because aphids and whiteflies often gain entrance to the garden on infested transplants. Remove the plants from the containers, and set the plants at the same depth they were growing in the containers. Firm the soil gently around each plant, and water in with a cup of transplant starter fertilizer mixed according to directions on the package. Homegrown transplants may become weak and leggy, but do not plant them deeper to compensate, or the roots will suffocate. Plant them on their sides, and lightly cover the long stems with soil. The tips of the stems will quickly turn upward, and the buried stems will sprout new roots.

## Care and Maintenance

Tomatoes are easy to grow, but various problems may affect them. Plant disease-resistant varieties to eliminate verticillium and fusarium wilts, and yellows. Control foliar diseases with maneb fungicide. Use insecticidal soap on aphids and mites; apply Sevin to take care of caterpillars and beetles. (See the pest control chart in the introduction to the vegetable garden.) Other troubles include blossom-end rot and lack of fruit set. Blossom-end rot appears as a leathery-brown spot on the bottom of a tomato. It is more common on certain varieties and on staked plants. It is not a disease, but a result of poor growing conditions. Usually, only the first few tomatoes show this problem, and the rest of the fruits are fine. Poor pollination may cause catfacing (malformed fruit). Unusually high or low temperatures or extremely wet weather can interfere with pollination. To help things along, tap flower clusters in early morning to shake pollen from the flowers onto the pistil. I usually use a pencil to tap the flowers.

Some means of support will keep the plants off the ground, reducing fruit spoilage and making harvesting easier. Tie indeterminate types to stakes, then prune these plants to a single stem by pinching off shoots that develop at each leaf axil. Grow determinate and semideterminate plants in cages. The tiny wire cages sold in garden centers are far too weak and the holes are too small to be worth the cost. Make cages from concrete reinforcing wire, which comes in 5-foot-wide rolls. A 10-foot piece, cut down the middle, will make two 2½-foot-tall cages about 3 feet in diameter. This wire has holes 6 inches square, so the tomatoes have plenty of room to come through the sides. As they grow, keep the shoots tucked in the cages. When the plants have grown above the tops, pinch them off to control them.

Tomatoes need sufficient water, about 1 inch per week. Fruit on plants that are under intermittent water stress are more likely to suffer from blossom-end rot and from fruit cracking. Drought-affected plants produce smaller and fewer tomatoes.

Mulch plants to maintain even soil moisture, but delay mulching early plantings until the soil warms up. Cold soils interfere with development of the plants. When the tomatoes bloom, or when they set the first fruit, is a good rule of thumb to indicate that the soils are warm. Mulching plants that are sprawling on the ground will keep the fruit out of the mud.

After the plants have set tomatoes about the size of golf balls, sidedress with a complete fertilizer. Use 10-10-10 at the rate of 1 pound per 100 square feet of bed. Repeat every 3 to 4 weeks until harvest is completed.

Harvest the fruit as it ripens. Overripe fruit attracts earwigs, yellow jackets, and picnic beetles.

## Focaccia with Cherry Tomatoes

*Cut the focaccia bread into single servings and place them on a large plate or on individual serving plates. Toss several cherry tomatoes with extra-virgin olive oil and season with salt and pepper. Top each slice of focaccia with tomatoes and garnish with basil leaves. Serve immediately.*

## VARIETIES

**Dwarf types** have been developed for container planting, and they are suitable for large pots, boxes, hanging planters, or patios where space is limited. Porches and galleries of high-rises often support crops of juicy, red tomatoes all summer. Because of the limited soil in a container, special attention to watering and fertilizing is essential. Containers may need watering as often as once or twice a day in warm weather. Use a dilute liquid fertilizer such as Miracle Gro, Peters, or something similar every 2 weeks. **Early variety plants** are usually more compact. Because the foliage is often sparse, sunburn can be a problem. Fruit is smaller than main-season varieties. **Extra-large tomatoes** are novelties, and they are often misshapen with catfacing and blossom-end rot. By the time you cut out the bad parts, you lose the advantage of the large size. **Main-crop varieties** should be preferred for most gardens. The plants are more vigorous, have better foliage, and are more easily trained to cages or stakes. The fruit is produced over a longer period of time, and it is of the best quality, essentially free from catfacing and cracking. All top varieties (including the AAS winners) are in this category. **Medium-early varieties** have normal-sized fruit and better-developed plants. They can serve as main-crop types if several plantings are made to spread out production. Best for processing, the **Roma types** are fleshy and drier than fresh-eating types. Lately however, Romas have become more popular for fresh eating. These plants set a lot of fruit that ripens at one time, so you need to do processing only once. Cracking is usually the biggest problem with **salad tomatoes**. One plant will usually be enough for a family; they come back from seed each year.

| Varieties | Days to Maturity | Comments |
|---|---|---|
| **Earliest Harvest** | | |
| Bush Early Girl | 52 days | VFNT; space saver, large fruit. |
| Early Girl | 54 days | VF; indeterminate, earliest of the full-sized tomatoes. |
| Jetsetter | 55 days | VFFNTA; this one is really something to try! |
| Quick Pick | 60 days | VFFNTA; indeterminate, good quality smooth fruit, popular among farm and community market producers, often grown staked and picked only once. |
| **Medium Early** | | |
| Mountain Spring | 65 days | VF; determinate, smooth and well rounded. |
| Red Sun | 65 days | Very large, beautiful fruit, fantastic production. |
| **Main Crop** | | |
| Better Boy | 72 days | VFN; indeterminate, most common variety in garden centers. |
| Burpee's Big Girl | 78 days | VF; indeterminate. |

## VARIETIES

| Varieties | Days to Maturity | Comments |
|---|---|---|
| **Main Crop** (continued) | | |
| Celebrity | 70 days | VFFNT; semideterminate, large fruit, very dependable; we rely on this variety for a crop, no matter what the weather; good for fresh use and processing. |
| Fantastic | 70 days | Indeterminate, has no proven disease resistance; it has been around a long time and is still worth growing if verticillium and fusarium aren't problems. |
| Floramerica | 75 days | VF; determinate, good red color, a reliable performer. AAS. |
| Mountain Delight | 70 days | VF; determinate, good where green shoulders are a problem. |
| Supersonic | 79 days | VF; indeterminate, never cracks, one of the best for staking. |
| **Dwarf** | | |
| Husky Gold Hybrid | 70 days | Same as Husky Red and Husky Pink but with yellow fruit. AAS. |
| Husky Pink Hybrid | 72 days | VF; indeterminate, same growth habit as Husky Red, pink fruit. |
| Husky Red Hybrid | 68 days | VF; indeterminate, large fruit, producing over a longer period. |
| Patio Hybrid | 65 days | Determinate, nearly normal-sized fruit on a dwarf plant. |
| Tiny Tim | 45 days | Determinate, cherry type. |
| **Extra-Large** | | |
| Beefmaster | 81 days | VFN; indeterminate, old favorite, 1 big slice goes well on a hamburger. |
| Delicious | 77 days | OP; indeterminate, very large fruit, including the world record at nearly 8 pounds. |
| Supersteak | 80 days | VFN; indeterminate. |
| **Roma** | | |
| Roma | 75 days | VF; OP; determinate, the standard red plum tomato. |
| San Marzano | 80 days | OP; determinate, lots of meat, very little juice, cooks down easily. |

## VARIETIES

| Varieties | Days to Maturity | Comments |
|---|---|---|
| **Salad** | | |
| Christmas Grapes | 65 days | Indeterminate, productive through winter indoors with adequate light and warmth. |
| Jolly | 70 days | Clusters of pink crack-free fruits. AAS. |
| Juliet | 70 days | Indeterminate, elongated 1-ounce fruits in clusters like grapes. AAS. |
| Mountain Belle | 65 days | VF; determinate, crack resistant, ripens evenly. |
| Sun Gold | 70 days | Golden fruit, outstanding flavor. |
| Super Sweet | 70 days | VF; indeterminate; large clusters, cherry-sized, red. |
| Sweet Million | 65 days | FNT; indeterminate, crack resistant. |

**Colored**

Yellow types may be less acidic than reds, and people who have trouble eating the red types may be able to enjoy yellows without difficulty. Yellow tomatoes for canning will need added acid; check the recipe or contact your county cooperative extension service for recommendations.

| Varieties | Days to Maturity | Comments |
|---|---|---|
| **Pink** | | |
| Brandywine | 80 days | OP; indeterminate, heirloom, large but rough with ridges and furrows. |
| Pink Girl | 76 days | VF; indeterminate, smooth pink. |
| **Yellow** | | |
| Jubilee | 70 days | OP; indeterminate, orange. |
| Lemon Boy | 72 days | VFN; indeterminate, lemon yellow. |
| Mountain Gold | 70 days | VF; OP; determinate, deep orange. |
| Vita-Gold | 70 days | Determinate, golden orange, unusually high in beta-carotene. |
| **Other** | | |
| Evergreen | 82 days | OP; indeterminate, green at maturity, the original for fried green tomatoes. |
| Green Zebra | 80 days | OP; heirloom, green and white at maturity. |
| Long Keeper | 80 days | OP; keeps for months. |

Abbreviations for disease resistance: V = Verticillium wilt; F = Fusarium wilt; FF = Fusarium wilt races 1 and 2; N = Nematodes; T = Tobacco mosaic viruses; A = Alternaria. Other abbreviations: AAS = All-America Selections; OP = Open pollinated (versus hybrid).

# TURNIP

***Brassica rapa*** var. ***rapifera***

Turnips are cool-weather members of the cabbage family, which includes broccoli, cauliflower, Brussels sprouts, and kohlrabi. Turnips are familiar, but not commonly grown vegetables in the U.S., although they are staples of Eastern European diets. Gardeners grow them for their roots, which they eat cooked or raw, and for the tops as greens. This crop has been cultivated since ancient times, and it is reported to have originated in Russia or Siberia. In this country, early settlers were growing turnips in Virginia in 1609.

## When to Plant

The turnip roots develop better in cooler weather. In the cooler parts of the Midwest, grow turnips for a spring or a fall crop. Sow seeds directly in the garden in March or early April for a spring crop; sow seeds in July for a fall crop.

## Where to Plant

Plant turnips in a full-sun location (8 to 10 hours will suffice) that has well-prepared, well-drained, fertile soil. Poorly prepared or rocky soil results in poorly formed roots.

## How to Plant

Apply a complete garden fertilizer, such as 10-10-10, at a rate of 1½ pounds per 100 square feet of garden. Spade or rototill the soil. (See "Soil Preparation" in the introduction to the vegetable garden.) To plant in rows, sow seeds ½ inch deep 8 to 10 per foot, in rows 12 inches apart. To plant in beds, sow in rows 10 to 12 inches apart across the beds. If root maggots have been a problem in the past and your previous crops have suffered damage, cover rows with screening or floating row covers after planting and leave them in place until plants are sizeable, because fly larvae may damage roots or stems. As soon as seedlings are 4 inches tall, thin them to about 3 inches apart, and use the extra ones for greens.

## VARIETIES

| Varieties | Days to Maturity | Comments |
|---|---|---|
| **Greens** | | |
| Alltop | 35 days | Regrows quickly. |
| Seven Top | 40 days | Dark green. |
| Topper | 35 days | Vigorous, slow to bolt. |
| **Roots** | | |
| Purple Top White Globe | 55 days | The standard, purple and white. |
| Tokyo Cross | 35 days | Uniform white roots, slow to become woody. AAS. |
| White Lady | 50 days | Sweet and tender, slow to become pithy. |

## Care and Maintenance

For the best-quality turnips, water as necessary to keep the plants vigorous and growing. Usually, about 1 inch of water per week is sufficient. Rapid growth results in the best quality.

### Additional Information

Harvest turnip greens about 5 weeks after sowing. Cut them just above the root so that they may regrow. Varieties grown for greens do not usually make satisfactory roots for harvesting. Harvest turnips grown for the roots when they are about 2 to 3 inches in diameter. If they are allowed to grow beyond maturity, the roots will be tough, woody, and poorly flavored. Don't throw the tops away; use them for greens. Turnips are quite hardy and will stand a freeze. Store late crops in the ground, and they will become sweeter with the cold. Protect them with heavy straw mulch to prolong the harvest into the early part of the winter, but dig the remaining roots before they are exposed to a hard freeze. Turnips also store well under refrigeration, but they may wilt. Protect them from wilting by dipping them in warm paraffin wax or storing them in plastic bags.

# WATERMELON

*Citrullus linatus*

Summertime celebrations would be incomplete without watermelons. Children of all ages love the sweet, juicy fruit of these hot-weather plants. As is the case with other summer melons, watermelons need a long, hot season to develop. Watermelons are vine crops closely related to cucumbers, squashes, and pumpkins, and like most vine crops, watermelons can take a lot of room. If you are reluctant to plant them because your garden has restricted space, you can plant smaller-fruited kinds, often called icebox watermelons. These can be grown on trellises if there is adequate support for the fruits so they do not pull down the vines.

## When to Plant

Do not plant watermelons too early because they cannot stand a frost. They need warm soil to develop and may rot off if weather is cool and wet. Sow seeds indoors under lights about 1 month before the latest date of last frost. Set out started plants or sow seed directly in the garden after any danger of frost has passed.

## Where to Plant

Plant watermelons somewhere with lots of room (they need about 25 to 30 square feet per hill), full sun (8 to 10 hours will suffice), and well-drained soil. If space is restricted, grow bush types in beds or containers, or train the vining types on a trellis, making sure that the structure is strong enough to support the plants. Icebox-type melons can weigh 6 to 12 pounds each, and several may develop on a vine. Standard and seedless melons at 25 pounds or more may be too heavy to grow on a support.

## How to Plant

Apply a complete garden fertilizer, such as 10-10-10, at a rate of 1½ pounds per 100 square feet of garden. Spade or rototill the soil. (See "Soil Preparation" on page 44.) Because vine crops do not tolerate root injuries common to transplanting, indoors under lights sow seeds in peat pots that can be planted without disturbing the tiny roots. Keep the lights on for 18 out of every 24 hours, and maintain the temperatures during the light period around 80 degrees Fahrenheit. After danger of frost has passed, carefully set 2 or 3 transplant seedlings in hills about 36 inches apart. In beds, space the plants 36 inches apart down the middles of the beds. In containers, plant bush types. Set the plants at the same depth they were growing. Black plastic mulch can get watermelons off to a good start since it traps the sun, warming the soil. Cut holes in the plastic with a small can from which you have cut off the rim. Be careful; it will be sharp. You could use a knife or scissors, but a can cuts the right-sized hole with a single effort. Then plant the seedlings in the holes.

## Care and Maintenance

From the minute watermelon seedlings are planted, cucumber beetles will threaten them. These pests will damage the leaves and scar the stems. Apply Sevin insecticide to eliminate the beetles, or cover the plants with floating row covers, being sure to tuck in the edges and ends, to keep the beetles out. When the plants begin to vine, remove the covers, and stop the spraying. In cooler areas, use floating row covers to warm the plants. When flowers appear, remove the covers so that bees may pollinate them. Watermelons, like all vine crops, have both male and female flowers. (See page 78.) The male flowers usually appear first and are smaller than the females. Many times new gardeners are dismayed that the flowers fall off without any melons. Usually, that happens because the flowers are all males. Female flowers have tiny melons below the flowers themselves; male flowers have only slender stems. The flowers are pollinated by bees that feed on the male flowers and then on the females, carrying the pollen from one to the other. Without bees, there will be no melons. If the weather is unfavorable for bees (that is, cold, wet, or dark), pollinate the melons by hand. Clip a male flower and dust the pollen from it on the pistils of the female flowers. Protect the foliage from diseases by applying maneb or an all-purpose garden fungicide. Rotate vine crops to a different part of the garden each year to reduce dangers of diseases. (See the pest control chart in the introduction to the vegetable garden.)

### Additional Information

In a garden with restricted space, grow melons vertically on a trellis or on a fence. Make sure the supports are sturdy enough to bear the weight of the plants with fruits on them. The heavy fruits will need additional support to keep from pulling the vines down. Use a little net or cloth parachute under each melon, tied securely to the support. Harvest watermelons when they are ripe. That sounds logical, doesn't it? But determining just when watermelons are ready to pick can be an art. Many gardeners rely on thumping. They are listening for a dull thud, but some melons make that sound when they are overripe. The most reliable way is to check the color of the bottom where the melon is lying on the ground. It should be a good yellow color, and the little curlicue where the melon attaches to the stem dries up as the melon ripens. The skin becomes dull looking, rough, and hardened sufficiently that you cannot cut into it with your fingernail. Melons do not continue to ripen once they are picked. They will become softer, but not sweeter.

## VARIETIES

Watermelons vary in size from the small, 6-pound icebox types to giants of 100 pounds or more. For most gardeners, the smaller, early types offer the greatest chance of success; they mature in 70 to 75 days. Bush types are especially well suited to home gardens. Standard varieties take more room and produce fewer fruits in smaller gardens, and the season may be too short in the more northern parts of the area. Standard varieties mature in 85 to 90 days. You must plant seedless varieties with normal-seeded types for pollination. Mark these plants in the garden so the ones with seeds can be separated from the ones that are seedless. Seedless melons mature in 85 days. Most watermelons are red, but types with yellow flesh are gaining popularity.

| Varieties | Size | Comments |
|---|---|---|
| **Early** | | |
| Bush Sugar Baby | 6 to 8 pounds | Bush type. |
| Golden Crown | 6 to 10 pounds | Red flesh, but skin turns yellow as melon ripens. |
| Sugar Baby | 6 to 8 pounds | Red flesh. Favorite icebox type. |
| Yellow Baby | 6 to 10 pounds | Yellow flesh, the first of the popular yellow varieties. |
| Yellow Doll | 6 to 10 pounds | Yellow flesh, hybrid. |
| **Seedless** | | |
| Cotton Candy | 20 pounds | Red flesh, large, seedless. |
| Honey Heart | 10 pounds | Yellow flesh, convenient size. |
| Jack of Hearts | 11 pounds | Red flesh, similar to King and Queen, but the smallest of the group. |
| King of Hearts | 18 pounds | Red flesh, largest of the Hearts. |
| Queen of Hearts | 15 pounds | Red flesh, mid-sized Heart. |
| **Standard** | | |
| Charleston Grey | 25 pounds | Red flesh, popular with commercial growers. |
| Crimson Sweet | 25 pounds | Red flesh, for larger gardens. |
| Sweet Favorite | 20 pounds | Red flesh, smaller and sweeter. |

# Growing Herbs in the Home Garden

Gardeners grow herbs for many uses, including cooking, creating fragrances, making medicines, and having attractive plants in the ornamental garden. Within the scope of this book, the herbs described are those generally used for culinary purposes.

Herbs add flavor and interest to our foods. Without them, food would often be bland and not very appetizing. Most cooks know how to use more common herbs, such as thyme, sage, and basil, which have been readily available in the U.S. marketplace. Many other herbs which are used in other parts of the world have been introduced by people immigrating from those regions, and because of the recent interest in ethnic cooking are becoming available here. Gourmet cooking shows on television have taught us about new herbs too. Most gourmet cooks never use dried herbs, but insist on freshly grown and harvested materials. Growing our own herbs enables those of us cooking at home to have the freshest ingredients for our dishes.

Fortunately, growing herbs is quite easy, often easier than growing many familiar vegetables. In fact, many thrive on minimal care and infertile soils. With too much tender, loving care, they become rank and less flavorful. For most gardeners, growing a few of each kind of herb is sufficient. Some herbs such as thyme and oregano are perennials, but most are generally grown as annuals (that is, you plant them new each season). Some do well as potted plants (for example, chives and rosemary) and can be brought indoors for the winter where they can be used fresh throughout the cold part of the year. Growing them under lights has become a popular pastime. Even cliff dwellers with no yard but a taste for fancy cooking can grow their herbs indoors under lights. (See the section on pages 63 to 65 in the introduction to the vegetable garden, referring to growing transplants under lights.)

## Planting Herbs

Some common herbs, such as mint and oregano, are aggressive and will take over the garden if they are not restrained. Sometimes walling them off from the rest of the garden with timbers is a satisfactory solution. You could use 2-by-2-foot squares outlined with 2-by-4s on edge. Let your imagination go to work incorporating concrete blocks, bricks, clay tiles, or other masonry.

Planting seed is the way to start some herbs, but others are better obtained as started plants. Many garden centers carry herbs, but mail-order seed houses and specialty herb growers are excellent sources for the best varieties and selections of plants. You may also get herbs from fellow herb gardeners who are propagating their own plants. If you do, be sure to find out the correct name and properly label each plant, so you know how to grow it and how to use it.

Some wild plants are usable herbs, and if you know these plants, you can move them to your garden. *Be careful!* Many wild plants, especially members of the *Umbelliferae* family, look nearly identical to familiar herbs but are poisonous.

## Pest Control

Pests do not bother most herbs. If you are growing only a few plants, bugs or diseases have a hard time finding them. Usually, the best way to control pests is to pick off the infested sprig and discard it before the pests move to the entire plant. Some such as mites, aphids, or thrips can be controlled with insecticidal soap if they become troublesome. Always remember to carefully wash off insecticidal soap after you harvest the herbs.

## Harvesting Herbs

Most herbs are ready to be harvested just as the flowers begin to open because they have the most flavor then. Early in the morning after the dew has dried is the best time to pick them while they are still cool, fresh, and crisp. By later in the day they may be warm and wilted. Cut off leaves or sprigs with a pair of scissors as needed, and keep harvesting the plants to stimulate continuing growth.

## Drying Herbs

When the season begins to wind down, herbs can be harvested for drying. Note that dried herbs are usually 3 or 4 times as strong as fresh herbs. Leaves are best stored whole and crushed just before use. Seeds, too, should be stored whole and ground as needed. Cut annual herbs at the ground; cut perennial herbs about ⅓ of the way down. To prepare the herbs for drying, rinse them with cold water, and drain them on paper towels.

I tie some herbs loosely in bunches and hang them upside down in brown paper bags in a warm, dry place. In some homes the attic may be a good place. This method works particularly well for seeds. After they are dry, I shake them in the bags until the seeds fall into the bags. Then I store the seeds in airtight glass jars.

For other kinds of herbs, particularly fleshy-leafed ones such as sage, I pick them, spread the herbs on a screen, and turn them every few days until they are dry. Then I strip the leaves from the stems and store the leaves in airtight glass jars. They do not require a dark place for storage but should be placed out of direct sunlight.

You may prefer to dry herbs in the microwave, but you need to be aware of the downside of this method. Most shrink, and some—basil, chives, parsley, and French tarragon—lose up to 90 percent of their flavor. Others—rosemary, sage, and thyme—are unaffected by microwave drying. Prepare the herbs by rinsing, draining, and placing them between 2 layers of paper toweling. Dry only 4 or 5 sprigs at a time. Turn on the microwave for about 3 minutes, then examine the herbs. If they are still too moist, turn them over and turn on the microwave for another 2 minutes. Repeat the process until the herbs are dry. There are tables for microwaving herbs, but they are only guides and provide a good starting place. After a few tries, you can determine the proper times for various herbs.

It is possible to freeze some herbs, such as dill, parsley, chives, and basil, for later use without blanching. Freeze the herbs quickly on a cookie sheet, and store them in airtight freezer bags. The herbs will be good 6 to 8 months or until the new crop comes in the next season.

Now let's get into the herb garden!

# Angelica

***Angelica archangelica***

Angelica is a tall biennial plant that acquired the name from its supposed ability to prevent or cure plague. People considered it a "guardian angel." All parts of the plant are aromatic. Use the leaves in salads, add the seeds as a flavoring in cooking, cook the roots as a vegetable, and candy the stems. Essential angelica oil is used to flavor vermouth and Benedictine.

## When to Plant

Plant angelica in early spring, as soon as the worst of the freezing weather is over. It can tolerate frost but not temperatures that get down to the teens at night.

## Where to Plant

This tall-growing herb needs room because it will reach 5 feet tall and spread 2 to 3 feet. Angelica prefers a location with light, moist soil that is in partial shade (filtered sun all day or shade part of the day). These plants fit equally well in a perennial border and the vegetable garden.

## How to Plant

Buy started plants in the spring. Space the plants at least 2 feet apart in the garden in well-prepared soil. (See "Soil Preparation" in the introduction to the vegetable garden.) Usually, a couple of plants are sufficient for culinary needs. Since these are biennial plants, they flower the second year after planting and then die out. To have flowering plants each year, plant or sow seed each year. You may collect seeds in the fall and sow them immediately, or you may save seeds in an airtight jar in the refrigerator and sow them the following spring.

## Care and Maintenance

Control weeds until the plants are large enough to shade them out. Mulching is not recommended as weed prevention because of its potential to attract slugs. The plants prefer cool weather and moist soil; as with most aromatic herbs, these plants do better in soil with low fertility. Water angelica in dry weather. Giving them 1 inch per week is probably okay, but too lush growing conditions cause overly tall, weak plants.

### Additional Information

Harvest leaves as needed during the season. Pick pieces of fresh stem with the leaves for candying. At season's end, collect and dry the leaves. (See "Drying Herbs" in the introduction to the herb garden.) Harvest the seeds as they ripen in the flower heads. If flower heads are removed, these plants will last several years, growing as short-lived perennials. If the plant is allowed to flower and the seed is allowed to ripen on the plants and fall to the ground, angelica can become naturalized in the garden. Plant it where it can grow undisturbed by other gardening activities.

# ANISE

***Pimpinella anisum***

Many herbs, including anise, are members of the *Umbelliferae* family. Anise is a native of the Mediterranean area and has been used as a flavoring and as a medicinal there for centuries. It has a flavor similar to licorice.

## When to Plant

Anise is an annual. Sow seeds in the early spring as soon as the soil has warmed and the danger of a hard freeze has passed.

## Where to Plant

Plant anise in fertile, well-drained soil that receives full sun (8 to 10 hours will suffice). Give these plants plenty of room because they reach a height of 2 feet or more, with an equal spread.

## How to Plant

Sow seed in well-prepared soil, $^1/_2$ inch deep, and space it about 1 inch apart in rows 1 foot apart. (See "Soil Preparation" in the introduction to the vegetable garden.) Sow seed thickly because the seed germinates poorly, then thin the seedlings to 12 inches apart when they are big enough to handle. Buy started plants of anise, or start plants indoors under lights in early spring. Set started plants at 12 inches by 12 inches in beds.

## Care and Maintenance

Keep weeds under control by light cultivation; mulching is not recommended for weed control of herbs because of slug problems. Anise will stand dry weather, but water if it wilts, about 1 inch per week.

### Additional Information

The plants develop a low rosette of foliage early in the season, then quickly produce a tall flowering stem. Harvest the leaves when they reach full size. Cut the flower heads as soon as the seeds begin to turn brown. If the flower heads are left on the plant, they will shatter and the seeds will be lost. Dry the flower heads in brown paper bags so the seeds can be caught as they dry and fall from the heads. Use the leaves in fruit salads, apple salads, or applesauce. Flavor cookies or candies with the seeds.

# Anise Hyssop

*Agastache foeniculum*

Anise hyssop is a large perennial plant, a member of the mint family, with showy purple spikes that attract bees in abundance. The flavor and aroma are definitely licorice. The leaves are good for teas or garnishes.

## When to Plant

Finding started plants at garden centers is difficult, so you will need to grow your own if you prefer to set out transplants. Start anise hyssop indoors under lights in late winter. Then set out plants or sow seed when the danger of a freeze has passed and the soil has warmed.

## Where to Plant

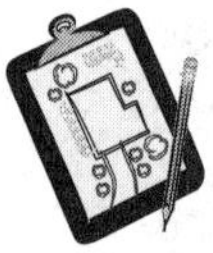

Locate these large plants in the garden where they will not shade out smaller plants and where they can be left undisturbed. Anise hyssop prefers well-prepared, moist soil in a sunny spot.

## How to Plant

Prepare the soil (see "Soil Preparation" in the introduction to the vegetable garden). For transplants, set them into the garden after the latest date of last frost, spacing the plants 2 feet apart in each direction. For seed, sow it ¼ inch deep directly in the garden in hills 2 feet apart in each direction or down the row, then thin to 1 plant per hill when the seedlings are big enough to handle.

## Care and Maintenance

The plants will bloom until frost if the spent flowers are removed. Leaving a few flowers to mature will allow the plants to reseed themselves, which is especially helpful where winterkill occurs.

### Additional Information

Harvest leaves when the plants are well established, and use the leaves fresh or dried. (See "Drying Herbs" in the introduction to the herb garden.) Remove flowers to become garnishes or to create bouquets. Anise hyssop is very attractive to honeybees, which make anise-flavored honey from the nectar. Bees attracted to the anise hyssop will stay around to pollinate other garden plants, too, such as the vine crops, which require bees for good production.

# Basil

***Ocimum basilicum***

A very familiar and popular herb, basil is the basis for pesto. Many cooks consider basil the premier culinary herb. Every gardener needs at least 1 basil plant to have the fresh leaves to toss into casseroles, sauces, and salads or to add to eggs, fish, pizza, spaghetti, and tacos.

## When to Plant

Basil will not tolerate cold weather. At temperatures below 50 degrees Fahrenheit, it suffers injury that looks similar to frost damage. Sow seeds indoors under lights about 2 months before the latest date of last frost. After the soil has warmed, move started plants into the garden, or buy and set out plants obtained from a garden center or mail-order nursery.

## VARIETIES

There are many basil selections and named varieties. Sweet basil is the best known and most commonly available. Lemon basil, *Ocimum basilicum* 'Citriodorum', has a fresh lemon flavor. 'Napolitano' has large, crinkled leaves. 'Cinnamon' provides a cinnamon flavor and fragrance. 'Dark Opal' AAS and 'Purple Ruffles' AAS have strong flavors and are better for bedding plants than for eating. 'Minimum' has small leaves and a compact form.

# Where to Plant

Plant basil in a full-sun location (8 to 10 hours will suffice) that has well-drained but moist soil.

# How to Plant

Prepare the soil (see "Soil Preparation" in the introduction to the vegetable garden). For direct seeding, sow seeds in warm soil in hills 12 inches apart, then thin seedlings to 1 plant per hill when the seedlings are big enough to handle. Growing from seed may get the plants off to a slower start than you want. You may prefer to use transplants; if you do, set them in the garden on a 12-by-12-inch spacing. Two to 6 plants are usually more than enough for a family.

# Care and Maintenance

When the plants are 6 inches tall and vigorously growing, pinch out the growing tips to stimulate branching. Basil plants cannot stand wilting, so be sure to apply water to keep the soil evenly moist. They need about 1 inch of water per week. Pests such as aphids and mites can infest basil. Pinch off affected shoots, or spray them with insecticidal soap. After harvesting, be sure to wash off the soap.

### Additional Information

Harvest sprigs as needed, but before flowers form. Cut each stem with a sharp knife or scissors, leaving 2 leaves on each stem to develop new shoots. You may harvest just the leaves, but harvesting the sprigs causes branching and more growth. If flowers have formed, pinch them off and let them regrow. Finish harvesting basil before the first frost. For winter use, trim the plants back, and pot up 1 or 2 plants. Dig the plants, shake off as much soil as possible, and set them in artificial potting soil. Place the pots indoors over the kitchen sink or in another bright, humid place.

# CARAWAY

### *Carum carvi*

Gardeners like caraway for the seeds, for the foliage, and for the roots, which are used like parsnips. Caraway joins carrots, parsnips, angelica, and anise as members of the *Umbelliferae* family.

## When to Plant

Caraway is a biennial plant, that is, it takes 2 seasons to produce seeds. Sow seeds in the spring as soon as the soil can be worked. Or sow seeds in the fall; fall-seeded plantings will not germinate until early the next spring.

## Where to Plant

These plants will be in the garden for 2 years, so plant them where they will not be disturbed or interfere with other garden activities. Grow caraway in a location with full sun (8 to 10 hours will suffice) and reasonably well-drained soil. It will tolerate clay soil.

## How to Plant

Prepare the soil (see "Soil Preparation" in the introduction to the vegetable garden). Sow seed directly in the garden in a place where you can leave the plants until they mature. Sow seed 1 inch apart in rows 2 feet apart, or sow seed in hills 1 foot in each direction. In hills, thin seedlings to 1 per hill; in rows, thin seedlings to 6 to 8 inches apart. Caraway will reseed itself readily. When it does, thin seedlings to the appropriate spacing. (The seed grows so readily that gardeners seldom use transplants.)

## Care and Maintenance

Keep weeds under control by hoeing or pulling; using mulch for weed control is not necessary. Water the planting when the weather is dry, providing about 1 inch of water per week.

**VARIETIES**

Some seed catalogs list selections, sometimes called annual caraway, that bolt easily and will set seed the first season if they are planted very early. In areas with mild winters, these varieties can be planted in early fall and will flower the next summer without fail.

### Additional Information

In the first season, caraway will make rosettes of low foliage, which will die down after the first freeze. During the first season, plants may be dug for the roots while they are young and tender, and then cooked like parsnips and served with butter and white sauce. In the second season, the plants will send up flowering stalks with heads of white flowers resembling Queen Anne's lace. After flowering, the plants die. Harvest the seedheads as they begin to turn from green to tan, before they shatter, and put them in paper bags to dry. Rub the dry seeds from the heads over a sheet of paper, and store the seeds in sealed glass jars in the refrigerator or a dry, dark place. A few plants will produce enough caraway seed for a year's supply. Many gardeners grow this herb when the supply gets low rather than every year.

# Chamomile, German Chamomile

***Chamaemelum nobile, Matricaria recutita***

Chamomile, sometimes called Roman chamomile, is a low-growing 4 to 6-inch tall perennial. German chamomile is a tall, erect, 3-foot annual. Both chamomiles are members of the composite (daisy) family, and the flowers of both are brewed for chamomile teas. The flavor is the same.

## When to Plant

Set out started plants from a garden center or catalog supplier in the spring, or sow seeds in the spring or fall. Freezing and thawing seem to improve germination, so planting when the weather is still cold doesn't pose a problem. For German chamomile, 1 to 2 plants are probably plenty. For Roman chamomile, which is smaller, more plants will be needed.

## Where to Plant

Both Roman and German chamomiles prefer a full-sun location (8 to 10 hours will suffice) that has dry soil.

## How to Plant

Because seeds of Roman chamomile grow well in cracks and crevasses and it has flowers, you may want to plant it in a rock garden if not the vegetable garden. Grow German chamomile in any open sunny spot in the garden. Be aware that after it is started, German chamomile will reseed easily, and may become a nuisance.

## Care and Maintenance

Roman chamomile will spread if the flowers are mowed off the first year. Pull or hoe out any weeds that appear. These plants need water only in a severe drought, otherwise they withstand dry weather well.

### Additional Information

Harvest the flowers when the florets begin to reflex (bend back). Remove the flowers from the stems because the stems will cause the flavors of the tea to be bitter. Air-dry the blooms on a screen tray, and store them in tightly sealed glass jars. Over the years, people have credited soothing, refreshing chamomile teas with all kinds of medicinal cures for things such as digestion, upset stomach, and nightmares. You'll need several flowers to brew the tea; the number will depend upon your taste.

# Chervil

***Anthriscus cerefolium***

Native to southern Russia, chervil is another member of the *Umbelliferae* family, along with angelica and anise. The plant grows to a height of 1 to 2 feet, sets seed, and dies within about 8 weeks. The leaves of chervil, which resemble parsley leaves, impart a delicate, aniselike (licoricelike) flavor to light dishes such as fish, poultry, soups, stews, and omelets, particularly those of French cuisine.

## When to Plant

Sow seed in early spring or late summer to take advantage of the plant's preference for growing in the cool weather of spring or fall. (Later seedings will germinate in the spring.) Because the plants are short-lived, make repeated sowings if you want to have a continuous supply.

## Where to Plant

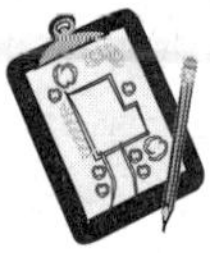

Chervil prefers cool, moist soil in a location that is protected from midday heat. You may plant it under a tree or on the north side of larger garden plants that will provide shade.

## How to Plant

Prepare the soil (see "Soil Preparation" in the introduction to the vegetable garden). Sow seeds directly in the garden in rows. Chervil seeds need light to germinate, but covering each row with a sheet of newspaper or a cloth that lets some light through will keep the soil moist and protect the seeds until they begin to germinate. Be sure to lift the cover every morning and evening to check whether the seedlings have emerged, then remove the cover immediately when you see any seedlings. When the seedlings are large enough to handle, thin them to about 6 inches apart. Chervil does not transplant well, and it grows so fast that most nurseries don't bother with transplants.

## Care and Maintenance

Few insects or diseases affect chervil. The plants grow so quickly, set seed, and die out so fast that few pests can find them. Keep soils moderately moist; water once a week if there is no rain, providing about 1 inch.

### Additional Information

Harvest the leaves as soon as they are full sized but still tender. Although the leaves have the most flavor when they are used fresh, they can be collected, dried, and stored in airtight containers. (See "Drying Herbs" in the introduction to the herb garden.)

# Chives

*Allium schoenoprasum*

Chives are perennial plants belonging to the onion family that produce foot-tall clumps of hollow, upright leaves. Allowed to go to flower, they make mounds of lavender-pink flowers. Chives add a delicate onionlike flavor to soups, stews, salads, omelets, and sauces.

## When to Plant

Spring is the usual time to plant chives, although they can be divided just about anytime during the season. Buy small plants that are available in garden centers in spring. Or purchase and sow seeds in early spring. Plants from seeds are not as uniform as those from plants; some will have larger or smaller leaves, so dig out the less desirable ones.

## Where to Plant

A few plants will probably meet your needs. Plant chives in a corner of the garden where they will not be disturbed and will not interfere with other gardening operations. Chives will tolerate shade, but choose a site in full sun (8 to 10 hours will suffice) to have the best growth. Chives do well in containers and are less likely to spread.

## How to Plant

Set started plants or divisions in well-prepared soil (see "Soil Preparation" in the introduction to the vegetable garden), spacing them 12 inches apart. Sow seeds on the soil surface, and cover them lightly.

## Care and Maintenance

Once started, chives need little, if any, care. They just grow. But you do need to watch out for the same problems that affect onions. To control thrips, use insecticidal soap—and remember to wash it off the chives after harvesting. If root maggots have been a problem in the past and your previous crops have suffered damage, cover rows with screening or floating row covers after planting and leave them in place until plants are sizeable, because fly larvae may damage roots or stems.

### VARIETIES

Garlic chives, *Allium tuberosum*, is another member of the onion family. It is a larger plant with flat leaves similar to those of a leek, and its flavor is reminiscent of garlic.

### Additional Information

As soon as the plants begin to grow, harvest the leaves. Snipping them off with a pair of sharp scissors works as well as anything. Keep the plants clipped to eliminate flowering, which is to be discouraged for at least 2 reasons. First, after a shoot flowers, the leaves become tough and unusable. Second, plants that are allowed to flower will reseed, the seedlings are seldom as good quality as the parent, and they become weeds. The plants will continue to make more leaves after flowering, but the ones that flowered will be lost. Divide clumps every 3 years so they do not become crowded. Separate them into bunches of 5 or 6 bulblets each, and discard the extras or give them to friends. To have chives all winter, dig a plant before the first frost, shake off as much soil as possible, and pot it up using artificial potting soil. Then set the plant over the kitchen sink where it will be convenient to take a snip. Some gardeners insist to have the best chives indoors in pots they must be frozen several times before digging and potting them up. Try them both ways and see which works the best for you. Remember, these plants do take a nap in December.

# Cilantro-Coriander

***Coriandrum sativum***

Cilantro and coriander are 2 stages of the same annual plant. The parsley-like foliage, which is picked before the seed stalk forms, is called cilantro. Mexican and Asian cuisine often calls for cilantro, and among U.S. consumers, salsa is the number one use of cilantro. Mature seeds, which are collected and dried for use in cooking and baking, are called coriander. Coriander is a major ingredient in curry powder.

## When to Plant

Cilantro is a short-lived 2-foot-tall annual. Plant seed directly in the garden, starting in early spring as soon as the worst of the freezing weather has passed. Make repeated sowings every 3 weeks to have a continuous supply of cilantro. Summer sowings may bolt (send up flower stalks) before the rosettes of leaves form and can be left to mature into coriander. Seeding is preferable to using transplants because transplants bolt too quickly.

> **VARIETIES**
>
> Quick-bolting varieties will produce seed early in the season. For cilantro, the slower-bolting varieties, such as 'Santos' or 'Long-Standing', will provide an extra week or so of harvest before the bolting begins.

## Where to Plant

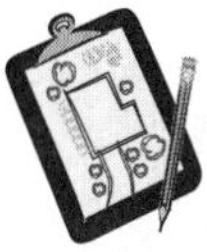

Plant seeds in a full-sun location (8 to 10 hours will suffice) that has well-drained, well-tilled soil.

## How to Plant

Prepare the soil (see "Soil Preparation" in the introduction to the vegetable garden). Sow seeds 1 inch apart in rows 2 feet apart. Or if you have raised beds, sow the rows across the beds. Do not thin the seedlings.

## Care and Maintenance

Few pests find cilantro before it is harvested. Water weekly during dry weather to provide about 1 inch. Hoe or pull weeds that appear. If mites become troublesome, spray them with insecticidal soap—and remember to wash it off after harvesting foliage.

### Additional Information

The plants will bolt very quickly in hot weather. For cilantro, harvest fully developed rosettes of the foliage as soon as you notice evidence of seed stalks, and cut individual leaves from the seed stalks. For coriander, allow the seed heads to develop and harvest them as they turn tan and before they begin to shatter. Don't be too hasty to harvest the seeds because immature green seeds have poor flavor. Sometimes, tying a paper bag over the flower clusters to catch the seed as it drops will result in mostly mature seed. Be sure to clean out and dispose of any immature seed and foliage before storing the seed.

# Dill

***Anethum graveolens***

Dill is a common herb that has a place in every garden because of its many culinary uses. Just a few plants provide enough dill for most households. The soft, fernlike foliage, called dill weed, is used fresh. Small plants that are harvested in spring and fall are known as salad dill. Dill weed and salad dill are great in soups, salads, eggs, or fish or poultry dishes. The flower heads and dried seeds are important for pickling processes, and the dried seeds may be added to rye bread. Mature plants are about 3 feet tall.

## When to Plant

Sow seeds or set out started plants in early spring. Make successive plantings throughout the summer to assure a continuous supply of dill weed. It gets old and tough when it goes to flower.

## Where to Plant

Plant dill anywhere in the garden that it can have well-prepared, moist soil. It thrives in either full sun (8 to 10 hours will suffice) or partial shade (filtered sun all day or shade part of the day).

## How to Plant

Prepare the soil (see "Soil Preparation" in the introduction to the vegetable garden). Sow seeds 1 inch apart in rows 1 foot apart. Then thin the seedlings when they are about 6 inches tall, and use the discarded seedlings as salad dill. Make more seedings every 2 weeks. Obtaining started plants from a garden center may be a good way to begin to grow dill. Set the plants 1 foot apart in beds or 2 feet apart in rows in well-tilled soil. The plants readily reseed themselves and can scatter throughout the garden. Dig up extraneous seedlings, and plant them where you want them in the garden.

## Care and Maintenance

Dill requires little care after it has started to grow. Water it when the weather is dry, providing 1 inch per week.

### ADDITIONAL INFORMATION

Harvest the salad dill when it is 6 to 10 inches tall. Keeping the plants cut back will extend the harvest of the foliage, but eventually, the plants will bolt and make flower stalks. Cut the flower heads when they are in full bloom, and use them either fresh or dried. For seeds, cut the heads when the seeds are mature but before they begin to shatter. Hang the heads upside down in brown paper bags to finish drying, catching the seeds as they shatter. Dry salad dill, flower heads, and seeds, and store them in airtight containers for later use. Late in the season, allow a few heads to mature and the seed to drop in the garden, which will produce seedling plants for the next year. If they grow where they are not wanted, transplant them into the proper places in the garden. Dill, along with fennel and parsley, is a favorite food of black swallowtail butterfly larvae. These large black-and-yellow-striped caterpillars do not eat much, but make spectacular butterflies. Collect the chrysalises that form and hatch them for a fun summertime project for kids.

**VARIETIES**

'Fernleaf' AAS is probably the best all-around selection for home gardens; it keeps producing side shoots all season. 'Bouquet' has excellent flavor. 'Dukat' is tall with high yields. Common dill is probably just as good as these other varieties for most home uses.

# FENNEL, FINOCCHIO

***Foeniculum vulgare, Foeniculum vulgare* var. *dulce***

Fennel is a European herb known for its aromatic seeds and tender, fragrant leaves. This herb has a wonderful aniselike or licoricelike flavor. Florence fennel, commonly called finocchio, develops a bulblike base used fresh or steamed. Common fennel develops a plant that can be 4 feet tall when it is in flower. Finocchio develops a bulblike rosette of foliage, which is harvested before it bolts. Both are tender perennials grown as annuals.

## When to Plant

You may start fennel or finocchio indoors under lights about 6 weeks before the frost-free date (average date of last frost) for a summer crop, and start them under lights in late summer for a fall crop. Or sow seed directly in the garden after the last heavy freeze. Seed can withstand a frost, but if plants are already up, they may be nipped. Started plants are not likely to be available in garden centers; they do not transplant well because they have tap roots. The number of plants depends on your tastes; you may want 6 or more if you like fennel or finocchio.

## Where to Plant

Plant fennel and finocchio in a sunny location with well-prepared soil. Since they get quite large and reseed vigorously, locate them where they will have room and will not shade out lower-growing plants.

## How to Plant

Prepare the soil (see "Soil Preparation" in the introduction to the vegetable garden). Sow seed directly in the garden. Then thin seedlings to about 8 inches apart when they are 4 inches tall, and use them in soups or sauces. Fennel and finocchio do not tolerate transplanting well because they have tap roots. Start them in peat pots, which you can plant without disturbing the roots. Sow several seeds per pot, and thin to 1 when they have germinated. Set the plants 8 inches apart in well-prepared soil.

## Care and Maintenance

After it has started to grow, fennel or finocchio require little care. Water them during dry weather, providing 1 inch per week.

### Additional Information

Harvest the tender leaves when the plants are 6 to 10 inches tall. Keeping the plants cut back will extend the harvest, but eventually, the plants will bolt and make flower stalks. To harvest seeds, cut the heads when the seeds are mature but before they begin to shatter. Hang the heads upside down in brown paper bags to finish drying, catching the seeds as the heads shatter. Tie harvested leaves into small bundles and hang them in a warm, dry place, or dry leaves on a screen. Store dried leaves and seeds in airtight containers for later use. Cover finocchio bulbs with soil to blanch them when they are 2 or 3 inches in diameter. Harvest the bulbs before they bolt in hot weather. In the cool weather of fall, production may be extended until freeze-up. Late in the season, allow a few flower heads to mature and the seed to drop, which will produce seedling plants for the next year. Since they do not transplant easily, harvest the tender leaves, and then hoe out the plants if they are in the way of other things. Fennel, along with dill and parsley, is a favorite food of black swallowtail butterfly larvae. These large black-and-yellow-striped caterpillars do not eat much, but make spectacular butterflies. Collect the chrysalises that form and hatch them for a fun summertime project for kids.

# Hyssop

***Hyssopus officinalis***

A native of southern Europe and Asia, hyssop has been used for centuries as a flavoring in soups, stews, or teas and may be used with sage in stuffings. It is also used as a cough medicine. It has a strong camphorlike fragrance, and a little goes a long way.

## When to Plant

Sow seed indoors under lights in late winter. Set out started plants in the spring as soon as the soil can be worked or seed directly in the garden. Plants are sometimes available at garden centers or nurseries about that time; buy ones that are a healthy green color and are short and compact.

## Where to Plant

Hyssop makes a good edging because it is attractive and can be kept trimmed to about 6 inches tall. It is a short-lived perennial that will be in the same place in the garden for 3 to 4 years. The plants prefer full sun (8 to 10 hours will suffice), but tolerate shade. Plants located in somewhat poor soil will have a more intense fragrance and taste.

## How to Plant

Prepare the soil (see "Soil Preparation" in the introduction to the vegetable garden). Sow seed ¼ inch deep in rows 1 foot apart, and thin the seedlings to a 1-foot spacing when they are big enough to handle. Set started plants 1 foot apart in each direction. Hyssop will do well in raised beds, too, if it is not overfertilized or overwatered. Divide overgrown plants, and replant in spring or fall.

## Care and Maintenance

Hyssop grows with little care. Few pests will damage hyssop in the garden. Generally, watering is not needed, but if no rain falls for a couple of weeks, apply 1 inch of water.

### Additional Information

Harvest flower spikes just as the blooms begin to open. Dry them quickly over a screen, and store the dried spikes in airtight jars. Grind the dried spikes as needed for use. After a few years, the planting will begin to decline; the plants will thin out and die out. Either divide the plants, or start a new planting.

# MINT

***Mentha* sp.**

Mints are easily grown perennial ground covers that are valued as flavorings in teas, ice cream, candies, and gum. There are many varieties, each with a distinctive flavor. The most commonly grown are peppermint (*Mentha* × *piperita*) and spearmint (*M.* × *spicata*). The plants can reach a height of 1 foot and spread rapidly to 2 feet or more.

## When to Plant

Set out started plants whenever they are available during the season. Certain specialty nurseries and garden centers carry them. Double-check that the plants are correctly labeled before you take them home.

## Where to Plant

Most mint varieties will thrive in full sun (8 to 10 hours will suffice) or partial shade (filtered sun all day or shade part of the day). Plant them where you can control them because they spread and will invade the rest of the garden, the lawn, or your neighbor's yard. The most damaging disease of the mints is verticillium wilt. Do not plant mint where solanaceous crops (tomatoes, potatoes, etc.) have been grown because they all carry the disease and infect the soil.

## How to Plant

Set out started plants in well-prepared soil. (See the introduction to the vegetable garden.) Separate the various types with barriers so they do not spread and grow together, or you will not know which one you are harvesting. Some gardeners construct elaborate barriers to help contain mint by using concrete blocks or timbers buried so that the tops are slightly above the soil surface, or planting in vertically placed 12-inch clay drain tiles. Space plants 2 feet apart in beds. For most gardeners, 1 or 2 plants of a kind are sufficient.

### VARIETIES

You may be more familiar with some varieties of mint than others. Spearmint (*M.* × *spicata*) flavors chewing gum. Peppermint (*M.* × *piperita*) does not come true from seed, so use only vegetatively propagated plants. Apple mint (*M. sauveolens*) has a fruity flavor and aroma; pineapple mint (*M. sauveolens* var. *variegata*) bears green and white variegated leaves and has a pineapple flavor; Corsican mint (*M. requienii*) carries a crème de menthe fragrance; and English pennyroyal (*M. pulegium*), with a menthol-like aroma, is sometimes used as an insect repellent. Make sure that you take home the variety of mint that you desire; check that the label and the plant match. Pinch a leaf and check the fragrance, then buy the plants with the strongest aroma. Unless you can trust your local supplier, order from a reliable producer or catalog.

## Care and Maintenance

Care of mint consists of controlling weeds by pulling them, keeping the soil moist but not wet—about 1 inch of water per week—and restricting the spread of the plants. Commercial growers renew the growth of their plantings by plowing the beds each fall to a 6-inch depth. Doing this cuts up the underground stems and stimulates new growth in spring. Some gardeners add 3 or 4 inches of straw mulch to protect the plantings over winter. The mulch must be removed before plants begin to grow in the spring.

### Additional Information

Harvest the sprigs of mint when flower buds first appear. Cut sprigs 6 to 10 inches long as needed, and use them fresh in drinks. Or dry them by hanging small bunches in a warm, dry place or placing them over a screen. Strip the leaves from the dry stems, and store the leaves in airtight containers. Use dried mint in teas, flavorings, and potpourri.

# OREGANO, GREEK

***Origanum heracleoticum* (True Greek Oregano)**

Oregano is an easily grown semihardy perennial that will reach 18 inches in height. Cooks flavor Mexican and Mediterranean dishes with the leaves. The most familiar use may be in pizza.

## When to Plant

Set out plants in early spring; they can stand a freeze. Divide them in spring or fall.

## Where to Plant

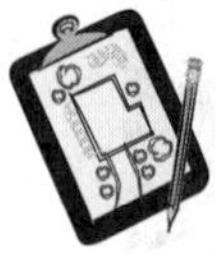

Oregano needs a full-sun location (8 to 10 hours will suffice) with reasonably good garden soil; it should drain well and should not be puddled or compacted. This is one instance where too much of a good thing can be a drawback because too-fertile soil results in rank growth and reduced flavor. Oregano can be grown in a pot or other container with an artificial potting soil or soil that you make at home. (See "Soils for Container Gardens" in the introduction.)

## How to Plant

Buy plants of the varieties you need from a garden center or nursery that grows the real thing. The best varieties even though they are rarely named are vegetatively propagated, which maintain the richness and flavor that you want in these herbs. Seedlings may be flavorless. The common oregano, *Oregano vulgare*, sold in many garden centers, and virtually all oregano seed, will grow into invasive plants with little, if any, flavor. When you find a selection that has good, intense flavor, propagate it yourself by dividing it to make sure you are growing plants that you can actually use in cooking. Prepare the soil (see "Soil Preparation" in the introduction to the vegetable garden). Set plants in the garden 18 inches apart in 18-inch rows. For many households, 1 plant is probably enough.

## Care and Maintenance

You will not have to spend a lot of time caring for oregano in the garden. It needs little water—about 1 inch per week—and is vigorous enough to squeeze out most weeds. In the colder areas of the Midwest, winter survival may be aided by applying 6 to 8 inches of straw mulch. Remove it in the spring before plants begin to grow.

### VARIETIES

Selections of Greek Mountain oregano, which is the best for flavor, have white flowers and dark-green leaves and are the kinds to have in your garden. Pot marjoram (*Origanum onites*) is actually an oregano that has a bite to it. Common oregano (*Origanum vulgare* subsp. *vulgare*) is a weedy plant with purple flowers and no discernible flavor. If the variety you are growing has purple flowers, kill it and replace it with something worth growing.

### Additional Information

Harvest oregano as soon as the first blossoms appear, usually in May. Cut the tops back several inches, and keep them cut to stimulate more production. Only the newer leaves are tender and flavorful. If the plant goes to seed, the growth of new leaves stops. Use the leaves fresh, or dry the plants quickly over a screen, strip the leaves from the stems, and store the leaves in airtight containers. (See "Drying Herbs" in the introduction to the herb garden.)

# Parsley

***Petroselinum crispum***

Virtually everyone recognizes parsley, a frequently appearing garnish on plates served in restaurants. Parsley leaves are also used in various dishes, soups, and sauces. Cooks add parsley root, which is grown in the same way as carrots, to soups and stews. Although parsley is a biennial member of the *Umbelliferae* family, gardeners grow it as an annual.

## When to Plant

You may sow seed indoors under lights in midwinter, or you may wait until the soil can be worked and sow parsley seed directly in the garden. Set out transplants as soon as the soil can be worked in the spring.

## Where to Plant

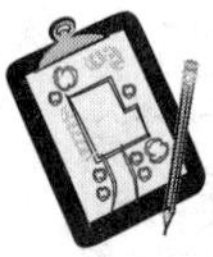

Parsley grows well in full sun (8 to 10 hours will suffice) or partial shade (filtered light all day or shade part of the day) in soil that has been prepared deeply and well. The plants reach only 1 foot or so in height, so plant them wherever they fit. Planting them at the end of a bed makes them easily accessible to be clipped as needed. Regular clipping of leaves permits you to use them before they deteriorate. Usually, 6 or 8 plants are sufficient for a family.

## How to Plant

Prepare the soil (see "Soil Preparation" in the introduction to the vegetable garden). The seed takes a long time to germinate outdoors, sometimes 4 or more weeks. Sow it 1 inch apart in rows 1 foot apart, then thin seedlings to a 5- or 6-inch spacing. Sown indoors under lights at 70 degrees Fahrenheit and covered with plastic wrap, seed will germinate in 1 week or less. Transplant seedlings into peat pots when they are large enough to handle for setting directly into the garden. Space plants 1 foot apart in each direction in beds, or 1 foot apart in rows 2 feet apart.

## Care and Maintenance

Parsley takes little care in the garden. Apply 1 inch of water per week if there is insufficient rainfall, and hoe or pull weeds as they appear. The plants are susceptible to mites, especially under lights. Spray with insecticidal soap to control them, and rinse the treated leaves before use.

### Additional Information

Harvest parsley leaves as they mature. Clip the oldest leaves as needed, or clip the entire top off and let the rest regrow. A plant can be harvested this way several times during the season. Dig parsley roots (*Petroselinum crispum tuberosum*) when they are $1\frac{1}{2}$ inches in diameter, usually in late summer. Parsley bolts and produces a seed stalk the second year. If parsley is protected from cold, it will continue to produce all winter. Dig up 1 or 2 plants before the first frost, shake off as much soil as possible, and pot them in artificial potting soil. Then set them over the kitchen sink where they will be convenient to take a snip to flavor your cooking all winter. Or you may grow parsley under lights. Parsley is grown as an annual because it will bolt immediately in spring.

## VARIETIES

There are 2 kinds of parsley, curled and flat. Curled parsley (*Petroselinum crispum crispum*) is used primarily as a garnish; it is seldom eaten, even though it has a good flavor in cooked dishes. Flat parsley (*Petroselinum crispum neapolitanum*) is preferred for the better flavor. Both the leaves and the roots of flat parsley are used. Root parsley (*Petroselinum crispum tuberosum*) is grown strictly for its roots, which are used like carrots or parsnips.

| Varieties | Days to Maturity | Comments |
|---|---|---|
| **Curled Leaf** | | |
| Banquet | 75 days | For garnish or salads. |
| Forest Green | 75 days | Gentle flavor. |
| Moss Curled | 75 days | The standard curled type. |
| Triple Curled | 75 days | Tightly curled. |
| **Flat Leaf** | | |
| Catalogno | 78 days | Italian type, dries well. |
| Giant Italian | 78 days | Larger than Single Italian. |
| Single Italian | 78 days | Glossy dark-green leaves used fresh or dried. |
| **Root** (grow the variety available in your area) | | |
| Early Sugar | 84 days | Long, tapered root similar to those of parsnips, sweet parsley flavor. |
| Hamburg | 84 days | Long, tapered roots similar to those of parsnips, sweet parsley flavor. |
| Short Sugar | 84 days | Long, tapered roots similar to those of parsnips, sweet parsley flavor. |

# Parsley Hints

*To make your dried herbs taste fresher, mince them together with a sprig of fresh parsley, then add to your recipe.*

*To keep purchased parsley fresher longer, snip the tips off their stems, removing the rubber band. Submerge the parsley in a half inch of water in a glass; cover with a plastic bag and store in the refrigerator.*

# Rosemary

***Rosmarinus officinalis***

Rosemary is a small, woody shrub, marginally hardy north of zone 6. Even so, gardeners grow it as a perennial, dutifully lifting and potting the plant for overwintering indoors. The needlelike leaves add a distinctive, vaguely pinelike flavor to a variety of dishes. It can be trimmed to any size and shape, but is usually kept about 1 foot tall. Leaves are used in soups, stews, and sauces, as well as with poultry and other meat dishes.

## When to Plant

Set started rosemary plants in the garden after danger of frost has passed.

## Where to Plant

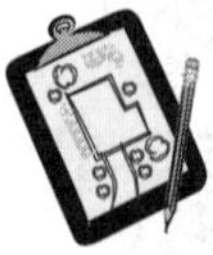

Grow potted plants on the patio, or set the plants directly in the garden. On the patio or in the garden, rosemary prefers a location in full sun (8 to 10 hours will suffice) or partial shade (filtered sun all day or shade part of the day), and the soil should be well drained. Choosing a spot near the end of a bed is ideal because it makes the plants more easily accessible to snip off a piece anytime it is needed.

## How to Plant

New plants may be started from cuttings or fresh seed, but plants from seed may develop more variation in flavor. Start seed indoors under lights in early winter, or start seed in a cold frame in early spring. Prepare the soil well (see "Soil Preparation" in the introduction to the vegetable garden). Set the plants in the garden at the same depth they were growing, and place them 18 inches apart in both directions in beds. The number of plants you set out depends on your use—1 may be enough for adding to food dishes, but you may want more if you use some in an ornamental way as well. Use artificial soil mixes in containers, setting the plants at the same depth they were growing. One plant per 12-inch container is about right.

## Care and Maintenance

Rosemary requires very little attention in the garden. It does well in soil with low fertility, and it will stand all but the most severe drought. Plants in pots require more care: see that they have enough water on a regular basis, making sure that they never dry out completely, and add dilute liquid fertilizer (mixed according to label directions) once in spring and again in summer. Before the onset of freezing weather, dig up 1 or 2 plants, shake off as much soil as possible, and pot them up using an artificial potting soil. Move plants indoors that are already potted. No significant insects or diseases affect rosemary. Poorly drained soil may cause root and stem rots to develop; correcting the drainage cures the problem.

### VARIETIES

The varieties 'Arp' and 'Hill's Hardy' may stand cold weather better than the common types. 'Prostrata' is a creeping type, which may be used for a scent garden and for edging.

### Additional Information

Harvest rosemary as soon as sufficient new growth has developed. Cut sprigs 8 to 10 inches long, and strip the leaves as needed. Or tie the sprigs in loose bunches, and hang them to dry or dry them over screens. Strip the leaves from the dried stems, and store the leaves in airtight jars. In milder parts of the area, rosemary may be overwintered in the garden if you treat the plants like hybrid tea roses. Hill up 12 inches of soil over the plants, and cover them with rose cones. Uncover them before growth begins in spring. Rosemary plants make attractive potted shrubs when you keep them trimmed to shape, and they make interesting topiaries as well. Some gardeners have plants that they have maintained for many years, producing sizable shrubs and providing the desirable leaves for culinary uses. They produce bright white or blue flowers in summer.

# SAGE

*Salvia officinalis*

Sage is a hardy, semiwoody perennial plant that makes a loose shrub about 2 feet tall. The leaves are harvested and used fresh or dried in stuffings, sausages, and dressings. One or 2 plants is usually sufficient for most gardeners.

## When to Plant

Start sage indoors under lights in late winter. Sow seed in peat pots, and thin seedlings to 1 per pot. Or buy started plants from garden centers or mail-order suppliers. Set out started plants as soon as the ground can be worked in the spring; they can withstand a frost.

## Where to Plant

Choose a site to plant sage where it can have well-drained soil and receive full sun (8 to 10 hours will suffice). The plants will eventually become quite big, so place them where they will not shade other plants and where they will not interfere with other garden operations.

## How to Plant

Work the soil deeply and well. (See "Soil Preparation" in the introduction to the vegetable garden.) Set out the started plants in the garden 15 to 18 inches apart so they have room to develop.

## Care and Maintenance

After it is established, sage is a low-maintenance herb requiring only a bit of weeding and pruning. Keep weeds under control by pulling or hoeing them. Prune established plants each spring to remove dead or damaged branches and to develop more compact plants. Although sage tolerates dry soil, you may need to apply 1 inch of water if there is no rain for 1 or 2 weeks. Mites can become troublesome, but using insecticidal soap controls them. (Always remember to wash it off after harvesting sage.) During wet seasons, diseases may damage some stems; cut them out before other stems are infected. To combat severe diseases, destroy the old planting, and start a new planting elsewhere in the garden.

### VARIETIES

There are many ornamental varieties of culinary sage, but they are not as hardy and winter survival is poor. Pineapple sage (*Salvia elegans*) has a delightful pineapple flavor. It is not hardy and should be treated as an annual or potted up and moved indoors for the winter.

### ADDITIONAL INFORMATION

Harvest leaves when they are fully developed in spring. Clip off sprigs 8 to 10 inches long, dry them, strip the leaves from the stems, and store the leaves in airtight containers until needed. Leaves can be used fresh, but dried leaves are usually used. Plants need no special care for winter. Do not prune them too severely before the onset of winter, however, or their survival will be adversely affected.

# SALAD BURNET

***Sanguisorba minor***

Salad burnet is a graceful perennial plant that forms a 15-inch mound of compound leaves. The leaves taste and smell like fresh cucumbers and are much more flavorful than many more commonly used herbs. This herb is a pleasant addition to salads, salad dressings, vinegars, beverages, sandwiches, and a variety of other foods. Salad burnet should have a more prominent place in trendy gourmet foods.

## When to Plant

Sow seeds directly in the garden in late fall or in spring. These hardy plants will withstand frost. Established plants can be divided in spring.

## Where to Plant

Salad burnet prefers a location in full sun (8 to 10 hours will suffice) or light shade (a little shade from a distant tree or some shade in the middle of the day), and it tolerates alkaline soils quite well. A well-drained but moist soil is best.

## How to Plant

Prepare the soil (see "Soil Preparation" in the introduction to the vegetable garden). Sow seeds in hills 12 to 15 inches apart, then thin to 1 plant per hill when the seedlings are big enough to handle. If necessary, divide established plants in spring before growth begins. A half dozen plants are probably sufficient for most gardeners.

## Care and Maintenance

Once established, salad burnet takes little care. Remove the flowers to encourage more foliage. If flowers are allowed to develop and drop seed, salad burnet may become weedy spreading throughout the garden. Pull or hoe seedlings that appear. Apply 1 inch of water when there is no rain for a week.

### Additional Information

Harvest tender new leaves once the plants are well established and before they begin to flower. Older leaves left on the plants will become bitter. Salad burnet makes an attractive mound of foliage that is appropriate for the ornamental perennial border as well as the vegetable garden.

# Savory

***Satureja hortensis, Satureja montana***

Both summer savory and winter savory are available to gardeners. Summer savory (*S. hortensis*), an annual of the mint family, is the more commonly grown of the two. The plant reaches 15 inches tall and 1 foot wide. Winter savory (*S. montana*) is an evergreen perennial that makes a mound of foliage about 1 foot high and 2 feet wide. Savories have been used to flavor wild game and meats for centuries. In a notable story found in the biblical book of Genesis, Jacob prepared savory game when he outwitted his brother, Esau, to gain their father Isaac's blessing. Savories have a pungent, peppery flavor, and winter savory is the more intense of the two.

## When to Plant

Sow summer savory seeds in starter trays or peat pots indoors under lights in March; do not cover the seed. Set started plants in the garden after the last hard freeze. Sow summer savory seeds directly in the garden after the frost-free date (average date of last frost). Start winter savory from cuttings in the spring or from divisions; winter savory doesn't need to be brought in for the winter. Set out winter savory 2 weeks before the frost-free date. Plants of either type may be available in garden centers in early spring.

## Where to Plant

Savories prefer well-drained soil in a full-sun location (8 to 10 hours will suffice), and they produce more intense flavors in soils of low fertility. Grow perennial winter savory in a part of the garden where it will not be disturbed and will not interfere with other garden activities.

## How to Plant

Prepare the soil (see "Soil Preparation" in the introduction to the vegetable garden). Space summer savory plants about 8 inches apart. Set winter savory plants 12 to 15 inches apart. A half dozen plants are more than enough for most gardeners. Or sow seeds of summer savory a few inches apart directly in the garden. The seed is very tiny and needs light to germinate, so do not cover it with soil. Thin the seedlings to 6 inches apart.

## Care and Maintenance

Savories require little care after they are established. Keep weeds under control until the plants are large enough to shade them out. Apply 1 inch of water per week if nature does not cooperate.

### Additional Information

Harvest or pinch off shoot tips of summer savory to stimulate bushy growth. Cut back winter savory to a low mound after flowering and in the spring before growth begins. Harvest leaves as needed, or harvest 6- to 8-inch stems, and hang them to dry in small bunches or dry them on a screen. Strip the leaves, and store them in airtight jars. Most people use only dried leaves, but there is no reason not to use fresh leaves. Winter savory provides a much longer harvest season than summer savory. It will stand a freeze and may be harvested well into winter. Severe trimming will keep the plants bushy and dense within the boundaries you have established for them. Some people consider winter savory to be too heavy and prefer the less intense flavor of summer savory. Winter savory is hardy to zone 5a, but it may overwinter even farther north if it is protected by adequate snow cover or 4 to 6 inches of straw. Green savory leaves crushed and rubbed on bee stings are said to take out the pain almost immediately.

# Sorrel

***Rumex acetosa (scutatus)***

Sorrel, commonly called garden sorrel, produces leaves with a sharp, lemony flavor. A high oxalic acid content, which may be troublesome for persons subject to gout, causes the sharpness. Although sorrel leaves are used in salads or cooked as greens, sorrel is best known for its use in French sorrel soup. This hardy plant can become a weed in the garden if it is not contained. Plants spread 2 feet and send up a 2-foot seed stalk if it is not cut off.

## When to Plant

Finding sorrel in garden centers may be difficult. If you prefer to work with transplants instead of seed, you may want to plan ahead and start your own. Sow seed in starter trays indoors under lights in March. Sow seed or set out started plants as soon as the soil can be worked in the spring. Sorrel can stand a light frost, so plants may be set out at least 2 weeks before the frost-free date (average date of last frost).

## Where to Plant

These plants are quite adaptable to conditions in the garden, but choose a planting site with well-drained soil in full sun (8 to 10 hours will suffice) for the best production. Give them soil with a high fertility level, and they will be even more productive. Since sorrel is a perennial and will stay in the same place from year to year, plant it where it will not be disturbed by other garden activities. A half-dozen plants are probably adequate for most gardeners.

## How to Plant

Prepare the soil (see "Soil Preparation" in the introduction to the vegetable garden). Set started plants, or sow seed directly in the garden, spaced 1 foot apart in rows or beds.

## Care and Maintenance

Few, if any, pests bother sorrel. Mites may be the exception and affect the plants in hot dry weather. To combat mites, spray with insecticidal soap, and remember to rinse the leaves before using them in the kitchen. Control weeds until the plants are well established.

### Additional Information

Remove flower stalks to keep plants producing. Harvest tender green leaves as needed, and use them fresh. Divide the plants every 3 years.

### VARIETIES

Many cooks prefer French sorrel, *Rumex montanus*, which has a milder flavor than garden sorrel. 'Profusion' is a sterile form producing no flower stalks, which is available only as started plants. I have not seen these plants in garden centers, but they are available in some catalogs.

# Sweet Marjoram

***Origanum majorana***

Sweet marjoram is usually grown as an annual for its sweet-scented leaves. It is of Mediterranean origin and popular in dishes of that region. Cooks use sweet marjoram in seasonings, dressings, and meats. The plants are 1 foot tall and spread about 6 inches.

## When to Plant

Set out started plants or sow seed directly in the garden in spring after danger of frost has passed.

## VARIETIES

Common marjoram (*O. vulgare*), a perennial also known as wild oregano, is naturalized and grows wild along roadsides, in abandoned farmsteads, and in disturbed woods, often along with chicory. It is often sold as marjoram or oregano. It has purple flowers and no discernible flavor. If the variety you are growing has purple flowers, kill it and replace it with something worth growing.

## Where to Plant

Choose a planting site for sweet marjoram that has exposure to full sun (8 to 10 hours will suffice) and well-drained infertile soils. Too-fertile soil causes rank, tasteless growth.

## How to Plant

Prepare the soil (see "Soil Preparation" in the introduction to the vegetable garden). Set started plants, or sow seed and thin seedlings to 6 or 8 inches apart. Sweet marjoram can be grown in pots or other containers using an artificial potting mix or a soil mix that you make yourself. (See "Soils for Container Gardens" in the introduction.)

## Care and Maintenance

Sweet marjoram takes little care in the garden. Control weeds until the plants are well established. Water sparingly, and trim the foliage to keep plants in shape.

### Additional Information

Harvest as soon as the first blossoms appear. Cut the tops (blooms and lengths of stem) back several inches, and continue to cut the tops to stimulate more production. Use the leaves fresh. Or dry the stems quickly over a screen, strip the leaves from the stems, and store the leaves in airtight containers. To have fresh sweet marjoram all winter, lift plants from the garden, pot them, and move them indoors. Set the plants back in the garden in the spring when weather has moderated (after the frost-free date). Shake off the excess soilless mix before planting again.

# Tarragon, French

*Artemisia dracunculus*

True French tarragon is a vegetatively propagated, 2-foot-tall perennial herb of outstanding character. There are only a few herbs that deserve to be grown in every garden, and this one is essential in every kitchen. It is the most important herb in French cuisine, used in Béarnaise, tartar, rémoulade, and hollandaise sauces; in salad dressings, mayonnaise, and soups; and in egg, pork, or chicken dishes. It also makes an outstanding vinegar. A half dozen plants are enough for most gardeners.

## When to Plant

Set out started plants or divide plants in your garden in early spring; they can stand a freeze. The plants spread by underground stems. Dig established plants, and separate the new offshoot plants.

## Where to Plant

Plant tarragon in full sun (8 to 10 hours will suffice) or light shade (filtered sun all day or shade part of the day) in fertile, well-drained soil. Set it to one side of the garden where it will not be disturbed by other gardening activities.

## How to Plant

True French tarragon is available from garden centers and mail-order suppliers only as plants. The herb does not come true from seed. Seed types are available but are of vastly inferior quality and not worth growing. Buy plants, or divide existing plants. Prepare the soil (see "Soil Preparation" in the introduction to the vegetable garden). Space plants or divisions 1 foot apart in each direction in beds or in rows.

## Care and Maintenance

Pinch newly started plants to encourage branching. Water to keep plants from wilting; 1 inch per week is sufficient. Use caution with fertilizing because it will produce rank, floppy plants. Repeated harvesting throughout the season will encourage the development of fresh, new leaves. Divide the plants every 3 or 4 years. Pests seldom bother tarragon, but indoors, mites may become troublesome. Spray the plants with insecticidal soap, and be sure to rinse the leaves thoroughly before using them in cooking.

### Additional Information

As soon as the plants are vigorously growing, begin to harvest leaves as needed. Tarragon loses most of its flavor when it is dried. To have fresh tarragon all winter, lift a few plants in the fall before they begin to go dormant. Clip them back to a convenient size, pot them, and move them indoors to a cool, bright place. Move them back to the garden in the spring. Tarragon is often seen growing in pots on balconies where it is easily available to the cook. Grow it in artificial soil mix, and be sure that the pot has adequate drainage because having wet feet causes more "winterkill" than the cold does.

# Thyme

***Thymus vulgaris***

This traditional perennial herb grows as a ground cover up to 12 inches high and spreading many times as wide if it is not contained. Thyme is a popular herb used in many kinds of dishes including salads, stocks, stews, stuffings, vinegars, pork, beef, fish, sausages, vegetables, breads, and honey.

## When to Plant

Spring is the time to plant thyme. Use plants that have been grown in containers, or divide existing plants. Or start plants from seed sown indoors under lights. Be aware that named varieties (that is, cultivars, or selections that have been made for quality) are generally superior to seed-grown plants.

## Where to Plant

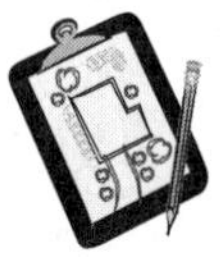

Plant it in full sun (8 to 10 hours will suffice) or partial shade (filtered sun all day or shade part of the day) in well-drained but not overly fertile soil. Thyme grows well in containers and makes an attractive plant for the porch or patio. A single plant of a variety is sufficient for fresh use; you may want to grow several varieties because each variety has a different taste. The plants make attractive edging, and more may be used more for that than for harvesting.

**VARIETIES**

English thyme has flat green leaves. French is known for its superior flavor. 'Orange Balsam' has a distinctive citrus fragrance. Lemon thyme (*Thymus × citriodorus*) is lemony, and there are several cultivars of lemon thyme.

## How to Plant

Prepare the soil (see "Soil Preparation" in the introduction to the vegetable garden). Set plants on 12-inch centers in rows or in beds. If several varieties are to be planted, separate them with barriers, such as timbers, bricks, or tiles, to prevent them from becoming an indistinguishable, tangled mess.

## Care and Maintenance

Trim thyme to keep it in bounds. Thyme may become contaminated by weeds, and after a few years the plants decline, becoming messy and woody. Most growers restart the thyme planting after 3 or 4 years. Take cuttings from old plants and just stick the cuttings in the ground; they root easily. Or divide old plants and replant them in another part of the garden. Excess moisture easily damages thyme, so water only if rain has not fallen for several weeks. Low fertility results in the best flavor. Vigorously growing plants have much less flavor and spread quickly, taking over the garden. Mites may become troublesome indoors. Spray the plants with insecticidal soap, and wash them thoroughly before use.

### Additional Information

Harvest thyme by clipping off 6- to 8-inch stems. Use them fresh, or tie the stems in loose bunches to dry quickly on a screen. Strip leaves from the stems, and store the leaves in airtight jars. To have a supply of thyme all winter, lift a few plants before they are frozen in. Trim them to shape and pot them up. Move them into a cool, bright place indoors where they are accessible to the cook. Return them to the garden in spring.

# Growing Fruits in the Home Garden

Fruit production was an important part of the garden in earlier times when estates, farms, and even urban backyards were larger. There was room for large trees, a berry patch, and a thicket of brambles. Although I grew up in the city, we had raspberries, 1 cherry tree, 3 apple trees, 2 peach trees, and 1 pear tree. We did not seem to have as much trouble growing things in those days as we do now either. The arrival of new pests, for example, gypsy moths, Japanese beetles, and apple maggots, has made it harder to grow clean fruit and necessitates more intense spraying.

After World War II, the sizes of lots for homes became smaller as land values climbed. The pace of life quickened, people had less time to spend taking care of demanding backyard orchards, and they regarded falling fruit a nuisance. The trees and berry patches fell into disrepair and were abandoned. But as the baby boomer generation has matured, gardening again is in favor, and many are looking for a challenge. New fruit varieties, new methods of growing smaller trees, and new cropping methods have renewed interest in this hobby.

Growing small fruit, and especially tree fruit, adds another dimension to backyard gardening. Because all fruit plants are perennials and stay in the garden from a few years to a person's lifetime, planning a fruit garden is more important than planning a vegetable garden, which can be moved every year if necessary. After a fruit planting is started, it may take from one season to as many as several years to see results. Fruit gardeners must have patience to wait for a fruit harvest, and while the plants are developing, they need a lot of care. Before starting a fruit garden, you must carefully consider your time available to do all the pruning, fertilizing, watering, and controlling pests required to develop productive plants and to have clean, wholesome fruit.

Fruit plantings can fit into most backyard gardens, but each plant must have enough room to develop to its full size. Much like vegetable plantings, small fruits such as strawberries can be grown in beds, matted or spaced rows, or hills. Strawberries can easily be squeezed into any available spot in the garden.

Strawberry Bed—Spaced Row

Strawberry Bed—Matted Row

Strawberry Bed—Hills

Blueberries and brambles will need more space, developing into bushes spreading 4 to 6 feet. Fruit trees recommended for backyard gardens are all dwarf types, and space requirements depend on the category. For example, standard apple trees will grow to 30 feet tall and wide, but semidwarfs will grow only to 15 feet tall and wide, full dwarf apple trees will spread 8 feet tall and wide, and extreme dwarfs are half that size. Dwarf trees will need to be staked, and must remain staked throughout their lives. Where space is severely limited, fruit plantings can be incorporated into the landscape. Properly maintained, they will produce fruit while adding to the beauty of the landscape.

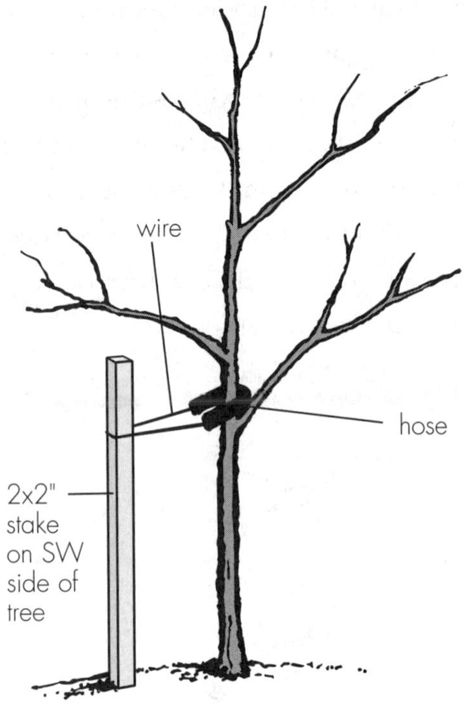

Staking a Fruit Tree

Choose a location for the fruit garden in full sun where it will not be disturbed by other activities in the yard. Also keep in mind that certain cultural necessities, such as spraying and pruning, may interfere with other things going on in the yard. For instance, fruit trees probably should not be planted where materials sprayed on them will cover other garden plants or will drift into the house.

## Planning the Fruit Garden

### Size

A home fruit garden needs to be large enough to produce the kinds of fruits you want, but not so large that it becomes a burden.

If it does, it will be neglected and soon become a liability instead of an asset. Produce needed for your family will determine the size of the garden; smaller rather than larger should be your gauge. Do not make it big unless you have an outlet to sell the excess, or you intend to do some preserving.

## Location

Draw a plan of your yard to scale on graph paper, and indicate the existing features. Evaluate the part of the yard where the fruit planting could be located: an area in full sun, where the soil drains well and where there is good air movement.

For large plantings, air drainage is important so that plants dry off quickly. This reduces disease problems and minimizes the chances of a late-season frost which could kill blossoms. Cold air sinks into the lowest areas, so it will be colder in a low valley than on a hilltop or hillside. Planting in a valley is not recommended for this reason. Low winter temperatures are not as damaging as a freeze when the plants are in full bloom.

Allow adequate space for the plants. As I noted, fully dwarf trees are recommended for backyard gardens. Leave enough room for trees so that they do not grow into each other, and so you can walk around them for tending and harvesting. Also make sure they will not grow into buildings or cover the driveway.

Planting the fruit garden in raised beds as described in "Growing Vegetables in the Home Garden" (see pages 58 to 59) maximizes the efficiency of the garden. You apply water and fertilizer only to the beds, weed control is easier, and brambles don't escape. Even extreme dwarf apples can be grown in raised beds.

## Varieties

For a continuous supply of fresh fruit, select varieties that ripen during different times throughout the summer. On the plan of your yard, indicate the kinds and varieties you want to plant. Keep in mind that some plants will need spraying when others are being harvested. Make sure that the ones being harvested are in separate parts of the planting, or it may be impossible to avoid getting spray on them too.

Some fruit types require 2 different varieties for pollination. Sometimes this can be accomplished by grafting 2 or more varieties on a single tree. 'Jonathan' apples will not set a full crop unless pollinated by another variety such as 'Red Delicious'. 'Seckel' and 'Moonglow' pears will pollinate each other and most other varieties.

Fruits can present special problems. Keep red and black raspberries separated to avoid disease problems. Because red raspberries and blackberries sucker and spread, plant them where you can mow down the emerging suckers. Also consider that blackberries need supports such as trellises or the hill system. Grapes also need a support system so set them at the side or end of the garden where they will not shade out other plantings.

A large part of a suburban backyard dedicated to growing fruit might support 2 dwarf apples, 2 pears, 2 peaches, 1 cherry, and some plums, as well as strawberries, grapes, brambles, and blueberries. For most families, 1 tree each of apple, pear, peach, and plum, a few feet of brambles, grapes on the

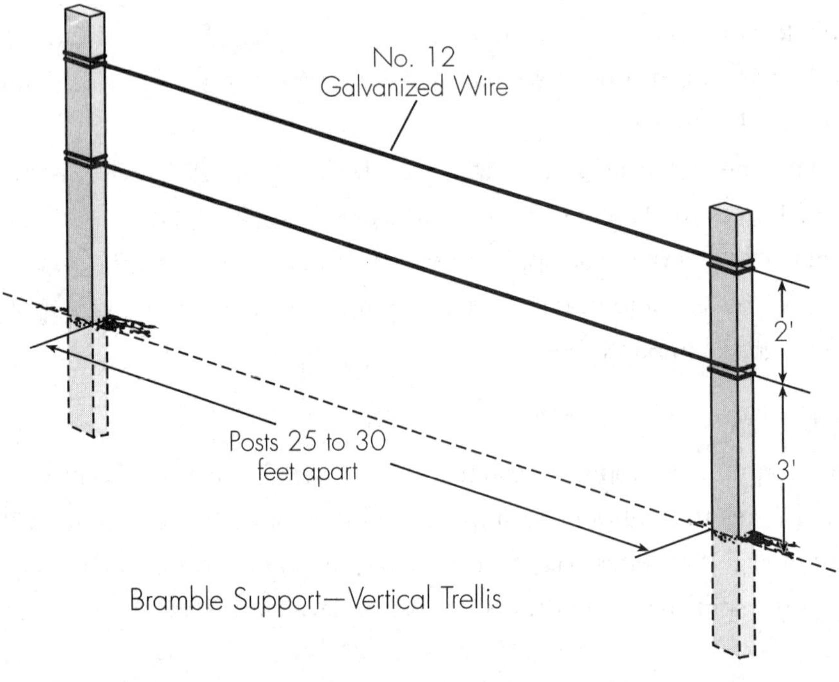


Bramble Support—Vertical Trellis

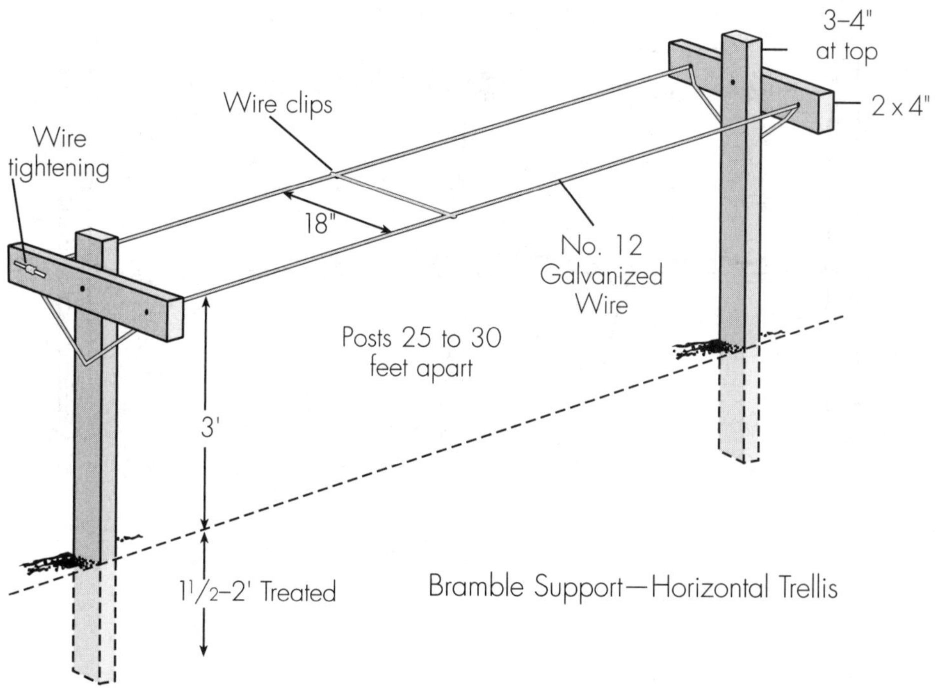

Bramble Support—Horizontal Trellis

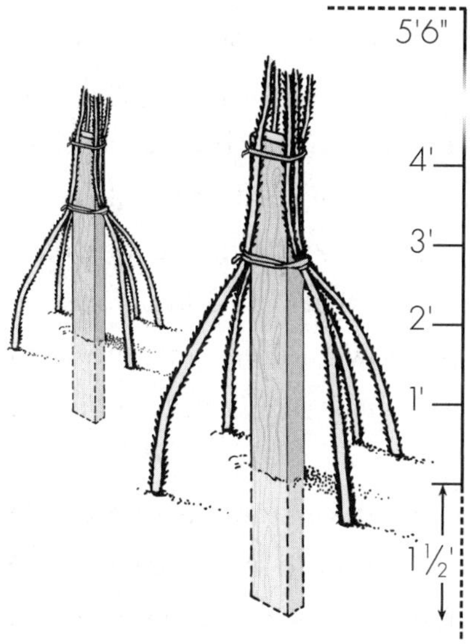

Bramble Support—Hill

back fence, and strawberries in the vegetable garden would suffice.

## Planting the Fruit Garden

Spring planting is the preferred time for most fruit plants, just as the soil has dried enough to be worked. Fruit plants are usually sold bare root, and you'll have to protect the roots from drying out by keeping them moist, refrigerating them, or healing them in. Soak mail-order plants in a bucket of water for several hours before planting to rehydrate them. Immediately set out plants from local nurseries. If there is to be a delay in planting, store the plants in plastic wrap in a cool place, but do not let them freeze. You can store

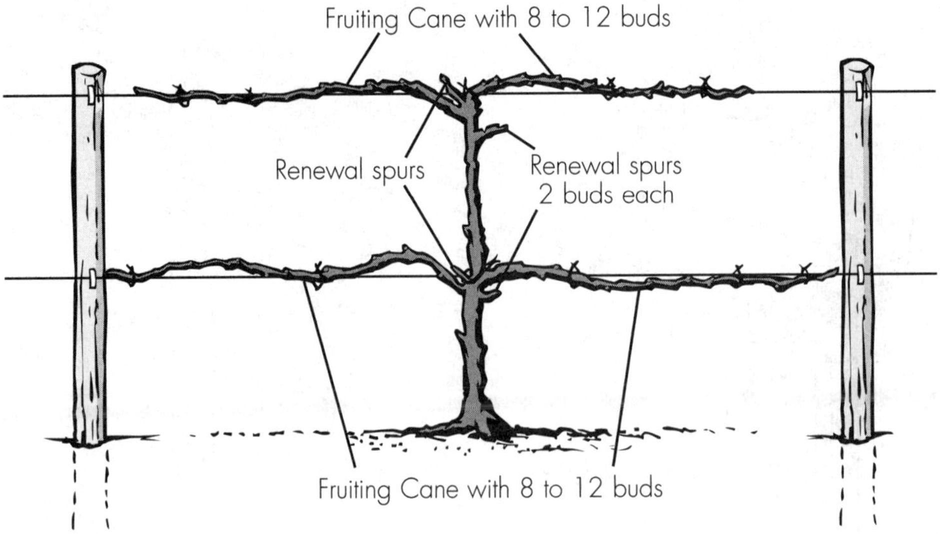


4-Cane Kniffen Training System-Grapes

the smaller fruit plants for up to a week in the refrigerator. Or heal in the plants by digging a shallow trench in a shaded place, opening the bundles of plants, separating them, and setting them so the roots are in the trench and the tops are at a 45-degree angle. Cover the roots with loose soil, and soak the area. Healed-in plants can be left for several days before planting.

Since fruit plants will occupy the same spot for several years, take your time preparing the soil. If possible, start a year ahead of the planting date by killing off all vegetation. Regularly till the soil that year, adding organic matter such as compost, or seed and plow down a green manure crop such as annual rye. Taking this extra trouble will significantly reduce a weed problem.

To plant, till the soil the same as you would for planting a vegetable garden (see "Soil Preparation" in the introduction to the vegetable garden). Space the plants according to their mature sizes, and apply remedial fertilizers as indicated by soil tests. Set the plants at the depth they grew in the nursery. Backfill with good topsoil, firming as you go. Soak thoroughly to settle the soil and force out any air pockets.

## Caring for the Fruit Garden

### Watering

For maximum production, fruit plants need adequate water, at least 1 inch of water per week. If rainfall is inadequate, apply a measured inch of water. To determine that amount from sprinklers, set out a coffee can to measure the output. When 1 inch of water collects in the can, turn off the water, or move the sprinkler. If you aren't using a sprinkler, dig down to make sure soil is wet at least 8 to 10 inches deep.

### Fertilizing

Soil tests taken before planting will identify deficiencies, and applying a corrective fertilizer prior to planting will remedy them. Routine fertilizer applications are necessary each season. Timing of these applications varies with the kind of fruit and is discussed in the specific entries.

### Pruning

Pruning and renewal of fruit plantings are essential for maximum production. Annually prune fruit trees to develop fruitful wood. Prune brambles to remove old canes, and prune grapes to develop vigorous new growth each year. Shear back strawberries to remove old foliage and open up the crowns to develop new foliage.

Here is the proper way to prune trees: cut small branches with hand shears, use lopping shears on larger branches, and cut limbs 1 inch or more in diameter with a tree saw. Make 3 cuts with the saw. Undercut about 1 branch diameter from the trunk until the saw begins to bind, then cut from the top another branch diameter farther out. The undercut will prevent splitting and tearing of the bark. Make a final cut to remove the remaining stub.

Central Leader Tree—Apple

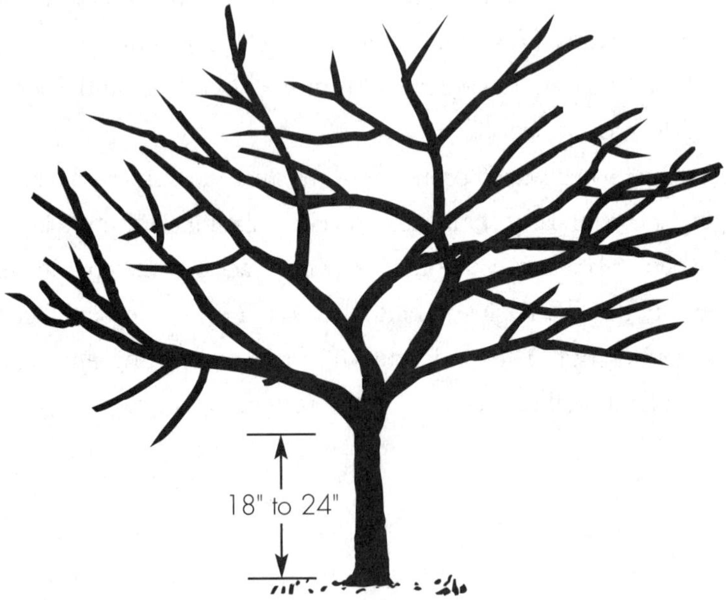


Open Center Tree—Peach

### Pest Control

Insects: The days when wholesome fruit could be produced without insect control measures have long passed away. Persistent treatment with the correct materials at the optimum times is essential.

Diseases: New fruit cultivars are being developed to eliminate certain disease problems. When you select varieties for planting in your garden, choose those with enhanced disease resistance. Growing the plants in a well-drained soil and keeping foliage dry are most helpful. Fungicide applications are necessary to control some diseases.

Be sure to read and follow directions on pesticide labels. Keep all pesticides in their original containers with l labels attached. Keep pesticides in locked storage, out of the reach of children. See the Suggested Controls of Major Fruit Pests chart on page 252.

## Weed Control

Starting the garden with the weeds under control reduces the problem, but controlling weeds is a constant chore. Keep a small garden weed free by regular hoeing. Using black plastic or organic mulches applied over weed-free soil will reduce the numbers of weeds and conserve moisture. Several herbicides are available to prevent emergence of weeds in fruit plantings. The various fruit types require different materials. Please note: *there are no herbicides that can be used on every kind of fruit.*

## Bird Control

Birds are probably the most difficult pests to control in fruit plantings, and most devices to frighten them are temporary remedies at best. As soon as the birds discover that the things won't hurt them, they are back. For home plantings, the most effective treatment is netting to cover the plantings (see a list of suppliers of netting in the back of the book). A few fruit trees or berry plantings do not take much netting

## Suggested Controls of Major Fruit Pests

| **Insects** | **Controls** |
| --- | --- |
| Aphids, mites, thrips—tiny, slow-moving insects that affect shoot tips or foliage of nearly all fruit plants. | *Apply insecticidal soap or multipurpose spray when noticed.* |
| Apple maggots, fruit worms, coddling moths, plum circulio—larvae mine their way through the fruit, destroying its value. | *Apply multipurpose spray following regular 10- to 14-day schedule beginning at petal fall.* |
| Crown borers—white grubs infest crowns of strawberry plants, which die at soil line. | *Apply multipurpose spray at 7- to 10-day intervals until 3 days before harvest begins.* |
| San Jose Scale insects—small immobile insects cause leaf drop and dead branches, and damage surface of tree fruits. | *Apply dormant oil before leaves emerge in spring, and apply multipurpose spray every 10 to 14 days after petal fall.* |
| **Diseases** | **Controls** |
| Mildew—white powder-like fungus covers surfaces of apple leaves. | *Apply sulfur when mildew appears.* |
| Rust—fungus causes orange spots on leaves, damages fruit. | *Apply multipurpose spray beginning as leaves emerge in spring and every 7 to 10 days until 2 weeks before harvest.* |
| Scab—fungus disease causes spots on tree fruit leaves and fruit, and severe leaf drop. | *Apply multipurpose spray beginning as leaves emerge in spring and every 7 to 10 days until 2 weeks before harvest.* |
| Verticillium wilt—causes branches or whole plants to wilt and die. | *Buy certified, disease-free stock. Plant in soil that has not grown solanaceous vegetables. Destroy infected plants.* |
| Virus diseases—cause undersized leaves and small, distorted fruit. | *Buy certified, disease-free plants. Destroy infected plants.* |

## Multipurpose Orchard Spray

| **Material** | **Amount per Gallon (Tablespoons)** |
| --- | --- |
| Sevin® | 2 |
| Malathion 25% WP | 2 |
| Captan 50% WP | 1½ |

Imidan® or Diazinon™ may be substituted for the combination of Malathion and methoxychlor. Imidan is labeled only for tree fruits and grapes. Do not use Diazinon on brambles. Azadirachtin (Neem®, etc.), insecticidal soap, or *Bacillus thuringiensis* Kurstaki (*B.t.*) may be substituted for the insecticides listed above. *B.t.* is effective against foliage-eating caterpillars.

and the expense is not too exorbitant, especially considering the time and effort expended in getting the fruit up to harvest time. Losing it when you can almost taste it is extremely discouraging.

## Fruit Explorers

Anyone involved in growing fruit in the home garden should be a member of the North American Fruit Explorers. These are backyard gardeners with tremendous knowledge of what to grow and how to grow it. The Midwest Fruit Explorers have a Web site (www.midfex.org) that posts informative articles, and they entertain questions from other gardeners.

Now let's get into the fruit garden!

# APPLE

***Malus* cv.**

Today, with the availability of dwarf trees, nearly any backyard can accommodate some fruit trees. Standard-sized apple trees reach 30 feet or more tall and wide. Semidwarfs reach 15 to 20 feet, and dwarfs grow to 7 to 10 feet. The severe-dwarf trees or minidwarfs can be kept to about 5 feet. Growing apples isn't difficult, but combating pests that want to destroy the apples can be a challenge. Be prepared to spray to save the fruit, although the amount can be moderated by selecting pest-resistant varieties, by following good cultural practices, and by keeping the orchard clean.

## When to Plant

Plant apple trees in the early spring as soon as the soil can be worked.

## Where to Plant

Select a full sun spot (8 to 10 hours will suffice) with well-drained soil because an apple tree will not tolerate wet feet. Leave sufficient room, depending on the type you are planting, so that you will be able to walk around the mature tree to spray it.

## How to Plant

Spacing is determined by the kind of trees you plant. Space standard trees at 35 feet, semidwarfs at 20 feet, and fully dwarf trees at 7 to 10 feet. Plant the minidwarfs in beds, spaced about 6 feet in each direction. Fully dwarf or minidwarf trees are recommended for backyard orchards. It is a good idea to decide on the kind you want to plant before you go to a nursery to make your purchase; do some calculations so that you buy the appropriate number of plants for the "apple" area in your yard. (See the varieties listed; some need a pollinator, so at least 2 are necessary.)

Apples are generally available as bare-root, 2-year-old whips. As soon as you get the trees home, plunge the roots in a bucket of water for a couple of hours to rewet them and keep them from drying out. If planting is to be delayed, heal-in the trees until you can plant them. To plant a tree, dig a hole twice as wide as the spread of the roots and deep enough that the plant will be at the same depth it grew in the nursery. Trim off excessively long and damaged roots (roots should not be long enough to wrap around the hole), and spread the roots out in the bottom of the hole. Supporting the tree, begin to backfill with soil, and firm it with a blunt stick, such as a 2-by-4. When the hole is half filled, fill it with water. After the water has drained out, replace the remaining soil, and fill with water again. Dwarf trees need staking and must remain staked throughout their lives. Set a 4-foot-tall post on the southwest side of the tree, 1 foot from the trunk, and fasten the tree with a wire run through a piece of garden hose to protect the trunk. (See illustration on page 220.)

## Care and Maintenance

Annual pruning is necessary to train the trees, and the ideal time is mid- to late winter. (See page 226.) Train dwarf apples to a 5- to 8-foot central trunk, with 6 to 12 horizontal branches (called scaffold branches) in whorls around the trunk. Begin the process by cutting off unbranched trees at 30 inches tall.

Branched trees are bigger and older, and they may allow selection of scaffold branches at an earlier age. For the first scaffolds, select 3 or 4 branches that are evenly spaced around the trunk and arise 18 to 24 inches from the ground. Cut these branches back to 10 inches long. Cut the leader (central vertical shoot) 15 inches above the top scaffold branch. If there are no suitable branches for scaffolds, remove all the branches, and cut the leader at 30 inches above the ground.

After the first year, select 3 or 4 scaffolds, cut them back to 10 inches, and remove all other branches. Clip the leader 15 inches above the top scaffold. In the subsequent 3 or 4 years, select 3 or 4 more scaffolds each year, cut them to 10 inches long, and clip the leader 18 inches above the top scaffold. By the end of the fourth year, the framework of the tree should be completed and the tree should be producing fruit.

Each winter thereafter, prune to remove dead or damaged branches, water sprouts (vigorous vertical sprouts growing from the base of the tree or from scaffold branches), vertical suckers, and branches touching the ground. Also remove branches growing into the center of the tree and those rubbing on others. Clip out weak, nonproductive branches. Do not treat cut branches with a sealant.

Some varieties try to make ascending scaffold branches with narrow crotches. Tie them down or brace them so they are about 90 degrees from the trunk. Several kinds of ties or spreaders can be made to do this: for example, tiedowns can be made of wires run through pieces of hose to protect the branches and staked to the ground. Spreaders can be made from narrow boards braced between trunk and branches to force them out. Set sharpened nails in the ends of the boards to keep them from slipping out.

Apple trees require water in dry weather, especially when they are growing in light soils that dry out quickly. Apply 1 inch per week if nature does not cooperate. Control weeds beneath the trees by hoeing or using herbicides. Apply 2 or 3 inches of mulch.

Young dwarf apple trees should grow 1½ to 2 feet each year. If they do not seem to be growing, fertilize with 10-10-10, at a rate of 1½ pounds per 100 square feet of ground beneath the tree. If they are growing too vigorously, do not fertilize because excessively vigorous trees do not set fruit.

Protect nonbearing apple trees from diseases with appropriate fungicides that are labeled for the particular disease on apples. Disease-resistant varieties require less spraying. Regularly apply pesticides to bearing trees to produce blemish-free fruit. Your local extension office can provide you with a spray schedule, which is essential to follow rigorously to prevent attack by insects and diseases. Do not stop spraying in midsummer because some of the worst pests arrive about that time. Make the last application 14 days before harvest. (See the pest control and spraying charts in the introduction to growing fruit.)

## Additional Information

Many apple varieties tend to produce large crops 1 year and none the next, and thinning the crop reduces this tendency of alternate bearing. When the developing apples are nickel sized, thin them to average 1 apple every 6 inches. For example, leave 2 apples on a branch 14 inches long even if they are close together; if there are 3 apples on that branch, remove 1. The resulting apples will be larger, and the tree will have the energy to produce a crop the following season. When the apples have developed their characteristic coloring, taste a few; the taste test is the only reliable test for ripeness. If they are ripe, harvest them. Guides are available from your local extension service and the North American Fruit Explorers to tell you the approximate date that certain varieties are ripe, but the dates vary from year to year. Animals may severely damage apple trees. Install wire or plastic guards to prevent rabbit damage, and pull back mulch so that voles can't hide next to the trunk. Sometimes various repellents stop aggressive deer. Many repellents are sold in garden centers or in catalogs; try some until you find one that works in your location because deer tastes vary.

## VARIETIES

In the spring, nearly every garden center stocks some apple trees chosen from the thousands of apple varieties. Before you buy any of them, make sure that the variety is tagged correctly, and that you know what rootstock the tree is grafted on. All apples are grafted—not all are dwarfs. Apple trees are produced by inserting buds or twigs called scions of named varieties into already growing rootstock plants. Various rootstocks impart different characteristics to the scions growing on them. Minidwarfs will be on M27 or P22 roots; dwarfs on M9. Semidwarfs will be on M7 or M26 interstems; slightly dwarfed trees on MM106 or MM111. Spur-type trees on M7 or MM111 will be true dwarfs. If you are serious about growing apples, you may want to contact a propagator who will provide the kinds of plants you need.

Many apple varieties require another variety for good pollination. This is called cross-pollination. For instance, most of the varieties listed here will pollinate each other, but 'Winesap' has sterile pollen, and it cannot pollinate anything. If you are short of space, more than one variety can be grafted onto the same tree. (To learn how to graft trees, contact members of the North American Fruit Explorers.) When you buy plants, check to see which varieties are needed for cross-pollination. Bees are necessary for pollination, so be sure not to spray insecticides when the flowers are open and bees are working.

An excellent resource for descriptions of apple varieties is the Applesource catalog (see the suppliers listings in the back of the book). Request a sampler of varieties you may be interested in growing, and taste them before you invest 5 years in growing them only to find out they aren't exactly what you had in mind.

Nearly all growers determine the ripening time for apples based on when 'Jonathan' apples ripen. 'Jonathans' ripen from early September in the southern parts of the Midwest, to the last week of September in the northern parts. Actual dates of ripening can vary a week or so earlier or later depending on the season. The following are listed in the order of ripening, from early to late:

| Varieties | Days to Maturity | Comments |
|---|---|---|
| Lodi | 6 weeks before Jonathan | Tart, greenish flesh. |
| Redfree | 4 weeks before Jonathan | Similar to Jonathan, but not as good for pies, early. |
| Prima | 3 weeks before Jonathan | Jonathan-like, with excellent disease resistance. |
| Gala | 1½ weeks before Jonathan | Good keeper, excellent quality. |
| McIntosh | 1 week before Jonathan | Old-time favorite. |
| Jonathan | | Another reliable oldie. |
| Red Delicious | 2 weeks after Jonathan | Many selections; the cardboard flavor often associated with this apple is due to long storage. |
| Cortland | 2 weeks after Jonathan | The best for pies and for fresh eating too. |
| Empire | 2 weeks after Jonathan | Keeps well; crisp, "cracks" when you bite into it. |
| Golden Delicious | 3 weeks after Jonathan | One of the best, versatile, sweet. |
| Jonagold | 3 weeks after Jonathan | Good quality, versatile. |
| Mutsu (Crispin) | 4 weeks after Jonathan | Large top-quality dessert apple. |
| Stayman Winesap | 5 weeks after Jonathan | Tart, makes good pies. |
| Fuji | 6 weeks after Jonathan | Delicious. |

# Blackberry

***Rubus* cv.**

Blackberries are very similar to raspberries. They are brambles that grow on biennial canes emanating from perennial roots. The canes grow the first year, fruit the second year, and die. Blackberries come in 3 types: upright, semiupright, and trailing (usually called dewberries). The upright varieties grow like red raspberries whereas the dewberries make long vines that need to be supported to keep the berries off the ground and to simplify harvesting. The main difference between blackberries and raspberries is that raspberries separate from the receptacle and come off as a fragile cup. Another difference is that blackberries are not as hardy as raspberries, and thornless varieties are less hardy than the thorny varieties. Blackberries are seldom grown for the market, so growing them in the home garden is just about the only way to enjoy them. A few pick-your-own operations do grow them, however.

## When to Plant

Plant blackberries in the spring as soon as the ground is dry enough to work without destroying the structure. (See the discussion of soils in the introduction.)

## Where to Plant

Choose a site for blackberries that has well-drained soil and receives full sun (8 to 10 hours will suffice). Leave enough room so that you can mow around the beds to control the suckers. Blackberries are susceptible to verticillium wilt, a fungus disease that infects the soil and kills susceptible plants growing in it. Do not plant blackberries where solanaceous crops (potatoes, tomatoes, peppers, etc.) have been grown in the last 5 years.

## How to Plant

Blackberries are sold as 1-year-old, Grade No. 1 plants or tissue-cultured plugs. (Plugs are plants grown in plugs of soil, small pots, or plug trays.) Buy only certified virus-free plants or tissue-cultured, disease-free plants from reliable nurseries. Prepare the soil as you would for a vegetable garden. (See "Soil Preparation" in the introduction to the vegetable garden.) Be sure to kill off perennial weeds such as quackgrass or bindweed using Roundup herbicide. Roundup is deactivated as soon as it hits the ground or is absorbed by the weeds, so there is no danger to plants later on.

Cut off broken roots, and soak bare-root plants in a bucket of water to rehydrate them and to keep them from drying out while you are planting. Plant blackberries in rows or in hills. Blackberries sucker extensively and will develop into a hedgerow on their own. Grow trailing blackberries and semiupright types on stakes in hills. (See page 247.) Space the plants 2 feet apart in rows 8 to 10 feet apart, or space the plants in hills 4 or 5 feet apart.

Dig the planting hole at least the diameter of the root spread. Spread out the root system of the bare root, or slice roots circling the ball of the container-grown plant before placing it in the planting hole. Set a bare-root or container-grown plant at the same depth it grew in the nursery. Then carefully cover and firm with soil. Fill the hole with water to firm the soil and force out any air pockets. Set plugs just deep enough that the roots can be covered with soil.

## Care and Maintenance

After planting, cut back handles (canes) of conventional blackberries (not tissue-cultured types) to about 1 foot tall. Burn these prunings or dispose of them in the trash to prevent diseases. If you are using tissue-cultured plants, you don't need to prune them because they do not carry diseases. Mulch well to conserve moisture and reduce weed competition.

Although blackberries will grow and fruit without support, they are much more attractive and easier to care for when they are trained up in some manner on a support. You could try the hill system, or you could construct trellises. For the hill system, drive a sturdy stake, such as a 6-foot-long wooden 2-by-2 or a steel fence post, into the ground. Tie 6 to 8 canes to the stake in the spring after you have completed pruning; you can use twine, long twist ties, or strips of cloth. You have to tie the plants regularly to keep them in order because they keep getting longer. For horizontal trellises, suitable for upright blackberries, place 1 sturdy treated wooden or steel post every 25 feet; the post should be 5 feet above the ground. Add cross pieces at the top of each post to support 2 wires spaced 2 feet apart. Then train the plants into the trellis so that they maintain a solid hedgerow about 2 feet wide. No tying is needed with this system, although ties can be used to prevent the trellis wires from spreading from the weight of the plants between the posts. For vertical trellises, suitable for semiupright and trailing blackberries, set posts, and string 2 rows of wires, the first row at 2 feet and the second row at 5 feet above the ground. Tie the canes of the plants to the wires after spring pruning. (See pages 222 to 223.)

Use these guidelines for pruning and training blackberries:

### Care for Trailing and Semiupright Blackberries

In early spring, remove all weak canes, and thin the remaining canes. Leave the best 4 to 8 canes on semiupright varieties. Leave the best 8 to 16 canes on trailing varieties. Save only the largest canes. On stakes, wrap the canes around each stake, and tie them in several places; then cut back canes even with the tops of the stakes. On vertical trellises, tie the canes to the wires. As soon as fruiting is completed, remove all canes that bore fruit. Be careful not to injure developing shoots that will bear the next year. Dispose of all trimmings to reduce chances of diseases.

### Care for Upright Blackberries

In early spring, remove all weak canes, and leave 4 or 5 of the most vigorous canes ($1/2$ inch or more in diameter) per plant. Thin out and cut back laterals (canes that grow horizontally from vertical canes); leave them about 15 inches long with 15 buds each. In summer, pinch back all new canes as they attain the desired height. Pinch unsupported erect blackberries at 36 inches. Leave plants 6 inches taller if they are supported by trellises or stakes. As soon as fruiting is completed, remove all canes that bore fruit. Be careful not to injure developing shoots that will bear the next year. Dispose of all trimmings to reduce chances of diseases.

Blackberries sucker profusely. Each spring, rototill the perimeter of the planting to eliminate all suckers that have grown outside the row. Hoe out suckers that develop during the season. Healthy blackberry plantings should produce for 10 or more years if they are properly maintained. Usually, plantings deteriorate prematurely because of virus diseases. If any plants begin to develop misshapen leaves, get rid of them immediately. If the planting begins to produce small berries, consider replacing it. There is no cure for virus diseases. Viruses are carried by sucking insects that feed on the plants infecting them, or they may be brought in with plants from a noncertified source. That is why I recommend getting only certified, disease-free plants. A delayed dormant application of an all-purpose orchard spray or liquid lime sulfur will prevent damage from mites, scale insects, anthracnose, and spur blight. Apply cover sprays of Sevin or Malathion insecticide, plus ferbam, as new growth reaches 6 inches tall, just before bloom, and again just after bloom. (See pest control and spraying charts in the introduction to fruit gardening.) Weed control, especially grass control, is important. Apply mulches to clean plantings, then hoe or pull weeds as they appear. Use Casoron® granules to eliminate weeds in berry plantings and prevent germination of weed seeds. Apply the granules only to well-established plantings.

## VARIETIES

Blackberries have varying hardiness. Some varieties tolerate severe cold if they are protected; others are only semi-winter hardy. Thornless varieties are recommended only for plantings in hardiness zone 6b or higher. Check with your county cooperative extension service for recommended blackberry varieties for your area. All blackberries mature in late summer, about the same time, which is 60 to 70 days following bloom.

| Varieties | Comments |
|---|---|
| Chester Thornless | Semierect, needs support; harvest can extend 6 weeks. |
| Darrow | Thorny, erect. |
| Illini Hardy | Thorny, long harvest season, dependable. |
| Shawnee | Erect, good flavor. |

### Additional Information

Harvest the berries as they ripen. Color is the primary indicator of ripeness: reds are red, and blacks are black. They deteriorate rapidly, so don't leave them on the plants. Birds, squirrels, and insects will harvest them if you do not.

## Blackberry Preserves

*Combine 1 pound blackberries, 1 pound sugar, and 2 tablespoons lemon juice in a medium bowl; cover and let stand for 1 hour.*

*Place ingredients in a pot over medium heat and cook until the mixture bubbles and thickens. Strain through a large strainer to remove the seeds. Follow manufacturer's directions for canning, or place in jars and store in the refrigerator.*

# Blueberry

## *Vaccinium corymbosum*

Blueberries are very specific in their soil and cultural requirements. They must be grown in an acidic soil, with a pH of 4.5 to 5.6. This may mean modifying the soil if it is alkaline, and in some parts of the Midwest, the soils are too alkaline to successfully grow blueberries without heroic means.

### When to Plant

Buy blueberries from plant nurseries for spring planting. Plant them as soon as the soil is dry enough to work without damaging the structure. (See the discussion of soils in the introduction.)

### Where to Plant

Before planting blueberries, have your soil tested. Many soils are alkaline, and trying to adjust them to a pH of 5 is nearly impossible. If the soil pH is 6.2 or higher, modify it by digging out the planting hole 2 feet deep and wide. Mix the soil, adding an equal amount of acidic peat moss, then use this mixture to backfill the planting hole. If your soils are decidedly alkaline, you can still grow your own blueberries by planting them in half barrels or half 55 gallon drums. Make sure that the containers have holes in the bottoms for drainage, and that they are placed in a well-drained area. Burn any residue out of the drums to avoid damaging the roots of the plants. Bury the barrels or drums, and fill them with a 50 percent soil, 50 percent acid peat soil mix. (Have the pH of the soil mix tested before planting.) Because the pH of these soil mixes will tend to rise, apply sulfur each spring to counter this tendency. Plant blueberries in full sun (8 to 10 hours will suffice) in well-drained soil. For large plantings, setting plants on a slope will improve air drainage, and a north-facing slope will often delay flowering, avoiding injury to flowers from late-season frost.

### How to Plant

Blueberries are available as bare-root, containerized, or balled-and-burlapped plants. All 3 types are satisfactory planting choices. The latter 2 are more expensive, but can be used where only a few plants are being installed. Vigorous 2-year-old plants are recommended. Dig the holes for planting shallower than the depth of the roots and at least twice as wide. Space the plants 4 to 6 feet apart in rows 8 feet apart. Trim broken roots from bare-root plants. Knock containerized plants out of their containers, and if the soil on the roots is much different from that in the holes, shake some off, being careful not to injure the roots. Mix some soil from the containers with that going back into the holes to avoid an interface problem. (For more detail, see the discussion of soils in the introduction.) Remove the burlap from balled-and-burlapped plants, and stuff it in the planting holes. Set the plants in the holes, keeping them higher than they grew in the nursery. Deep planting or poor drainage may cause root or crown rot and plant loss. Replace half the soil, and fill the holes with water. When the water has drained out, fill the holes the rest of the way with the remaining soil. Soak thoroughly to settle the soil with water to which you have added a transplant starter fertilizer, such as 10-52-17 or 10-30-10, mixed according to the directions on the label. Mulch the plants with 2 to 3 inches of shredded bark or compost.

## Care and Maintenance

After planting, remove all flower buds and all weak or broken wood from the plants. In the second year, remove only dead or damaged branches. In subsequent years, remove a few of the oldest canes to develop a plant with 7 or 8 young, vigorous canes. If plants are too vigorous, making long canes, pinch the tips out when the canes are 4 to 5 feet tall to force laterals that will bear fruit the following spring.

Watering, mulching, and fertilizing are important parts of blueberry care. Watering will be needed about once a week in dry weather. Blueberries are shallowly rooted with fine, fibrous roots, and drought easily damages them. The beds of modified soil and the soils in containers will not rewet from still-moist soil beneath the planting; the water will not move upward into the lighter soil above. Apply 1 inch of water each time, or irrigate with soakers to avoid wetting the foliage and fruit because wetting developing fruit can cause it to crack. Reapply 2 to 3 inches of mulch in the spring and again in the fall. Fertilize 4 weeks after planting with 10-10-10 or a similar fertilizer, 1 handful spread evenly under each plant. The next year, apply double the amount per plant in the spring just before buds begin to swell. Increase the amount to 3 handfuls the next year. Then apply about 1 pound per plant each year thereafter, about half in early spring and half 6 weeks later. Test the soil for pH every 2 years, and apply sulfur if it is needed to keep the soil acidic. Yellowing of young leaves, chlorosis, is an indication that the soil pH is too high.

## VARIETIES

Blueberries are self-fruitful, not needing a separate variety for pollination. Planting a couple of varieties improves pollination and increases yields, however. Where late frost may kill flowers, later varieties may be more reliable. Many other varieties are available in addition to the ones listed here. Check with local suppliers and with your county extension service office for additional recommendations for your area.

| Varieties | Comments |
|---|---|
| Bluecrop | A standard cultivar, widely planted, midseason. |
| Bluetta | Adaptable, early. |
| Collins | Dependable, early. |
| Herbert | Tops in flavor, dark blue, late. |
| Patriot | Early to midseason, new. |

Competition from weeds can severely stunt blueberries. Hoe out any weeds, and apply 4 to 6 inches of mulch. The mulch will discourage weeds and conserve moisture. Research has shown the importance of mulching blueberries in developing and maintaining vigorous, productive plants.

Blueberries are susceptible to a few diseases and some insects. Apply dormant oil in early spring for scale insects; apply all-purpose fruit spray at budbreak (as buds begin to open in the spring); apply Captan every 7 to 10 days to control stem blight, anthracnose, and mummy berry; and apply Malathion or Sevin insecticide to control mites or fruit worms as needed. (See the pest control and spraying charts on page 228.)

Birds are the most troublesome pests in blueberry plantings. Noise devices and scare objects such as "hawk eye" balloons are often recommended, but the only sure way to prevent loss of the crop is to cover the plants with netting. (See the list of suppliers in the back of the book.) If voles are gnawing on the stems, pull the mulch back from the bases of the plants in early fall. Doing this will prevent the voles from taking up residence next to the stems of the plants and will reduce the chances of feeding injury. Use chicken wire fencing around the planting to prevent rabbit damage.

### Additional Information

Harvest blueberries when they are fully blue colored and are sweet to the taste. Some varieties do not attain full flavor for several days after attaining full color. The taste test is best until you become familiar with the variety being grown. Blueberries mature 60 to 75 days after bloom, about the end of June in the southernmost parts of the Midwest, and in late July to the far north. Since all berries will not ripen at the same time, several pickings may be necessary at 5-day intervals.

# Cherry

***Prunus avium*** **(Sweet Cherry)**
***Prunus cerasus*** **(Pie Cherry)**

Cherries are probably the easiest tree fruits to grow. Pie cherries grow throughout the Midwest; they are hardy into zone 3. Sweet cherries can be grown in the southern portions of the Midwest, and on the lee side of the Great Lakes where the winters are moderate; they are cold-hardiness zone 6 or 7 plants.

## When to Plant

Plant cherry trees in early spring as soon as the soil is dry enough to work.

## Where to Plant

Dwarf cherry trees will achieve a spread of 10 to 15 feet. Plant them in an area that receives full sun (8 to 10 hours will suffice) and has well-drained soil.

## How to Plant

Natural dwarf trees and spur types are recommended for backyard orchards. Natural dwarfs are not grafted; they grow that way. Dwarf trees of apples, for instance, are grafted on dwarfing rootstock. Doing this is not necessary with the natural dwarf cherries and solves some problems such as graft incompatibility or excessive sprouting from the rootstock (suckers) that must be pruned off continuously. Spur types produce an abundance of shortened, compact fruiting stems (spurs) along the scaffold branches. Cherry trees are generally available as bare-root, 2-year-old whips. As soon as you receive the trees, plunge the roots in a bucket of water for a couple of hours to rewet the roots, which are often dried out in shipping. If planting is to be delayed, heal-in the trees until you can plant them. To plant, dig a hole twice as wide as the spread of the roots and deep enough that the plant will be at the same depth it grew in the nursery. Trim off excessively long and damaged roots, then spread the roots out in the bottom of the hole. Supporting the tree, backfill the hole with soil, firming it with a blunt stick, such as a 2-by-4. When the hole is half filled with the soil, fill it with water. After the water has drained out, replace the remaining soil, and fill with water again.

## Care and Maintenance

The central leader training system is preferred for natural dwarf types of cherry trees. This is the same system described elsewhere for apples, but cherries do not require the intensive pruning needed by apples. Annual pruning is necessary to train the trees, however. The goal is to train dwarf cherries to a 5- to 8-foot central trunk, with 6 to 12 horizontal branches (scaffold branches) in whorls around the trunk. Begin the process at planting by cutting off unbranched trees at 30 inches tall. On branched trees, you may be able to select branches for the first scaffolds.(Branched trees are bigger than unbranched trees, but the branches may not be where you want them for scaffolds.) Select 3 or 4 branches that are evenly spaced around the trunk and arise 18 to 24 inches from the ground. Cut these branches back to 10 inches long, and cut the leader 15 inches above the top scaffold branch. If there are no suitable branches for scaffolds, remove all the branches, and cut the leader at 30 inches above the ground. (See page 226.)

After the first year, select 3 or 4 scaffolds on pie cherries, cut them back to 10 inches, and remove all other branches; then clip the leader 15 inches above the top scaffold. Do not cut back the leader or scaffold branches of sweet cherries during this first year. Let them grow. Sweet cherries do not need as much pruning as pie cherries, and if they are pruned excessively, they will be more susceptible to winter damage. In the subsequent 3 or 4 years, select 3 or 4 more scaffolds each year, cut them to 10 inches, and clip the leader 18 inches above the top scaffold. By the end of the fourth year, the framework of the tree should be completed with 10 to 12 good scaffold branches selected, and the tree should be producing fruit. Each winter thereafter, prune to remove dead or damaged branches, water sprouts, vertical suckers, and branches touching the ground. Also remove branches growing into the center of the tree and those rubbing on other branches. Clip out weak, nonproductive branches.

Watering, weeding, and fertilizing are parts of caring for cherry trees. Cherry trees need water in dry weather, especially if they are growing in light soils. Apply 1 inch per week if nature does not cooperate. Control weeds beneath the trees by hoeing or by using herbicides, and apply 2 or

3 inches of mulch. Young dwarf cherry trees should grow 1½ to 2 feet each year. If they are not growing, fertilize with 10-10-10, at a rate of 1½ pounds per 100 square feet, beneath the trees.

**VARIETIES**

Pie cherries include 'Meteor' and 'NorthStar' (both are natural dwarfs); 'Montmorency' is a spur type of pie cherry. If your yard is in a protected location and you prefer sweet cherries, try 'Yellow Glass', 'Windsor', 'Black Tartarian', or 'Stella'. Sweet cherries are reliable in zone 6b or milder. In more severe climates, chances are that winter temperatures will kill the flower buds most years.

Cherry trees are not bothered by as many pests as those affecting apple and peach trees. But if pests do become a problem, spray as the husks begin to pull away from the base of the fruit. Use a multipurpose fruit spray, or use Captan and Malathion. Repeat in 7 to 10 days, and spray again after you harvest the fruit. (See the pest control and spraying chart in the introduction to fruit gardening.) Cherries are very attractive to birds, which will harvest your crop if you do not get to it first. If birds are enjoying more of your fruit than you are, consider covering the trees with netting available from garden suppliers for this purpose. (See some suppliers noted at the end of this book.)

### Additional Information

Cherries mature in July, about 2 months after they flower. Harvest when the fruit develops its full color.

## Tasty Cherry Salad

*Mix 1 beaten egg white, 1 tablespoon flour, 1 cup sugar and ½ teaspoon salt in a medium saucepan. Add 1 cup skim milk and cook until thickened, about 10 to 15 minutes on low heat. In a large bowl, combine 1 quart pitted cherries, 1 cup miniature marshmallows, and 1 cup walnuts. Pour liquid mixture over cherry mixture. Refrigerate. Chopped bananas and pineapple may be added if desired.*

# GRAPE

***Vitis* cv.**

American bunch grapes are popular fruits for the home garden. They can be grown in the garden as ornamentals, or just for the fruit. Unfortunately, most are grown on arbors suited for decoration, but not for the grapes. Usually the plants become terribly overgrown, fail to produce fruit, and eventually are considered strictly ornamentals. In nearly every case, severe pruning would have saved the plantings or could resurrect them, but too many gardeners are afraid to prune. To thrive, grapes need severe pruning, removing as much as 90 percent of the growth each spring. The reason is that grapevines fruit on 1-year-old canes. Removing the old canes stimulates the growth of new canes, which will then bear fruit.

## When to Plant

Plant grapes in the spring as soon as the soil is dry enough to work. The plants need time to become established before the stresses of summer afflict them.

## Where to Plant

Because grapes like hot weather, they are some of the latest plants to leaf out in spring. In cooler climates, plant them where they will warm up quickly, such as the south side of a building. Well-drained soil is essential, but grapes do not do well in extremely fertile soils. The plants grown in fertile soils produce lots of leaves and often low-quality grapes. Poor soils tend to produce moderate crops of grapes with excellent flavor. Hillsides are particularly good sites for grapes, promoting air drainage (cooler air drains down the hill). Air drainage reduces the chance of late-season frosts and dries foliage more rapidly, lessening problems with diseases.

## How to Plant

Prepare the soil the year before planting by killing the weeds and tilling the soil. Grapes do not compete well with weeds, so starting clean is a good idea.

Before planting, decide on the kind of support system you want. There are at least 3 in common usage, but the 4-Cane Kniffin (see page 224) is probably the easiest for a home garden. Plants trained to a 4-Cane Kniffen system consist of a permanent trunk and 4, 1-year-old fruiting canes supported by wires. (This system is described below.) Other systems include Umbrella Kniffin and Geneva Double Curtain, but these are more complicated. Because grape plantings last 50 years or more, make sure the structure is sturdy, and use treated wood to prevent rotting. Build the support using 1 heavy post every 25 feet or less. Grapevines are big, but if you don't have a lot of room, closer spacing is acceptable. The posts should be 8 feet long, set 2½ to 3 feet into the ground, and the end posts need bracing to prevent them from being pulled over by the weight of the vines. Run 2 wires about 3 feet apart on the posts; align the bottom wire 3 feet above the ground, and the top wire even with the tops of the posts.

Space the plants about 10 feet apart along the support. A typical garden may have room for only 1 row. Set the plants at the same depth they grew in the nursery. If you are using grafted plants for phylloxera resistance, make sure the graft is above ground. Do not fertilize the plants after planting unless they are low in vigor (that is, they have very little growth). Grapes should have a huge amount of growth each year, but overly vigorous plants may suffer winter damage.

## Care and Maintenance

Immediately after planting, prune the plants to a single stem with 2 buds. These buds should grow into 2 shoots. Tie the more vigorous shoot to the lower wire or to the top wire if it is long enough. Pinch back the tip of the other shoot. By the end of the first year, the longer shoot should be long enough to reach the top wire. The second spring, after the worst of the winter cold is over and before the plants leaf out, prune off all but the strongest cane. If it is tied to the lower wire, remove it and tie it to the top wire; it will become the permanent trunk. Remove all shoots that grow below the bottom wire that year. Tie laterals (canes growing horizontally from the permanent trunk) along the wires. Select at least 4 growing in each direction along the bottom and top wires. Remove any flowers that begin to develop. The third spring, select 4 laterals and prune them severely, leaving 2 buds on each. These buds will grow into the fruiting canes for the next year. Once vines are into production, prune them every spring. Select 4 moderately strong laterals, pruning them back and leaving

6 to 10 buds on each; these arms will produce fruit that year. Select 4 small laterals, cutting them back to 2 buds each; these are renewal spurs for the laterals the following year.

Proper pruning reduces the number of problems that grapes may have with insects and diseases. To maintain clean grapes, follow a regular spraying schedule. When new growth is 4 inches long, spray with an all-purpose orchard spray or with ferbam fungicide and Sevin insecticide. Repeat the application just before bloom. When the grapes have set, spray with Captan fungicide to prevent black rot. Add Sevin insecticide if insects are present. Repeat the Captan application 3 weeks later. (See the pest control and spraying chart in the introduction to fruit gardening.)

### Additional Information

On trellises, grow the main trunk over the top. Select 1-year-old laterals along the trunk every 3 feet; prune them back to about 10 buds each. Select renewal spurs at the same spacing; prune them to 2 buds each. A productive plant should have 50 to 60 buds left after pruning. Each spring, remove all the old wood that produced fruit the previous year—you will be impressed at the amount of prunings a grape vine will produce in a year. Proper pruning removes about 90 percent of the wood on a vine.

Grapes mature in late summer to early fall. Full color is not the only indicator of maturity. At maturity the seeds and the cluster stems turn brown, and the berries attain maximum sweetness. Harvest them then.

## Harvest Salad

*In a large bowl, combine 12 cups leaf lettuce, 1 pound green seedless grapes, 1 pound red grapes, and ½ pound cooked, peeled, and deveined medium shrimp. Break 1 package (3 ounces) Oriental Ramen noodles into small pieces (do not use the seasoning packet) and add to salad along with ½ cup raisins, ¼ cup sliced green onion, and ¼ cup toasted walnuts or sunflower kernels. Drizzle with salad dressing of your choice. Toss to coat.*

## VARIETIES

There are literally thousands of grape varieties. To try varieties that are commonly grown in your area, check with your local garden center. The following are readily available to the home gardener. By careful selection of varieties, grape harvest may extend from mid-August to late September.

| Varieties | Comments |
|---|---|
| **American Blue Grapes** | |
| Buffalo | Early, the best quality for juice and desserts. |
| Concord | Midseason, hardy and reliable. |
| Fredonia | Late midseason, good for juice and pies. |
| Stark Blue Boy | Midseason, good quality. |
| Van Buren | Very early. |
| Worden | Early, vigorous. |
| **American Red Grapes** | |
| Brighton | Late. |
| Catawba | Late. |
| Delaware | Midseason, best of the reds. |
| Steuben | Early, superb quality. |
| Swenson Red | Midseason, dessert grape. |
| **American White Grapes** | |
| Cayuga | Excellent for winemaking. |
| Golden Muscat | Late midseason. |
| Niagra | Midseason, table use. |
| Ontario | Very early, productive. |
| **Seedless American Grapes** | |
| Candice | Late, small dessert type, red. |
| Concord Seedless | Midseason, blue. |
| Interlaken | White. |
| Reliance | Late, hardiest of the seedless, red. |

# Peach

***Persica vulgaris***
***Prunus persica***

Peach trees are challenging to grow. They are susceptible to several damaging pests. The flowers are killed by absolute winter temperatures of minus 10 degrees Fahrenheit, and they are easily killed by late-season frost. In some areas, commercial growers expect to get a crop only 1 year out of 5. Yet gardeners continue to defy the odds and grow peaches because the results are so gratifying. Some grow them in tubs that can be moved into a protected area for the winter. I agree that there is nothing like a juicy, ripe peach on a warm summer day.

## When to Plant

Always plant peach trees in the spring after any danger of severe cold weather has passed.

## Where to Plant

To choose a site, be sure to take into account the full-grown size of the trees. Peaches on dwarfing rootstock will spread 12 to 15 feet; standard trees will be twice that size. Peach trees prefer well-drained soil in full sun (8 to 10 hours will suffice) in an area that has protection from winter winds. The trees themselves are hardy, but the flower buds are not. If the garden is on a slope, plant the peach trees on the side of the hill so they are protected from wind, but not at the bottom where cold air will settle.

## How to Plant

Dwarf trees on St. Julian A dwarfing rootstock are recommended for backyard orchards. Peaches are generally available as bare-root, 2-year-old whips. As soon as you receive the trees, plunge the roots in a bucket of water for a couple of hours to rehydrate them and keep them from drying out. If planting is to be delayed, heal-in the trees until you can plant them. Peaches are self-fruitful (not needing another variety for pollination). The number you choose to plant depends on your available space and your love of peaches.

To plant a peach tree, dig a hole twice as wide as the spread of the roots and deep enough that the plant will be at the same depth it grew in the nursery. Trim off excessively long and damaged roots, then spread the roots out in the bottom of the hole. Supporting the tree, backfill the hole with soil, and firm the soil with a blunt stick, such as a 2-by-4. When the hole is half filled with soil, fill it with water. After the water has drained out, replace the remaining soil, and fill with water again.

In severe climates, peaches can be grown in containers such as half 55-gallon drums or half wine barrels. Make sure there are holes in the bottom for drainage. Use a soil mix of ⅓ sand, ⅓ peat moss, and ⅓ garden soil, and fill the container so the plant is set at the same depth it was growing in the nursery. Fill and firm with soil to 2 or 3 inches from the rim. Soak it thoroughly.

## Care and Maintenance

Pruning is essential to peach trees, and the open center system is recommended. (See page 226.) After planting, cut back the central leader of an unbranched tree to 30 inches above the ground. If a branched tree has well-developed and properly spaced branches, select 2, 3, or 4 that arise at least 15 inches but not more than 30 inches from the ground. Then remove all other branches. Cut back the selected scaffold branches, leaving 2 buds each. The second year, finish selecting the scaffold branches, and prune out suckers and any branches that are not selected as scaffolds. In each subsequent year, thin out extra branches and shorten the scaffolds. As the trees age, they will need heavier and heavier pruning. Prune peach trees in the spring, keeping the trees low and thinning them out well.

Move containerized peaches to a protected location where temperatures can be kept below 40 degrees but above 10 degrees Fahrenheit for the winter. Move them back out in spring when danger of severe cold has passed.

An application of fungicide in early spring is necessary to prevent peach leaf curl. Apply a multipurpose orchard spray, Captan, or liquid lime sulfur. Then apply Captan when the flower buds turn pink and again at full bloom. When husks begin to split away from the bases of the fruit, apply Captan and Diazinon, plus sulfur, or a multipurpose orchard spray plus sulfur. Repeat the last spray every 7 to 10 days until 4 weeks before harvest. Peach trees need an additional treatment to protect them from borers; when the mockorange bushes are in bloom or spirea finishes blooming, spray the trunk and branches with either Diazinon or Imidan.

## VARIETIES

The varieties include 'Compact Redhaven', a natural dwarf that can be grown as a severe dwarf if grafted onto St. Julian A rootstock; 'Freestone'; 'Madison', which drops the fruit when fully ripe; and 'Reliance', the most hardy peach recommended for hardiness zone 5 with some protection.

(See the pest control and spraying chart in the introduction to fruit gardening.)

### ADDITIONAL INFORMATION

Peach trees often produce huge crops 1 year, but none the next season. Thinning the crop prevents this alternate bearing. When the developing peaches are nickel sized, thin them to 1 peach every 5 inches. For example, leave 2 peaches on a branch 14 inches long, even if they are close together; if there are 3, remove 1. The resulting peaches will be larger, and the tree will still have the energy to make a crop the following season. Harvest the fruit when it is ripe or a few days earlier. Peaches continue to ripen after harvest. The taste test is the best means of determining ripeness. After a few seasons, experience will tell you when fruit is just about ripe.

## Grandma's Peach Cobbler

*Preheat oven to 450 degrees. Combine 1 cup flour, 1 cup sugar, 1 teaspoon baking powder and ½ teaspoon salt in a mixing bowl. Cut in 2 tablespoons shortening. Set mixture aside.*

*Combine 2 to 3 cups sliced peaches, ½ cup water and ¾ cup sugar in a non-corrosive saucepan. Bring to a boil. While the fruit is heating, stir ½ cup milk into the dry ingredients.*

*Pour batter into a 8- or 9-inch-square pan, and pour the boiling fruit over it. Bake for 10 minutes at 450 degrees, then decrease heat to 350 degrees; cook another 15 minutes. Serve warm.*

# Pear

*Pyrus* cv.

Pears would be as plentiful as apples were it not for the bacterial disease called fire blight. Most exotic pears are extremely susceptible to the disease, and commercial production is limited to areas remote from any concentration of the disease and where the weather is more reliable—in other words, California. Pears can be grown successfully in home gardens by selecting disease-resistant varieties and carefully pruning them to remove diseased branches.

## When to Plant

Plant pear trees in the spring as soon as the soil is dry enough to work.

## Where to Plant

Choose a planting site that receives full sun (8 to 10 hours will suffice) and has well-drained soil.

## How to Plant

Dwarf trees on dwarfing quince rootstock are recommended for backyard orchards, so buy them from a reliable nursery that can assure you get what you order. Pears grafted on dwarfing roots will attain a spread and height of 8 to 12 feet. Standard pear trees will be twice that size. Dwarf trees bear almost as much fruit as standard trees but occupy much less space in the garden. Recently, the U.S. Department of Agriculture genetically engineered a standard pear variety so that it grows as a true dwarf, and the process is being applied to other varieties as well. These trees should be available to home gardeners in a few years. Pears are generally available as bare-root, 2-year-old whips. As soon as you receive the trees, plunge the roots in a bucket of water for a couple of hours to rehydrate them and keep them from drying out. If planting is to be delayed, heal-in the trees until you can plant them.

To plant a pear tree, dig a hole twice as wide as the spread of the roots and deep enough that the plant will be at the same depth it grew in the nursery. Trim off excessively long and damaged roots, then spread out the roots in the bottom of the hole. Supporting the tree, begin to backfill the hole with soil, and firm the soil with a blunt stick, such as a 2-by-4. When the hole is half filled with soil, fill it with water. After the water has drained out, replace the remaining soil, and fill with water again.

## Care and Maintenance

Pear trees require less attention than peach or apple trees but still need annual pruning, ideally in mid- to late winter. The training system is the same as that for apples, the central leader system. (See page 226.)

Train dwarf pears to a 5- to 8-foot central trunk, with 6 to 12 horizontal branches (scaffold branches) in whorls around the trunk. Begin the process at planting by cutting off an unbranched tree at 30 inches tall. A branched tree may have branches that can be selected for the first scaffolds. Select 3 or 4 branches that are evenly spaced around the trunk and arise 18 to 24 inches from the ground, cut these branches back to 10 inches long, and cut the leader 15 inches above the top scaffold branch. If there are no suitable branches for scaffolds, remove all the branches, and cut the leader at 30 inches above the ground.

After the first year, select 3 or 4 scaffolds, cut them back to 10 inches, and remove all other branches; clip the leader 15 inches above the top scaffold. In the subsequent 3 or 4 years, select 3 or 4 more scaffolds each year, cut them to 10 inches, and clip the leader 18 inches above the top scaffold. By the end of the fourth year, the framework of the tree should be completed, and the tree should be producing fruit. Each winter thereafter, prune the tree to remove dead or damaged branches, water sprouts, vertical suckers, and branches touching the ground. Also remove branches growing into the center of the tree and those rubbing on other branches, and clip out weak, nonproductive branches. Most pear varieties try to make scaffold branches with narrow crotches that ascend. Usually, there is no need to do anything about it because the weight of the fruit will eventually bring the branches down.

Remove all evidence of fire blight by cutting at least 6 inches below evidence of the disease. Affected stems appear to have been burned, and cankers (dead areas in the bark) can form on branches. Overwintering cankers are the primary source of infection the next spring.

Other care of pear trees includes watering, weeding, fertilizing, and applying pesticides. Pear trees need water in dry weather, especially if they are growing in light soils. Apply 1 inch per week when nature does not cooperate. Control weeds beneath the trees by hoeing, and apply 2 or 3 inches of mulch. Young dwarf pear trees should grow 1½ feet each year. If they do not seem to be growing, fertilize them with 10-10-10, at a rate of 1½ pounds per 100 square feet of ground beneath each tree. Avoid overstimulating the trees because soft growth is very susceptible to fire blight. Bearing pear trees need regular applications of pesticides to produce usable fruit. Contact your local extension office for a spray schedule, and follow it rigorously to prevent attack by insects and diseases. Apply dormant oil before the buds swell in spring. Apply a multipurpose orchard spray plus sulfur, or Captan plus zineb plus sulfur, when the tips of the buds are green. Repeat the application when the flower buds turn pink and again when half the petals have dropped. Then apply the same mixture every 7 to 10 days until 2 weeks before harvest. When husks begin to split away from the bases of the fruit, apply Captan and Diazinon, plus sulfur, or a multipurpose orchard spray plus sulfur. Repeat the last spray every 7 to 10 days until 4 weeks before harvest.

Do not stop spraying in midsummer because some of the worst pests arrive about that time. (See the spray chart in the introduction to fruit gardening.)

## Additional Information

Many pear varieties tend to make large crops 1 year and none the next. Reduce the tendency to alternate bearing by thinning the crop. When the developing pears are nickel sized, thin them to average 1 pear every 6 inches. For example, leave 2 pears on a branch 14 inches long, even if they are close together; if there are 3, remove 1. The resulting pears will be larger, and the tree will still have the energy to make a crop the following season. Harvest pears before they are fully ripe. It will take some experience for you to know just when to pick your pears. Ripe pears are soft and particularly attractive to yellow jacket wasps and birds. Pears will continue to ripen after they are picked, so store them in a cool place such as a refrigerator. Set some out in a warm spot every few days to ripen. Asian pears mature as early as midsummer, and most European varieties mature from late August to mid-September.

## VARIETIES

Since you need to plant 2 varieties for cross-pollination, check with your supplier to make sure which varieties will cross-pollinate the others. Some are self-infertile and will not pollinate others either. 'Seckel' and 'Moonglow' seem to pollinate most other European varieties.

| Varieties | Comments |
|---|---|
| Golden Spice | Hardy to zone 4. |
| Maxine | Resists fire blight. |
| Moonglow | Early, cross-pollinates with Seckel. |
| Seckel | Best quality, cross-pollinates with Moonglow and with Starking Delicious; resists fire blight; matures in late August to mid-September. |
| Starking Delicious | Resists fire blight; matures in September. |
| Summercrisp | Good cold tolerance in northern areas. |

Asian pears are not as hardy as European pears, but some hobbyists grow them successfully. Most are natural dwarfs, reaching a height and spread of 6 to 8 feet. They are dessert-type pears maturing in midsummer to late September. Members of the Midwest Fruit Explorers are testing several varieties; for more information, contact them at their web site (www.midfex.org). Plant 2 Asian varieties for best pollination because European varieties are not completely reliable for pollinating Asian pears.

| Varieties | Comments |
|---|---|
| Hosui | Very early; ripen the fruit fully on the tree for best quality. |
| Shinsieki | Matures early; excellent flavor, self-fruitful. |
| Ya Li | A Chinese import of excellent quality. |

# Pear and Tuna Salad

*Dice 2 fresh ripe cored and sliced pears, reserving 3 slices. Drain one 7-ounce can water-packed tuna; break into large chunks. Combine diced pears, tuna, 1 cup green pepper strips and 1 cup shredded cabbage in a medium bowl. Toss with ⅓ cup Italian dressing. Serve in lettuce-lined bowl; garnish with reserved pear slices. Serve additional dressing if desired.*

# Plum

***Prunus* cv.**

Plums grown in the Midwest are usually divided into 2 classes, Japanese (*P. salicina, P. triflora*) and European (*P. domestica*). Japanese plums are grown for fresh eating. European plums are eaten fresh, too, but are often used for making jam or drying. Hybrids are usually classified with the Japanese types. The Japanese types and the hybrids are often not as hardy as the European types.

## When to Plant

Plant plum trees in the spring as soon as soils are dry enough to work.

## Where to Plant

Choose a planting site with well-drained soil and full sun (8 to 10 hours will suffice). Be sure to allow enough room to walk around the tree when it matures. Don't let plum trees grow into each other or into nearby structures.

## How to Plant

Trees on dwarfing rootstock are recommended for backyard orchards. They will spread about 8 feet while standard trees spread twice that or more. Plums are generally available as bare-root, 2-year-old whips. As soon as you receive the trees, plunge the roots in a bucket of water for a couple of hours to rehydrate them and keep them from drying out. If planting is to be delayed, heal-in the trees until you can plant them. To plant, dig a hole twice as wide as the spread of the roots and deep enough that the plant will be at the same depth it grew in the nursery. Trim off excessively long and damaged roots, then spread the roots out in the bottom of the hole. Supporting the tree, begin to backfill the hole with soil, firming it with a blunt stick, such as a 2-by-4. When the hole is half filled with soil, fill it with water. After the water has drained out, replace the remaining soil, and fill with water again.

## Care and Maintenance

Prune European plum trees to a single leader. (See page 226.) Annual pruning is necessary to train the trees, ideally in mid- to late winter. Train dwarf plums to a 5- to 8-foot central trunk, with 6 to 12 horizontal branches (scaffold branches) in whorls around the trunk. Begin the process at planting by cutting off unbranched trees at 30 inches tall. Branched trees sometimes have branches that can be selected for the first scaffolds. Select 3 or 4 branches that are evenly spaced around the trunk and arise 18 to 24 inches from the ground. Cut these branches back to 10 inches long, and cut the leader 15 inches above the top scaffold branch. If there are no suitable branches for scaffolds, remove all the branches, and cut the leader at 30 inches above the ground. After the first year, select 3 or 4 scaffolds, cut them back to 10 inches, and remove all other branches; clip the leader 15 inches above the top scaffold. In the subsequent 3 or 4 years, select 3 or 4 more scaffolds each year, cut them to 10 inches, and clip the leader 18 inches above the top scaffold. By the end of the fourth year, the framework of the tree should be completed, and the tree should be producing fruit. Each winter thereafter, prune the trees to remove dead or damaged branches, water sprouts, vertical suckers, and branches touching the ground. Also remove branches growing into the center of the tree and those rubbing on other branches, and clip out weak, nonproductive branches.

Prune Japanese and hybrid plums to the open center system. (See page 226.) After planting, cut back the central leader of unbranched trees to 30 inches above the ground. If branched trees have well-developed and properly spaced branches, select 2, 3, or 4 that arise at least 15 inches but not more than 30 inches from the ground. Then remove all other branches. Cut the selected scaffold branches back, leaving 2 buds each. The second year, finish selecting the scaffold branches, and prune out suckers and any branches that are not selected as scaffolds. In the following years, thin out extra branches and shorten the scaffolds every year. As the trees age, they will need heavier and heavier pruning. Always prune plum trees in the spring, keeping the trees low and well thinned out. Most of the training takes place the first 2 years.

Black knot is a fungus that causes large black galls on the stems of plums. Prune out any galls that form, and control the disease by applying dormant oil in spring before buds swell. Follow that with Captan fungicide just before budbreak to control plum pockets disease. Repeat the application when the buds are pink and again at full bloom. When husks begin to pull away from the bases of the fruit, apply Captan and Diazinon, or a multipurpose orchard spray. Repeat the application every 10 to 14 days until 4 weeks before harvest. Plum trees need an additional treatment to protect them from borers; when the mockorange bushes are in bloom or spirea finishes blooming, spray the trunk and branches with Diazinon or Imidan. (See the pest control and spraying charts in the introduction to fruit gardening.)

### Additional Information

Many plum varieties tend to make large crops 1 year but none the next. Reduce the tendency to alternate bearing by thinning the crop. When the developing plums are nickel sized, thin them to average 1 plum every 6 inches. For example, leave 2 plums on a branch 14 inches long, even if they are close together; if there are 3, remove 1. The resulting plums will be larger, and the tree will still have the energy to make a crop the following season. Japanese plums ripen in early to midsummer, usually in early July throughout the central Midwest (zones 5b or 6a), earlier or later in other parts. European plums ripen later, usually in August. Harvest plums when they are fully ripe. Plums do not all ripen at the same time, so it will be necessary to make several pickings. The fruit continues to ripen after the full color appears so the taste test is the most reliable means of determining when they are ready. Plums do not continue to ripen after harvest, so do not pick them too early.

## Preserving Plums

*Select firm, ripe plums soft enough to yield to slight pressure. Rinse plums; leave whole or halve and pit. Plums can be halved, sliced or chopped. Prepare using the following methods.*

*Dry Pack: Rinse and drain plums. Pack whole plums into plastic freezer bags or containers. Seal, label, and freeze.*

*Sugar Pack: Mix one part sugar to five parts plums. Allow to set until sugar is dissolved. Pack plums into jars or plastic freezer containers. Seal, label, and freeze.*

*Syrup: Pack plums into jars or plastic freezer containers. Ladle a mixture of 1¼ cups sugar and 5½ cups water over the plums, leaving ½-inch headspace. Seal, label, and freeze.*

## VARIETIES

Plant 2 varieties of plums for cross-pollination. (Be sure to carefully check the nursery tags for the varieties.) European varieties will not pollinate Japanese plums nor will Japanese plums pollinate European varieties. To pollinate, the trees need to be within 100 to 200 feet of each other. Japanese plum trees are not usually recommended for zone 5 or farther north, but several avid hobbyists have demonstrated that it can be done if proper precautions are taken for protection, such as planting in a sheltered spot or potting them up and moving them into shelter before winter conditions set in. Plums ripen in early to midsummer, usually in early July throughout the central Midwest (zone 5b or 6a), earlier or later in other parts.

**European Types** (Plant any 2.)

| Varieties | Comments |
|---|---|
| Bluefre | Large blue freestone with yellow flesh. Harvest is late, about the end of August in zone 5b. |
| Damson (Shropshire) | Shropshire is probably the most adaptable of the Damson types. Purplish-black with golden flesh. Midseason. |
| Green Gage (Reine Claude) | Greenish-yellow cling type, sweet. Midseason. |
| Mount Royal | Hardiest blue type. Smallish blue-black freestone fruit of top quality. Harvest end of August. |
| Stanley | Nearly as hardy as Mount Royal. Dark blue freestone with juicy, yellow flesh. Harvest early September. |

**Japanese Types and Hybrids** (Plant any 2 for improved pollination.)

| Varieties | Comments |
|---|---|
| Methley | Purple with red blush, very juicy. Early-ripening. Harvest about mid-July in zone 5. |
| Ozark Premier | Large red fruit, yellow flesh. Tart. Harvest mid-August. |
| Santa Rosa | Dark reddish-purple with red flesh, great flavor. Ripens mid-August. |
| Shiro | Yellow with pinkish blush, clingstone, very juicy. Harvest first week of August. |
| Superior | Fire red, cling type with yellow flesh. Japanese type hardy as far north as central Minnesota. Harvest early August. |

# RASPBERRY

***Rubus* cv.**

Raspberries are second in popularity after strawberries in home small fruit gardens. They are also very popular at pick-your-own farms. Fresh raspberries are nearly impossible to find in grocery stores because they deteriorate quickly after picking and do not ship well. Growing a few in your backyard is the best way to enjoy these delicious fruits. Other than the inconvenience of their thorns, raspberries are easy to grow, and they are the most productive of the small fruits you can plant in your garden.

Caring for raspberries is easier when you understand how these plants grow. You will have to do a lot of pruning, but the fruit is worth the effort. All brambles grow from biennial canes. These canes grow 1 year (primocanes), produce fruit the next summer (floricanes), and die. The crowns are perennial and remain in the ground for many years, sending up new shoots each spring. All raspberries bear fruit in the summer. Some kinds of red raspberries are double-cropping types and produce a crop in the fall, followed by a second crop on the same canes early the next summer. These are called "everbearing," but "fall-bearing" would be more nearly correct. Some growers handle the everbearing plants so that they produce only a large fall crop and no crop the next summer.

## When to Plant

Plant raspberries in the spring as soon as the ground can be worked.

## Where to Plant

Choose a planting site for raspberries that receives full sun (8 to 10 hours will suffice) and has well-drained soil. Leave enough room so that you can mow around the beds to control the suckers. Plant black and purple raspberries as far away from red raspberries as you can; 500 feet is recommended. Red raspberries carry virus diseases that do not affect them, but will destroy black or purple raspberries. Unless you have room to separate the 2 types, select 1 kind to grow. These plants are susceptible to verticillium wilt, a fungus disease that infects the soil and kills susceptible plants growing in it. Do not plant raspberries where solanaceous crops (potatoes, tomatoes, peppers, etc.) have been grown in the last 5 years.

## How to Plant

Raspberries are sold as 1-year-old, Grade No. 1 plants. Buy only certified virus-free plants or tissue-cultured, disease-free plants. Most reliable suppliers and catalogs specify that the plants meet these requirements. Prepare the soil as you would for a vegetable garden. Be sure to kill off perennial weeds such as quackgrass or bindweed using Roundup herbicide. Roundup is deactivated as soon as it hits the ground or is absorbed by the weeds, so there is no danger to plants later on. Spade or till thoroughly. (See "Soil Preparation" in the introduction to the vegetable garden.)

Raspberries may be grown in rows or in hills. Space the plants 2 feet apart in rows that are 8 to 10 feet apart, or space the plants in hills 4 or 5 feet apart. Red and yellow raspberries sucker extensively and will develop into a hedgerow on their own. Black and purple raspberries do not sucker and will remain in hills. Soak bare-root plants in a bucket of water to rehydrate them and to keep them from drying out while you are planting. Dig the planting holes at least the diameter of the root spread. Set red and yellow raspberries at the same depth they grew in the nursery, but set black and purple plants a little deeper. Cut off broken roots, then spread out the root system in the planting hole, and carefully cover it with soil. Fill the hole with water to firm the soil and force out any air pockets.

## Care and Maintenance

After planting, cut back conventional (not tissue-cultured) red raspberry handles (canes) to about 1 foot tall. Cut handles of black raspberries at the soil line. Burn these prunings or dispose of them in the trash to prevent diseases. No pruning is needed on tissue-cultured plants because they are disease free. Mulch well to a depth of 2 to 3 inches to conserve moisture and reduce weed competition.

Although the plants will grow and fruit without support, raspberries are much more attractive and easier to take care of when they are trained up in some manner on supports, such as stakes in hills or trellises. (See pages 222 to 223.) For the hill system, drive a sturdy stake, such as a 6-foot wooden 2-by-2 or a steel fence post, into the ground. With twist ties, pieces of cloth, or string, tie 6 to 8 canes to the stake in the spring after dormant pruning. Then tie plants regularly to keep them in order. For horizontal trellises, set sturdy,

3-foot treated wooden or steel posts every 25 feet in the garden. Add cross pieces to support 2 wires at the top spaced 2 feet apart. Then train the plants into the trellis so that they maintain a solid hedgerow about 2 feet wide. No tying is needed with this system, but ties can be used between the posts to prevent the trellis wires from spreading from the weight of the plants.

Maintenance pruning each year is the most important facet of growing raspberries. I prefer to use hand clippers for the task. Wearing heavy gloves and a long-sleeved shirt is a good idea.

### Red and Yellow Raspberries

In early spring, remove all weak canes (those that are falling over or less than pencil sized), and thin out the remaining canes, saving only the largest canes. Leave 1 cane every foot in rows; leave 6 to 8 canes per hill. Cut back all canes to 5 feet tall. (If the plants are not supported, cut them back to 3 feet.) As soon as fruiting is completed, remove all canes that bore fruit, being careful not to injure developing shoots that will bear the next year. Dispose of all trimmings to reduce chances of diseases. Everbearing red raspberries will produce a fall crop on the newly developing primocanes. Do not remove these canes after the fruit is harvested if you want a crop the next summer. If you do not intend to produce a crop the next summer, mow the entire planting down after the fall harvest with the mower set to a height of 2 to 3 inches. New primocanes will grow and produce fruit the next fall. Many commercial producers use this tremendous labor-saving system. Red and yellow raspberries sucker profusely and need to be controlled. Each spring, rototill the perimeter of the planting to eliminate all suckers that have grown outside the row. Hoe out suckers that develop during the season.

### Black and Purple Raspberries

In early spring, remove all weak canes. Leave 4 or 5 of the most vigorous canes (½ inch or more in diameter) per plant. Thin out and cut back laterals (side shoots growing from the main vertical cane) on black raspberries to 8 or 12 buds each; on purple raspberries, to 15 buds each. In summer, snap off the growing tips of the canes as they grow to the desired height. Snap off black raspberries at 24 inches; snap off purple raspberries at 36 inches. (Leave plants 6 inches taller if they are supported by trellises or stakes.) As soon as fruiting is completed, remove all canes that bore fruit, being careful not to injure developing shoots that will bear the next year. Dispose of all trimmings to reduce chances of diseases.

Properly maintained, healthy raspberry plantings should produce for 10 or more years. Plantings usually deteriorate prematurely because of

## VARIETIES

| Varieties | Comments |
|---|---|
| **Black Raspberries** | |
| Bristol | High yield, widely grown. |
| Haut | Excellent flavor, may be tender in the North. |
| Jewel | Large fruit, hardy. |
| **Purple Raspberries** | |
| Brandywine | Large fruit, good for jams. |
| Royalty | Pick either red for lighter flavor or fully ripe; suckers like reds; grow in hedgerows. |
| **Red Raspberries** | |
| Boyne | Hardy, productive. |
| Heritage | Everbearing, widely adapted, good flavor, grown commercially for excellent fall crops. |
| Latham | Few thorns, reliable. |
| Ruby | Everbearing, large fruit, may not be as productive as Heritage. |
| **Yellow Raspberries** | |
| Goldie | Everbearing, a mutation of Heritage. |

virus diseases for which there is no cure. Immediately rogue out any plants that begin to develop misshapen leaves. If the planting begins to produce small berries, consider replacing it.

Making a delayed dormant application of an all-purpose orchard spray or liquid lime sulfur will prevent damage from mites, scale insects, anthracnose, and spur blight. Apply cover sprays of Sevin or Malathion insecticide, plus ferbam, as new growth is 6 inches tall, just before bloom, and again just after bloom. (See the pest control chart on page 252.)

Weed control, especially grass control, is important. Apply mulches to clean plantings, then hoe or pull weeds as they appear. Use Casoron granules to eliminate weeds in berry plantings and prevent germination of weed seeds. Apply these granules *only* to well-established plantings (plantings that have been through 1 full season).

### Additional Information

Harvest the berries as they ripen. The berries will achieve full color when they are ready to pick. All summer-bearing raspberries mature in early to midsummer, June and July, at about the same time. Fall-bearing types mature in September. Berries deteriorate rapidly, so don't leave them on the plants. Birds, squirrels, and insects will harvest them if you do not.

# STRAWBERRY

*Fragaria* cv.

Growing your own strawberries means that you can have the makings for a tasty treat, especially with short cake and ice cream, on a hot summer evening. Strawberries respond to good treatment and reward your time and effort with plenty of high-quality fruit. Neglect them and the berry patch will rapidly deteriorate. You can choose from 3 types of strawberries: **June-bearing types** produce a heavy crop for 2 or 3 weeks in June; **everbearing types** produce 3 crops per season, a crop in June, in midsummer, and in fall; and **day-neutral types** produce flowers and fruit all season. To have sufficient berries at one time for freezing or preserves, grow June-bearing types. To have fresh berries all summer, choose everbearing or day-neutral varieties.

## When to Plant

Plant strawberries in early spring as soon as the soil dries enough to be workable. Do not try to plant in wet soil. (See the discussion of soils in the introduction.) Early planting allows the plants to become established before the arrival of hot weather.

## Where to Plant

Well-drained soil and full sun (8 to 10 hours will suffice) are essential for growing strawberries. Although strawberries will grow in shade, the production will be severely reduced, and diseases can become a major problem. Good air circulation is essential. Make sure the bed is not sheltered by a fence, shrub beds, or other taller garden plants. The bed will be in place for 3 years or more, so locate it where it will not be disturbed and will not interfere with other gardening operations. Strawberries are susceptible to verticillium wilt, a fungus disease that infects the soil and plants growing in it. Do not plant strawberries where solanaceous crops (potatoes, tomatoes, peppers, etc.) have been grown in the last 5 years.

## How to Plant

Prepare the soil as you would for a vegetable garden. (See "Soil Preparation" in the introduction to the vegetable garden.) Kill off perennial weeds such as quackgrass or bindweed with Roundup herbicide the fall before planting. Roundup is deactivated as soon as it hits the ground or is absorbed by the weeds, so there is no damage to plants later on. Apply $1\frac{1}{2}$ pounds of 10-10-10 fertilizer per 100 square feet of bed. Till the soil to make a fine seedbed, making sure the soil is finely broken up. If you do this work in the fall, the soil will dry more quickly and allow planting earlier in the spring. Buy certified virus-free plants if possible. When plants arrive from the supplier, protect them from drying out until you can plant them by refrigerating them or healing them in. Wrap them in plastic and keep them in the refrigerator for up to a week. To heal in the plants, find a protected place, dig a furrow deep enough to cover the roots of the plants, lay the plants in the furrow, cover the roots with topsoil, and then water. Plants can stay healed in for several days.

June-bearing strawberries are usually planted in matted rows: set plants 18 inches apart in rows at least 3 feet apart. (See page 219.) An alternative is the spaced row system: set plants at the same spacing for matted rows, but allow 2 to 4 selected runners in the row to grow, and remove the others as they appear.

Everbearing and day-neutral varieties are best planted in hills. I find raised beds to be ideal for growing strawberries using the hill system: set the plants 12 inches apart in 2 directions, which will usually be 3 plants across the bed. (See page 219.) Then just cover the roots with soil. If the crown (the part just above the roots from which the leaves grow) is buried, it will rot. If the roots are exposed, they will dry out. Water the planting thoroughly to settle the soil.

Everbearing and day-neutral varieties can be grown successfully in strawberry jugs or other containers. Place 1 plant in each opening in strawberry jugs; place 2 or 3 plants in a large pot. Use an artificial potting soil, such as Jiffy Mix or Pro-Mix, and again, just cover the roots with soil. If the crown is buried, it will rot. If the roots are exposed, they will dry out. Water the planting thoroughly to settle the soil.

## Care and Maintenance

For plants in matted rows, allow them to spread freely, and train the daughter plants so they stay in the row until they root. Keep the row about 2 feet wide. For plants in spaced rows, allow only a few selected runners to root. Space either 2 or 4 runners to root no closer than 4 inches from the mother plant. The result is a row that is less crowded and easier to pick and produces larger berries than a matted row. For plants in hills, do not allow them to send out runners. As runners appear, clip them out. Large plants with multiple crowns develop, resulting in more flower stalks and better production.

Do not allow strawberries to flower and fruit the first season. Any fruit that develops will seriously sap the strength of the plants and reduce the crop the following year. You may want to make an exception with everbearing and day-neutral varieties and allow them to flower in late summer the first season to produce a few berries for fall. There will be no reduced crop with everbearing or day-neutral the next year if plants are well developed before they are allowed to make berries.

Weeding and watering are important for berry production. Cultivate to keep weeds from getting a start in the berry patch. Grasses are especially troublesome, so hoe or pull them as soon as they appear. Apply 2 inches of straw mulch to deter weeds, to conserve moisture, and to keep the berries off the ground. Berries require about 1 inch of water per week when the weather is dry. Remember to water as the daytime temperature rises so the plants dry off before nightfall.

Renovate matted row plants immediately following harvest each year. Run the power mower over the bed, removing the leaves just above the crowns. Rake out and dispose of the old foliage. Then reduce the width of the rows to about 12 inches by rototilling or hoeing out the extra plants. If you cannot cut back the bed within 10 days of harvest, forget it until the next year. If the plants are cut back after 10 days, they will be stunted and next year's crop will be reduced. Fertilize matted rows immediately after cutting the plants back, using 2 pounds of 10-10-10 or the equivalent per 100 square feet of bed. Be sure to apply water if rain does not fall in a day or so, or the fertilzer may burn the plants.

Fertilize hill plantings in August with 10-10-10 at a rate of 1 pound per 100 square feet of bed. Be careful: avoid getting the fertilizer on the foliage where it will burn the plants. Band the fertilizer along the sides of the bed, or wash or brush off the plants after you have broadcast the fertilizer.

You will have few problems with growing strawberries if you start with disease-free plants and provide adequate air circulation and water. But if a planting does develop serious diseases, replace it. Most insect problems can be solved with timely applications of insecticides. Apply Sevin to control strawberry clippers and tarnish plant bugs, and use insecticidal soap to control aphids and mites. Try not to let bug problems develop by controlling weeds in the area surrounding the strawberry beds.

### Additional Information

Strawberries need winter protection, and covering them with straw is a way to do it. After several good freezes, apply clean straw 3 to 4 inches deep over the plants. If winter winds blow the straw off, rake it back. In the spring, begin to remove the straw when day temperatures are consistently in the 40-degree Fahrenheit range. Be prepared to reapply it if a late-season frost is predicted. The freezing of open flowers means that the berries will be killed. Other means of protecting blooms from frost include covering the planting with old sheets or blankets, or running the lawn sprinkler all night to keep free water on the plants. The plants may have ice on them, but the flowers will not freeze as long as there is free water on them too.

Matted row strawberry plantings last only 2 or 3 years. Then the production goes down and disease problems show up. Some gardeners overcome this problem by planting a bed on 1 side of the garden 1 year, and on the other side the next year. While 1 is in production, the other is becoming established.

Strawberries are ready for harvest about 30 days after the first bloom. Harvest the berries when they are fully red. Do not allow them to stay on the plants when fully ripe or something else will harvest them for you. Any spoiled berries must be picked off the plants to avoid rotting, which could spread to other berries. Snap the berries off with the cap and a small piece of stem attached, using your thumbnail if necessary.

## Strawberry Roll

*Boil 1½ cups sugar and 1½ cups water for 5 minutes. Set aside. Hull and slice 1 pint fresh strawberries. Mix 2 cups flour, 4 teaspoons baking powder, 1 egg, ½ teaspoon salt, 4 tablespoons shortening and ¾ cup milk in a medium bowl and form into a ball. Roll out dough. Spread with chopped strawberries. Roll up like a jelly roll. Cut in slices approximately 1 inch thick and place in a greased 13"×9-inch pan. Pour syrup over rolls. Bake at 450 degrees for 25 to 30 minutes. Let cool. Serve with whipping cream.*

## VARIETIES

Catalogs list so many varieties that determining how a variety will grow in your yard is difficult. Select some varieties that sound promising, and try a few of each to see how they perform. After some trials, you will be able to select varieties that do what you want in your garden. Your county extension office may be helpful in selecting varieties that do well in your particular locality.

Strawberries ripen between 30 and 45 days after flowering. June-bearing types can be expected to bear from early June to as late as early July if the weather is cool. Everbearing and day-neutral kinds will flower and fruit throughout the season with the first harvest about the same time as June-bearing kinds.

| Varieties | Comments |
|---|---|
| **Everbearing and Day-Neutral Strawberries** | |
| Ft. Laramie | Tolerates severe winters with protection. |
| Gem | Also known as Superfection; good production. |
| Ogallala | Good cold tolerance with protection. |
| Ozark Beauty | Late, very productive. |
| Tribute | Good disease resistance, late. |
| Tristar | Resistant to verticillium and red stele, early. |
| **June-Bearing Strawberries** | |
| Allstar | Very large, late, resistant to verticillium and red stele. |
| Catskill | Hardy. |
| Delmarvel | Large fruit, good disease resistance. |
| Earliglow | Early, good disease resistance. |
| Honeoye | Large fruit. |
| Midway | Good for freezing. |
| Sparkle | Excellent flavor. |

# Suppliers

This list of suppliers is not complete and is provided only for convenience. It does not imply endorsement of the firms listed, nor does it discriminate against firms not listed.

## Sources for Bird Netting

Bird-X, Inc.
300 North Elizabeth
Chicago, IL 60607

Forestry Suppliers, Inc.
P.O. Box 8397
Jackson, MS 39284-8397

Gemplers
211 Blue Mound Road
Mt. Horeb, WI 53572

Hummert International
4500 Earth City Expressway
Earth City, MO 63045

Indiana Berry and Plant Company
5218 West 500 South
Huntingberg, IN 47542

## Sources for Beneficial Insects

Rincon Vitola
P.O. Box 1555
Ventura, CA 93002
805-643-5407
Fax: 805-643-6267
E-mail: Bugnet@West.net

The Bug Store
113 West Argonne
St. Louis, MO 63122-1104
800-455-2847

## Catalog Mail Order Seed Suppliers

Alberta Nursery and Seeds
P.O. Box 20, Bowden, AB T0M 0K0
Phone: 403-224-3544
Fax: 403-224-2455

W. Atlee Burpee Co.
300 Park Avenue
Warminster, PA 18947
Phone: 215-674-4900
Fax: 215-674-0838

E & R Seed Co.
1356 East 200 S.
Monroe, IN 46772
No phone (Amish)
Write for catalog

Gurney Seed & Nursery
Gurney Building
Yankton, SD 57078
Phone: 605-665-4451
Fax: 605-665-6435

Harris Seeds
60 Saginaw Drive
Rochester, NY 14623
Phone: 716-442-0410
Fax: 716-442-9387

Holmes Seed Co.
P.O. Box 9087
Canton, OH 44709
Phone: 330-492-0123
Fax: 330-492-0167

Ed Hume Seeds, Inc.
1819 South Central Avenue, Bay 33
Kent, WA 98032
Phone: 253-859-1110
Fax: 253-859-0694

Johnny's Selected Seeds
R.R. 1, Box 2580
Albion, ME 04910
Phone: 207-437-4301

J. W. Jung Seed Co.
335 South High Street
Randolph, WI 53956
Phone: 920-326-3121
Fax: 920-326-5769

Lindenberg Seeds, Ltd.
803 Princess Avenue
Brandon, MB R7A 0P5
Phone: 204-727-0575
Fax: 204-727-2832

McFayden Seeds
P.O. Box 1060, Brandon, MB R7A 6E1
Phone: 204-725-7333
Fax: 204-571-7538

Nichols Garden Nursery
1190 North Pacific Highway
Albany, OR 97321
Phone: 541-928-9280
Fax: 541-967-8406

George W. Park Seed Co.
Highway 254 North
Greenwood, SC 29657
Phone: 864-223-8555
Fax: 864-941-4206

Pinetree Garden Seeds
Box 300, New Gloucester, ME 04260
Phone: 207-926-3400

Seed Savers Exchange
3076 North Winn Road
Decora, IA 52101

Seeds of Change
P.O. Box 15700
Santa Fe, NM 87506
Phone: 888-762-7333

R. H. Shumway
P.O. Box 1
Graniteville, SC 29828
Phone: 803-663-9771
Fax: 803-663-9772

T & T Seeds, Ltd.
P.O. Box 1710
Winnipeg, MB R3C 3P6
Phone: 204-895-9962
Fax: 204-895-9967

Thompson and Morgan
P.O. Box 1308
Jackson, NJ 08527
Phone: 800-274-7333

Tomato Growers Supply
P.O. Box 720
Ft. Myers, FL 33902
Phone: 941-768-1119
Fax: 941-768-3476

Totally Tomatoes
P.O. Box 1626
Augusta, GA 30903
Phone: 802-273-3400

Vermont Bean Seed Co.
Garden Lane
Fair Haven, VT
Phone: 803-273-2400

West Coast Seeds Ltd.
Unit 206—Ontario Street
Vancouver, BC V5X 3E8
Phone: 604-482-8800
Fax: 604-482-8822

## Fruit Plant Suppliers

Applesource
1716 Apples Road, Chapin, IL 62628
Phone: 217-588-3854

Bear Creek Nursery
P.O. Box 411, Northport, WA 99157
Phone: 509-732-6219

Brittingham Plant Farm
P.O. Box 2538, Salisbury, MD 21802
Phone: 410-749-5153

Hartmann's Plantation
310 Sixtieth Street
Grand Junction, MI 49056
Phone: 616-253-4281

Hilltop Nursery
P.O. Box 578, Hartford, MI 49057
Phone: 616-621-3135

Miller Nurseries
5060 West Lake Road
Canandaigua, NY 14424
Phone: 800-836-9630

Raintree Nursery
391 Butts Road, Morton, WA 98356
Phone: 360-496-6400

Stark Bros. Nursery
P.O. Box 10, Louisiana, MO 63353
Phone: 800-325-4180

# GLOSSARY

**AAS**: All-America Selections, awarded to plant varieties that have given outstanding performance in trial gardens throughout the country.

**annual**: a plant that starts from seed, grows, flowers, and produces a fruit and seeds in 1 season. Lettuce, corn, and beans are examples.

**anthracnose**: a fungus disease characterized by discolored, often dead, angular spots on leaves, stems, or fruit.

**artificial potting soil**: a commercial blend of peat moss, composted bark, perlite beads, or other materials used instead of soil for growing containerized plants.

**banding**: applying fertilizer or pesticide to the soil in a narrow strip alongside the plants as opposed to broadcasting over the entire planted area; similar to sidedressing.

**bare root**: plants lifted for transplanting with no soil attached to the roots.

**biennial**: a plant that requires 2 seasons to produce seed. It grows a rosette of foliage from seed the first year, produces a flower, fruit, and seed the second year, and dies. Examples include parsley, angelica, and carrots.

**blackleg**: a fungus disease characterized by black discoloration of the plant stem at and above the soil line.

**black rot**: a fungus disease characterized by black discoloration and rotting of the fruit, for example, of grapes or apples.

**blossom-end rot**: a leathery-brown spot that develops on the bottoms of tomatoes, or peppers or vine crops due to unfavorable growing conditions. It is usually limited to the first few fruits early in the season and is self-correcting.

**bolt**: to produce flowers or seed prematurely—generally referring to plants grown for their foliage such as lettuce, spinach or certain herbs.

**cane**: a woody, often hollow stem, usually unbranched, arising from the ground. Stems of brambles are referred to as canes.

**catfacing**: malformed fruit caused by poor pollination.

**chlorosis**: yellowing of young leaves due to failure to develop chlorophyll; often caused by high soil pH or nutrient deficiencies.

**clubroot**: a disease characterized by swollen, clublike roots on plants such as cabbage or broccoli.

**cold hardiness**: the ability of a plant to withstand the expected low temperatures in a location. Some vegetables are completely hardy and can stand winter weather; perennial vegetables and herbs such as asparagus and thyme are in this category. Some annual vegetables are semihardy and stand a freeze; peas and Brussels sprouts are examples.

**come true**: a characteristic of collected seed that produces a plant identical to the one from which the seed was collected. Hybrid varieties do not come true from collected seed.

**companion planting**: growing 2 crops in the same space or growing plants of several different varieties next to each other to reduce insect problems; for example, radishes are often sown in the same rows as carrots.

**composite**: plants characterized by flower heads consisting of petal-less disk flowers surrounded by ray flowers, each with a colorful petal. Sunflowers, daisies, and dandelions are composites.

**compound leaves**: leaves consisting of several to many leaflets attached to a single central stem.

**cross-pollination**: fertilization of a flower of one variety of a plant by the pollen of another closely related plant as opposed to self-pollination.

**crown**: the center part of a plant; the point at which the leaves and stems of a plant join the roots.

**cultivar**: the correct nomenclature for a variety that is developed and persists under cultivation.

**cup and receptacle**: the cup-shaped fruit of raspberry or blackberry consisting of tiny cohering fruitlets covering a buttonlike receptacle. Cups of raspberries separate from the receptacle; those of blackberry do not.

**determinate**: growth characteristic of tomato varieties that set terminal flowers, thus stopping further growth. Determinate plants form low bushes with all of the fruit formed about the same time; they are convenient for processing.

**dibble**: a small, hand-held, pointed stick used to make holes in the soil for planting seedlings. Also, to poke a hole in the soil with a dibble.

**dioecious**: plants bearing male and female flowers on separate plants.

**dormant oil**: a highly refined petroleum product used as an insecticide. Dormant oils kill insects by smothering them in a film of oil.

**drainage**: the capacity of a soil to drain away water.

**fallow**: to keep soil free of all plants for a season or more, thus reducing subsequent weed problems.

**fertilizer**: any substance used to add plant nutrients to the soil.

**foliage**: leaves of plants.

**frass**: a mass of shredded plant parts and often insect parts due to feeding by insect pests.

**frost-free date**: average date of last frost (as compared to latest date of last frost).

**full sun**: receiving all available sunlight from sunrise to sunset.

**germinate**: to begin growth as a plant from a seed.

**green manure**: temporary planting of fast-growing vegetation to be plowed into the soil, adding organic matter and improving soil condition.

**greensand**: glauconite, a naturally occurring potassium-bearing mineral used as a fertilizer.

**green shoulders**: a condition that develops on plants such as carrots when roots are exposed to light, or tomatoes when exposed to conditions unfavorable for ripening.

**growing season**: the number of days between the last freeze of spring and the first freeze of autumn.

**gynoecious**: refers to female flowers, as in gynoecious plants, which have only female flowers.

**harden off**: to gradually expose plants grown indoors or in a greenhouse to lower temperatures, making it possible for them to withstand colder conditions. Also applies to plants exposed to adverse conditions such as low fertility, low temperatures, or drying, which causes stunting and sometimes premature flowering.

**healing in**: a method of storing plants in the ground until conditions are favorable for planting. Plants are laid on their sides in a shallow trench and covered with soil so that only the tips of the plants are exposed.

**heirloom**: items handed down from generation to generation. Heirloom plants or heirloom varieties have been maintained by collecting and saving seed each year. They are available from seed specialists, have not been improved and may lack the disease resistance of newer varieties, but retain the wonderful characteristics that made them popular in the past. These varieties may do very well in your garden if it is free of certain diseases.

**hilling up:** mounding soil around the base of a plant for various purposes, for example, to blanch celery or Belgian endive, or to protect potatoes from the sun.

**hill planting:** setting several plants in close proximity in a "hill," and widely spacing the "hills" in rows. (In row planting the plants are evenly spaced along the row.)

**hybrid:** a cultivar resulting from a cross between two dissimilar cultivars, the ensuing cultivar being different from either parent.

**indeterminate:** growth characteristic of tomato plants that set flower clusters along a vining stem, never setting terminal flowers. They grow indefinitely, producing fruit throughout the season until killed off by frost. These varieties are excellent for growing on trellises or stakes.

**insecticidal soap:** highly refined liquid soap used as an insecticide.

**insecticide:** a pesticide to control insects and related pests.

**latest date of last frost:** the date after which frost does not occur in a locality.

**leader:** the central vertical shoot of a plant.

**leaf axil:** the angle between the upper side of a leaf or stem and the supporting stem.

**leaf spots:** localized disease infections producing spots on leaves.

**lifting:** digging up or pulling plants, as in harvesting or removing plants for transplanting.

**monoecious:** plants bearing separate male flowers and female flowers on the same plant (typical of vine crops).

**mosaic:** a virus disease causing a mosaic pattern of discoloration in plant leaves.

**mulch:** a covering of straw, compost, plastic sheeting, etc., spread on the ground around plants to reduce water loss, prevent weeds, and enrich the soil.

**mummy berries:** tiny, misshapen, useless fruits, usually the result of disease; often refers to brambles or grapes.

**open pollination:** refers to plants pollinated naturally by whatever pollen happens to blow onto them. These varieties come true from seed, that is, collected seed will produce a plant identical to the one from which the seed was collected. Hybrid varieties do not come true from collected seed.

**overwinter:** to survive winter; to tolerate the winter conditions without injury.

**partial shade:** filtered sun all day or shade part of the day.

**PCNB (Terraclor)**: soil fungicide used to prevent certain soil-borne diseases.

**peat pot**: small pot formed of peat moss.

**perennial**: a plant that grows from seed, developing a plant for the first year, and flowering and producing fruit and seeds each year thereafter. Rhubarb, strawberries, and apple trees are examples.

**pesticide**: a material used to control insects (insecticide), fungi (fungicide), or weeds (herbicide).

**pH**: Soil pH is a measure of acidity or alkalinity. Soil is neutral at a pH of 7.0. Above 7.0, the soil is alkaline; below 7.0, the soil is acidic. Most garden plants prefer a pH of 6.0 to 7.0.

**pinch back**: to remove the growing tip of a plant to stimulate branching.

**pistil**: the central, seed-bearing, female organ of a flower.

**plug**: a plant grown in a plug of soil, small pot, or plug tray.

**pollination**: fertilization of female part of a flower by pollen from the male part of a flower.

**reflex**: to bend, turn, or fold back.

**reseed**: to seed again; often refers to plants that spontaneously drop seed, thus perpetuating themselves.

**rogue**: to uproot or destroy things that do not conform to a certain standard.

**root cutting**: a small, thin section of root used for propagation.

**root division**: a section of a root system used for propagation.

**rosette**: a circular cluster of leaves.

**rototill**: to till the soil using a rototiller.

**row covers**: sheets, blankets, or plastic covers placed over susceptible plants to prevent frost damage or insect damage; for example, miners attacking Swiss chard or cucumber beetles feeding on vine crops. Floating row covers are mats of spun-bound polypropylene that are very light, needing no supports, and do not smash plants under them.

**rust**: a fungus disease characterized by masses of rustlike sores on plant surfaces.

**savoy**: crinkled or puckered leaves, for example, savoy cabbage or savoy spinach.

**scaffold**: a horizontal branch on a tree.

**scald**: a condition in which plant leaves dry out and become papery at the edges.

**seedbed**: finely tilled soil suitable for sowing seed; also a bed prepared in that manner.

**side-dress**: to apply fertilizer next to the rows of plants at about half the normal rate, thus avoiding damage from getting fertilizer on the growing plants. Sidedressing is usually applied about midseason after the preplant fertilizers have begun to run out.

**soil types**: sand, silt, clay, or loam, describing the coarseness or fineness of the soil.

**spur-type fruit tree**: a tree that has fewer lateral branches and shortened, fruit-bearing stems called spurs. It grows more slowly, usually bears earlier, and develops into a smaller tree.

**stamen**: the male part of a seed-bearing flower.

**suckers**: undesirable shoots arising from the roots of a plant near the base or a short distance from the base.

**tender perennial**: a perennial plant that is unable to tolerate the winter temperatures in a particular climate.

**till**: to work the soil by spading, digging, cultivating, or rototilling.

**tilth**: physical condition of the soil.

**variety**: a cultivar.

**vegetative propagation**: propagation by means of cuttings or divisions.

**water sprouts**: vigorous vertical sprouts growing from the base, trunk, or scaffold branches of a tree.

**whip (in relation to fruit tree)**: a small, single-stemmed, whiplike tree used to start a planting.

**wilt**: a fungus or bacterial disease that causes plants to wilt and die.

# Bibliography

*Apple Varieties and Their Uses*. University of Missouri-Columbia Agricultural Publication G6022, 1993.

Bailey, L. Hyde. *Standard Cyclopedia of Horticulture*. New York: Macmillan, 1963.

Berolzheimer, Ruth. *The Great American Cook Book.* Chicago, IL: Consolidated Book Publishers, Inc., 1940.

*Better Homes and Gardens Heritage Cook Book.* Meredith Corporation, 1975. Des Moines, IA.

*Big Book of Gardening Skills*. Garden Way Publishing, 1993. Pownal, VT.

Brady, N. C. *Nature and Properties of Soils*. New York: Macmillan, 1974.

Brickell, Christopher, ed. *Encyclopedia of Garden Plants*, the American Horticultural Society. New York: Macmillan, 1989.

Divoc, Rosemary. *Growing Herbs in the Midwest.* Amherst, WI: Amherst Press, 1996.

Fizzell, J. A. *Month-by-Month Gardening in Illinois*. Franklin, TN: Cool Springs Press, 1999.

Fizzell, J. A. *Month-by-Month Gardening in Indiana*. Franklin, TN: Cool Springs Press, 1999.

Fizzell, J. A. *Month-by-Month Gardening in Michigan*. Franklin, TN: Cool Springs Press, 1999.

*Fruits for Minnesota*. University of Minnesota Extension Service Publication FS-1104-GO, 1998.

Gordon, Don. *Growing Fruit in the Upper Midwest.* Minneapolis, MN: University of Minnesota Press, 1991.

*Growing Tree Fruits in the Home Garden*. University of Illinois Extension Publication 1013, 1987.

Hepper, F. Nigel. *Baker Encyclopedia of Bible Plants.* Grand Rapids, MI: Baker Book House, 1992.

*Home Fruit Production: Apples*. University of Missouri-Columbia Agricultural Publication G6021, 1993.

(*Bibliography continued on next page*)

*Home Fruit Production: Peach and Nectarine*. University of Missouri-Columbia Agricultural Publication G6030, 1997.

*Illinois Agriculture Pest Management Handbook*. Urbana: University of Illinois, 1997.

*Illinois Small Fruit and Strawberry Schools, Proceedings of*. Urbana: University of Illinois, 1999.

Oster, Maggie. *Ortho's All About Herbs*. Des Moines: Meredith Books, 1999.

*Small Fruits in the Home Garden*. University of Illinois Extension Publication 1343, 1997.

*Small Scale Fruit Production—A Comprehensive Guide*. Pennsylvania State University, 1999. State College, PA.

*Suggested Vegetable Varieties for Home Gardeners in Minnesota*. University of Minnesota Extension Publication FO-1425-GO, 1995.

Swahn, J. O. *The Lore of Spices*. Barnes and Noble, Inc., 1997.

Thompson, H. C., and W. C. Kelly. *Vegetable Crops*. New York: McGraw-Hill, 1957.

Tiedjens, Victor A. *Vegetable Encyclopedia and Gardener's Guide*. New York: New Home Library, 1943.

Voigt, C. E., and J. S. Vandemark. *Vegetable Gardening in the Midwest*. University of Illinois Extension Service, 1995.

*Weeds of the North Central States*. University of Illinois Agricultural Experiment Station, Circular 718, 1960.

# INDEX

# About the Author

James Fizzell

James Fizzell has more than 40 years of hands-on horticultural experience, making him the source that other experts turn to with their toughest turf, vegetable and landscape plant problems. Fizzell has been featured often on television and radio and in leading trade journals, and has become a celebrated guest speaker at industry seminars and horticultural associations throughout the Midwest.

Fizzell was the horticultural advisor for the University of Illinois Cooperative Extension Service for nearly 35 years. In 1991, he founded James A. Fizzell and Associates, Ltd., which provides services to professional horticulturists, arborists, municipalities, sports turf managers, media, and other plant experts needing specialized help. Wrigley Field, home of the Chicago Cubs, is one such facility that has turned to Fizzell for landscaping and turf aid.

Fizzell is well known to Midwest gardeners through numerous radio and television appearances and gardening articles. He is a frequent guest on the WGN "Farm Show" radio program, and in 1998 through 1999 hosted his own garden radio show on WYLL. He often appears on WGN-TV and was the host of "Garden Street USA" from 1998 through 1999 on Direct TV. He writes frequently for neighborhood weekly newspapers such as the *Pioneer Press,* and is a contributor to *The Landscape Contractor, The Landscape Buyer, Common Interest,* and *On Course* magazines.

Fizzell attended Pasadena California City College and California State Polytechnic College and received his B.S. in Floriculture and his M.S. in Horticulture from the University of Illinois. He participated in advanced studies at the University of California, Colorado State University, the University of Minnesota, Duluth, and Loyola University Law School.

Other titles Jim Fizzell has written for Cool Springs Press include *The Illinois Gardener's Guide, Month-by-Month Gardening in Illinois, Month-by-Month Gardening in Indiana, Month-by-Month Gardening in Michigan,* and as co-author, *My Illinois Garden: A Gardener's Journal.* Jim and his wife Jane currently reside in Park Ridge, Illinois.